# LOST
# DEVON

✳

*This book is dedicated to my father Stephen Goodall,*
*who helped imbue me with a love of history.*

First published in 2007 by
Birlinn Limited
West Newington House
10 Newington Road
Edinburgh
EH9 1QS

www.birlinn.co.uk

Hbk
ISBN13: 978 1 84158 552 9
ISBN10: 1 84158 552 1

Pbk
ISBN13: 978 1 84158 648 9
ISBN10: 1 84158 648 X

British Library Cataloguing-in-Publication Data
A catalogue record for this book is available
from the British Library.

Editor Katy Charge
Design Andrew Sutterby

Printed and bound in China by 1010, China

# LOST DEVON

## Felicity Goodall

BIRLINN

# CONTENTS

# ACKNOWLEDGEMENTS

Local history is the province and enthusiasm of many, both amateur and professional. Organisations such as the Devon Archaeological Society bring the two sets of enthusiasts together, and enable excavations such as those of the Taw and Torridge fish weirs to take place and subsequently to be published. It was thanks to volunteers such as Derry Bryant from the North Devon Archaeological Society that those excavations were even started. Under the auspices of archaeologists Chris Preece and Colin Humphreys of South West Archaeology the weir remnants were surveyed, recorded and researched.

Peter Weddell, Richard Parker and colleagues past and present at Exeter Archaeology have been responsible for rescuing our knowledge of the past as the bulldozer moves in, and recording pieces of the jigsaw.

Archaeologists, archivists and librarians are the unsung heroes and heroines of local history, and many have shared unstintingly their knowledge and expertise. Ian Maxted, now retired from Devon Library Services, was generous in his time and pointed me towards the lost medieval books of Exeter Cathedral, with help from the cathedral Library. Staff at the West Country Library in Exeter; Plymouth and West Devon Record Office; Barnstaple Local Studies Library; Torquay Library Services; Newton Abbot Library; the Railway Studies Library, and my local librarians in Kingsbridge have all been willing and able to answer my queries or point me elsewhere.

Our local museums are the guardians of so much of the county's heritage and my thanks go to volunteers at the Cookworthy Museum in Kingsbridge; Totnes Museum; Felicity Cole at Newton Abbot Museum; Maureen Attrill at Plymouth City Museum and Art Gallery; Andrew Fielding at the Lions Saltworks Trust in Cheshire for sharing and discussing the salt trade; Ted Gosling at Seaton Museum; Sir John Soane Museum in London; Clive Grenfell, voluntary archivist at Morwellham Quay for lending me publications and giving me his time; the Institute of Mechanical Engineers; and to Sandra and Chris at the Permissions Department of the British Museum for making it possible for me to use the illustration from the Luttrell Psalter. Special thanks go to Ruth Spires at the Museum of Barnstaple and North Devon for letting me interrupt her unannounced, and giving me access to items from the display including photographs of the men of the Devon Regiment at the Battle of Wagon Hill, and for bringing to life the lost county regiment, I am grateful to Tony Cox.

In my search to find information about Kipling's alma mater at Westward Ho! I turned to the archives at Haileybury where Toby Parker helped with documents, and photographs. The National Trust gave permission to quote from Rudyard Kipling's accounts of the school. Pat Slade and other history enthusiasts in Westward Ho! helped to fill in the picture.

Richard Evans was kind enough to share his research into Tuckenhay Mill, and present owner Peter Wheeler lent me photographs and gave me every help. Thanks to Endsleigh House Hotel, Michael Taylor, His Grace The Duke of Bedford and the staff at Woburn Abbey for help with the story of Endsleigh House, and permission to reproduce part of the diary of The Flying Duchess; I am also grateful to Steve Mulberry at the National Trust's North Devon Property Office for information and pictures of that lost gem Dunsland House.

Tony Manley shared pictures of the Hartland Chronicle; Dick Bird kindly let me use pictures of a sight few people have ever seen, the workings of what was once the greatest copper mine in Europe; Gerald Smallacombe gave me his memories of the railways in the pre-Beeching era; Anne Whitbourn of the Dartmoor Tinworking Study Group for her enthusiasm and pictures; and Len Copley allowed me to borrow some of his superb collection of slides of Dartmoor.

Thanks to the family of the late Eric Dott; St Peters Convent; Ann Lidstone and Percy Moysey ; the Patey family for sharing their Hallsands archive; and a huge thank you to David Clarke for spending an evening to teach me fishlore.

Finally I would like to thank all the members of my family who have allowed me to pick their brains and plunder their resources of patience and support.

# CHAPTER 1

# LOSSES TEMPORAL
# AND SPIRITUAL

The Church of St Peter the Poor Fisherman at Revelstoke stands a few yards back from the beach, where the land's edge gives a little more to the sea each year. Its location offers the tempting idea that it could be the last remnant of a drowned medieval village, whose cottages once stood on the crumbling cliffs. Gravestones surrounding it commemorate retired naval captains, fishermen and farm workers. Before the caravan park was built behind it, the little church stood solitary, the nearest house half a mile away among the trees. A perfect spot to assuage the soul. The church lies abandoned now, not because the congregation was daunted by walking a mile or two from nearby villages but, thanks to a storm in 1868, it was left partially ruined. Burials in the little graveyard continued, but a new church was built in Noss Mayo to serve the needs of the community.

The redundant Church of St Peter the Poor Fisherman dates back to Saxon times. At Parracombe on the edge of Exmoor, another redundant church, St Petrock's, is thought to have been the last church in Devon where hymns were accompanied by a band of musicians rather than an organ. There is even a pew where a piece of wood has been carved out to allow for the bow of the bass viol. Just like the little chapel at Revelstoke, St Petrock's Church stands outside the village it served. In the high Victorian period it was threatened with demolition, and owes its continued existence to a campaign led by John Ruskin. A new church was built in the centre of the village to serve the congregation.

Devon's most iconic redundant place of worship is the ruined Charles Church destroyed in the 1941 Plymouth Blitz. It was built exactly three centuries earlier. Despite Plymouth's staunch Parliamentarian stance during the English Civil War, the church was named after that troublesome monarch Charles I, perhaps in deference to the Puritan abhorrence of saints! The skeletal church walls have been left standing in memory of the 1,200 people who lost their lives in the Second World War bombing of Plymouth.

Bombs had direct hits on the cathedral and several churches in the county's spiritual capital, Exeter. The vicar of St Sidwell's Church risked his life to rescue the parish registers and silver from the vestry as the church blazed around him. But the most extraordinary ecclesiastical loss to the city and diocese happened long before the Second World War.

## Bishop Leofric's Curse

When Bishop Leofric left Crediton to become the first Bishop of Exeter in 1050, he brought his library with him. In this era before the printing press, every book had been copied by hand in a scriptorium. During the twenty years that followed, Leofric added to this collection, so that by 1072 a catalogue of Leofric's donations to the cathedral library included sixty-six titles. This was a valuable collection by the standards of the eleventh century. Bibliophiles today paste 'ex libris' plates into the front of treasured books to ensure their safe return. Bishop Leofric went a step further. In nine of the manuscripts to have survived from his library is a curse written in Latin and Old English:

> Bishop Leofric gave this book to the Church of St Peter the Apostle
> in Exeter for the use of his successors; if anyone bears it away from
> here he will be eternally cursed.

Despite the curse, all nine of these books were spirited away from Exeter. Some were to become the basis of one of the most famous libraries in the world: the Bodleian.

In fact Leofric's curse was mild by the standards of the day. It was a malediction as opposed to a benediction. It could have been worse; some surviving medieval manuscripts are inscribed with a similar curse, which threatens the borrower with excommunication.

The only book from Leofric's donation to have survived in the Exeter Cathedral Library is The Exeter Book: ironically no curse has been inscribed on its pages, but then the first page is missing. It is one of only four books of Anglo Saxon poetry to have survived into the third millennium, and The Exeter Book contains a third of that poetry. Of the 131 folios in the book, 75 of the poems are readable, but amongst these is evidence of the reverence with which books were regarded at the time The Exeter Book was written. In Riddle 24 the laborious tenth-century publishing process is expounded –

from stripping the skin from a newly-killed animal, to the repetitive process of dipping a quill pen in ink made from oak gall. As a result, most of these books were holy books, as only the Church could afford the labour required. In the tenth century, a book was tantamount to a shrine containing the word of God.

Tastes and fashions change, and the Old English vernacular in which The Exeter Book was written went out of favour. Latin was the language of choice, and as the English vernacular changed to what we now know as Middle English, the language of Chaucer, fewer and fewer people would have been able to read it. At one time in its life, this beautiful manuscript was not even included in the inventory of the cathedral library. In the catalogue of 1327, a total of 350 volumes are listed. At the end of the list, a fourteenth-century librarian dismissed the remainder of the books as 'Worn out by age, written in French, English or Latin, which are not assessed because they are accordingly of no value'.

One of these would have been The Exeter Book, which is referred to as 'an mycel Englisc boc be gehwilcum thingum on leothwisan geworht', in other words a large book on various subjects written in verse. The book bears the scars of the disdain with which it was regarded. As a large, bulky object which no one was able to read, held in a corner of the scriptorium, it came in handy as a chopping board. When monks were cutting up the skins to cover manuscripts, they used the 'mycel Englisc boc'. Glue stains on the front cover have soaked through several pages, and the back has been burnt. It was also a useful store for the gold and silver leaf, which the monks used to illuminate later manuscripts, and some pages are spotted with flecks of gold and silver.

Book-loving Bishop Leofric, born in 1016, established the first library at Exeter Cathedral. His life bridges the turbulent transition between Saxon and Norman rule, and he is said to have offered sanctuary to King Harold's mother after the Battle of Hastings. So the story goes, when William the Conqueror arrived to besiege the city of Exeter in 1067, Harold's mother was smuggled out of one gate, while Leofric greeted the storming Normans at another. He certainly managed to negotiate a peaceful truce with the new King of England.

Tucked inside one of the volumes to have survived from Leofric's collection, is a document that gives us some idea of the man's reputation. It states:

> A man of modest life and conversation who, when he proceeded to
> his see, went about his diocese studiously preaching the Word of God
> to the people committed to him and instructing the clergy in learning.

*This is believed to be the tomb of bibliophile Bishop Leofric.*

Leofric was obviously a practical man. Until 1050 the bishopric had been based in Crediton, at the time little more than a village. Devon was a constant target to Danish raiders, so Leofric wrote to the Pope asking if he could move his see to the walled city of Exeter, which would be safer. He was duly installed there by England's King Edward the Confessor and Queen Edith. Leofric and Edward had met in Bruges in 1039, and Leofric had been the King's priest earlier in his career. His see was set up at the existing monastery in Exeter. The remaining eight monks were moved to Westminster, so that the new bishop could set up home. But this erstwhile monastery had a mere half a dozen books. What the new bishop established was a reference library that he and his successors could consult on matters ecclesiastical and practical.

By the fifteenth century Exeter was an established seat of learning, and the growing cathedral library needed dedicated premises. In 1412 a reading room over the east cloister was converted into a library, and the books and manuscripts were so valuable that they were chained to the desks to prevent theft. By 1506 there were 625 volumes in the cathedral library, although not all of them were in the library building itself. Some 43 per cent of these were Bibles and service books, very few of which have survived. There were also law books, which were essential for diocesan administration, as well as history, astronomy and mathematics books, but no literature.

Today 135 volumes have survived from the medieval library used by Leofric and his successors. Among those that have been lost through the centuries are medieval encyclopaedias. These were not encyclopaedias in the modern sense, but rather a motley collection of knowledge divided into subject areas, and rarely sorted alphabetically. There are also known to have been medical reference books, which had been translated into Latin from Arabic. The rudimentary medical techniques described were probably acquired from the Moors, during their rule of Spain.

Records of the fate of some of Leofric's library have survived. The first known culprit was the dean-elect Gregory Dodds, who presented the Archbishop of Canterbury Matthew Parker with Leofric's Old English Gospel. This was a sweetener, so that the Archbishop would look favourably on his bid for promotion. Matthew Parker was a noted Anglo-Saxon scholar. But the main culprit was Thomas Bodley, born at a house on the corner of High Street and Gandy Street, Exeter, on 2 March 1545. He went on to use about eighty books from the cathedral library's collection to found one of the first public libraries in the world.

Thomas Bodley grew up in a world of religious division and persecution. As a toddler he and his family fled to Geneva to escape the persecution of Protestants when Queen Mary came to the throne. During his education abroad, Bodley developed a passion for books and learned ancient Greek, Hebrew and Latin. On his return at the age of thirteen he went up to Magdalen College, Oxford, later becoming the first lecturer in ancient Greek at Merton College. Thomas was a gifted linguist, and after a short time at Elizabeth I's court he became a diplomat charged with several secret missions to cement alliances with other Protestant princes. It was in 1596 that he hung up his diplomatic hat and offered to build a library for his old university. No doubt using his diplomatic skills, and the same powers of persuasion with which he had formed alliances on the continent, Thomas leaned on a cousin who was a canon at Exeter Cathedral. He persuaded him to part with a large proportion of the cathedral's collection to help set up the new Oxford library. But perhaps it was just as well. During the upheaval of the English Civil War (1642–51), the cathedral became part of the collateral damage. On

*A relic from the time of Bishop Leofric, St Martin's Church Exeter was
founded in 1065, the fabric is still largely Anglo-Saxon.*

the eve of the Civil War, the city of Exeter was split just as the nation was.
Many of the population were by nature Royalist, and none more so than the
clergy of Exeter Cathedral. But the city council was packed with puritans,
and gradually the Parliamentarian cause took over the city. The Dean and
Chapter were abolished. Eventually, the city found itself under attack from
all sides. But a huge Parliamentarian army under the Earl of Stamford was
on its way, and the Royalists decided to beat a retreat to Cornwall. When
Stamford arrived, those who were sympathetic to the King and his cause
were disarmed.

Stamford's men were religious extremists, the Taliban of their day.
Rampaging through the cathedral buildings, these Parliamentarian soldiers
smashed stained-glass windows and statues, and ripped apart the cathedral
organ. The cloisters, including the library room built in 1412, were destroyed,
and it was only thanks to the efforts of an Exeter doctor, Robert Vilvaine, that
any part of the library was saved. Tradition has it that books looted from the

library were sold on the streets. In other parts of Devon, Parliamentary forces certainly burned and destroyed libraries and collections in the hands of members of the clergy. Dr Vilvaine was horrified as the library room was torn apart and the books vandalised. He organised the removal of the surviving books to St John's Hospital, and managed to persuade the city council to let him rebuild a library. He chose the site of the dismantled Lady Chapel and cared for the remainder of the books with an assistant.

The last remnant of Bishop Leofric's library, The Exeter Book, is one of the greatest treasures in the county.

Four centuries later this treasure was under threat again as the nation prepared for yet another war. In August and September 1939 a special committee met to discuss the safekeeping of the 'mycel Englisc boc' and other priceless manuscripts. There was no suggestion that Exeter would be a target of German bombers, but precautions were taken nonetheless. It was stored for safekeeping throughout the Second World War, in a fire-proof box in a strong room at Feniton Court, Honiton, home of the Acland family.

At 1.36 on the morning of 4 May 1942 air-raid sirens sounded in Exeter. Luftwaffe bombers flew up the Exe estuary to bomb the city in what became known as the Baedeker raids, instigated by Hitler in revenge for the bombing of the ancient German town of Lubeck. The first bombs fell on Newtown, at 1.51. Exeter Central Library was the control centre for the city's civil defence teams. That night incendiary bombs rained down on the library roof and 80,000 books went up in smoke. In a separate fire at the Probate Registry, most of the 100,000 wills and inventories for the years prior to 1858 were destroyed.

In an apposite postscript to the story of Exeter Cathedral's lost medieval books, the Bodleian Library today, requires every new reader to sign the following pledge when they are given their reader's card.

I hereby undertake not to remove from the library, nor to mark, deface or injure in any way any volume, document or other object belonging to it or in its custody.

Bishop Leofric would have approved.

### The Tavistock Twenty

It is Monday, 3 March 1539. A group of strangers ride into a small western town. People watch from their doorways, silent, as the riders head for the town's main building. Their arrival is an event that affects the future of every citizen, and will change the face of Tavistock forever. The arrival of royal commissioner Dr John Tregonwell and his companions at Tavistock Abbey has been anticipated. News has already reached the monks of the results of Tregonwell's visits to the other major Devon monasteries at Plympton, Tor, Buckland and Buckfast: orchestrated, state-licensed vandalism, which has been recorded in history as the Dissolution of the Monasteries.

Three years earlier in far-off Lincolnshire, two abbots were executed for opposing the royal decision to end the rule of Rome, and seize the riches belonging to its monasteries and abbeys. Thomas Cromwell, mastermind of this campaign, had conducted a war of nerves ever since, picking off the smaller religious houses while their bigger brothers watched in fear. Tavistock's thirty-ninth – and last – abbot, John Peryn, gently but publicly expressed his opposition to the King's campaign against the monasteries, but despite the wealth and status of the abbey within the local community, opposition to this revolution was pointless.

Tregonwell and his companions were looking for evidence of sodomy, sex and scandal to justify their actions. The act of parliament that legitimized what became known as the Dissolution, made it clear what the authorities wanted:

> Possessions of such spiritual religious houses, now being spent, spoiled and wasted for increase and maintenance of sin, should be used and converted to better uses, and the unthrifty religious persons so spending the same to be compelled to reform their lives.

The religious community at Plympton Priory justified all their expectations; it was certainly 'spoiled'. In 1535 the churchwardens at the nearby village of Wembury were forced to put their grievances into writing. Despite paying Prior John Howe and his eighteen canons the considerable sum of £50 a year, many parishioners had not had the services of a priest. The churchwardens even included a list of those who had died without receiving the sacrament. To devout sixteenth-century minds this was tantamount to condemnation to purgatory. Another parish complained that the prior would not send anyone to bury the dead for less than 7d. Yet another parish did have the services of a priest, but only on a Sunday, and he said mass, matins and evensong before noon, and got home in time for his dinner! One kindly priest had ministered to a parish without wages for ten years – the prior had forbidden the tenants to pay.

So the sixteenth-century Church had indeed acquired a reputation as a corrupt and depraved institution, where monks and nuns behaved with impropriety. But all Tregonwell's men found to apparently justify their moves to make twenty Benedictine monks homeless and unemployed was a quarrel with the local vicar; letters written without the abbot's permission; the throwing of private dinner parties; and gossip with the lads over a pint of beer at the pub – Tavistock Abbey was not the den of depravity the riders were hoping for.

*The south tower of the abbot's lodging house, known as Betsy Grimbal's Tower.*

Abbot John Peryn and his monks gathered in the octagonal, carved-stone chapter house, to listen to the details of their redundancy package. The abbot was given a pension of £100 a year, less than the abbot at Plympton, but enough to live quite comfortably in Tavistock for the rest of his life. However, unlike his predecessors, when he died ten years later, he was not buried in clothes decorated with gold thread, his head enfolded in a hollowed-out pillow stone, silver penny on the mouth, the tools of his trade beside him ready to say Communion at the Resurrection.

Monks such as John Wele and John Peke were given a pension of two pounds a year, until they died or found another job. They had been used to a

*Remains of the cloister in the graveyard of St Eustace's Church.*

menu of mutton, game and mead, flushing toilets and running water, and the services of a washerwoman. Their disciplined but comfortable monastic lifestyle was at an end, as was the intellectual life enjoyed by the monks. The abbey was home to the first printing press in the South West, and only the seventh in England. Thanks to the Dissolution no book was printed in Devon for another half a century. Nearly a century later antiquarian Tristram Risdon recorded with regret what was completely lost. In his *Survey of Devon* he describes how the monks:

> ...by a laudable ordinance, had lectures read in the ancient Saxon tongue, and so continued to our grandsire's days, to preserve the antiquitie, laws, and histories formerly written in that language, from oblivion; a thing almost now come to pass.

Eleven abbey servants who had brewed beer, cooked food, and tended the cloister gardens, also had to find new jobs, and travellers looking for bed and breakfast were no longer able to stay at the abbey. Free medical attention and care of the elderly provided by the monasteries also vanished. Thus this sacking of the monastery affected the whole town – after all when hardship and hunger hit, the locals no longer had anywhere to turn for a free meal or a loaf of bread.

*The exterior wall and Still Tower Tavistock Abbey.*

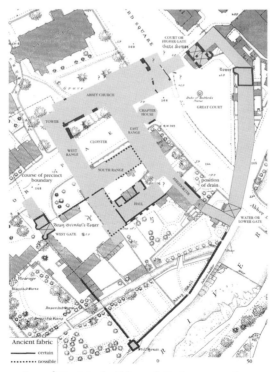

*Known remains of Tavistock Abbey plotted on a modern street map.*

The building that had been at the heart of the town for nearly five centuries was systematically destroyed: lead was stripped from the roof, opening the building to the elements; the shrine of St Rumon, the obscure Cornish patron saint of the abbey, was dismantled, its gold, silver and jewels prised off and added to the treasure in the Tower of London. The six huge bells, which had called hundreds of Benedictines from their beds to chant the liturgy, were sold. Churchwardens bought the choir stalls, candelabra and paving stones for the parish church of St Eustace just outside the abbey walls. It did not take long for the abbey, which was once said to have eclipsed every religious house in the county in the extent and magnificence of its buildings, to become a ruin.

In the immediate wake of the Dissolution, John Leland went on a mission to salvage surviving manuscripts from the monasteries. He described Tavistock Abbey's church as 126 yards long, so it was not surprising that when construction materials were needed in the town, it was an obvious source of stone. The ruined building was razed to the ground in 1670 to build a schoolhouse. Many of the other abbey ruins would have been recycled in this way. The abbey stood in a commanding position by the river so the site was also reused. In 1736 a house was built for the steward to the Duke of Bedford, subsequently replaced by the Bedford Arms Hotel. Today Bedford Parade and Bedford Square straddle much of the abbey site, but set back

*The plaque commemorating the successful defence of Exeter during the Great Western Rebellion.*

from the modern streetscape, as if retreating from the world, is the old refectory, used since 1691 as a Nonconformist chapel.

There is no record of people's reaction to the destruction of the abbey at Tavistock, but it was the hub of an estate valued at over a thousand pounds at the time of the Dissolution. Under the monks' leadership, farmers produced brilliant crops of wheat, rye and barley, on land that has since been considered of poor arable quality. Dairy herds grazed in the water meadows giving milk, butter and cheese; sheep provided wool; and in line with the Benedictine policy of riparianism, salmon and other fish were caught in weirs on the Tavy and Tamar rivers. The abbey was at the centre of economic and spiritual life in the Tavistock area.

In a remarkable display of forethought, the clever abbot made some attempt to cushion the tenants against the worst physical effects of this revolution. Instead of selling the lambswool at market in the autumn of 1538, the wool was woven into blankets and clothes for the abbey labourers. Leases were renewed, so that tenants should keep their homes for sixty years, or three lifetimes. Under their new landlord, the King's favourite John Russell, this was later cut to two lifetimes (although Russell is only known to have evicted one tenant). Although some rents were put up, Russell was canny enough to try not to antagonise the people of Tavistock.

There's no doubt that the authorities had anticipated trouble. In 1536, the year the act was passed to dissolve the monasteries, a Devon nobleman put quill to parchment. Sir Peter Edgcumbe, a former sheriff of the county, tried to diplomatically convey the mood of the county in a letter to Sir Thomas Cromwell:

> To advertysse yow that here ys moche comunycacyon and bruts that all abbays, pryorys and nunrys...shall be suppressyd nottwtstondynge hyt ys nott as yet in these parties uponly known the occacyon off suppression nor who shall take most benyffyte thereby nor to whate usse hyt shall rest at lengthe.

What was about to hit Devon and the rest of England, was a tsunami of change to the social order and fabric of life. Naturally people were worried, but it would take another change more pertinent to their daily lives before the people of Devon were roused. At some point during this period Tavistock must have earned itself a reputation for being a haven for potential troublemakers, because of what followed a decade later: in 1548, riots broke out in Cornwall just across the River Tamar. The riots were crushed and the leaders hanged, drawn and quartered. But one grisly quarter of one of the ringleaders was despatched to Tavistock as a warning. Its effect was short-lived.

The flame that lit the fuse of the rural population of Devon burst into life the following year. The loss of the monasteries had brought lower wages. But spiritual life still went on in the parish church, in the form of the familiar, if incomprehensible, Latin Mass. When the King dictated that the mass was no longer to be said in Latin, but in English, it was as if he had declared war on the people's souls. Whit Sunday 1549 was the day designated for this new revolution. That June morning the people of a village on the northern edge of Dartmoor were astounded when their vicar complied. Father Harper, priest of Sampford Courtenay, was known to be a sympathiser of the Catholic queen-in-waiting, Mary Tudor. The mob persuaded him to say the Latin Mass the following day. William Hellyon was one of the unlucky magistrates who tried to call the religious rebels to order but tempers were running high and he was hacked to death on the steps of the Church House. Breaking a law enforcing religious conformity was one thing, but murder of a magistrate was a different matter. The rebels had nothing to lose: this marked the start of the Western Rebellion of 1549.

Devonians joined rebels from Cornwall and marched on Exeter. Carrying a banner showing the five wounds of Christ, backed by a chorus of priests waving incense and chanting, the rebels tried to win the city with this religious propaganda. It did not work.

On the west gate by the old city wall, there is an ornate plaque commemorating the siege of the city by an army of some 10,000 peasants and a handful of like-minded gentry. Cornish tin miners attempted to tunnel under the city walls, but were foiled when a Devon miner, who happened to be in Exeter, dug a counter tunnel to their shaft. Every household then emptied a hogshead of water down into the tunnel, flooding the Cornish mine.

Historian John Vowell, who wrote under the alias John Hooker, was in Exeter, and here describes the dangers posed by rebel snipers during the siege:

> The rebels would keep themselves close in sundry houses in the sub-
> urbs near the walls and would so watch the garrets that if any within
> the city would look out at the garrets they with their shot did
> shrewdly gall and annoy as also killed divers of the city watching and
> warding within upon the walls which was the cause that some part
> of the suburbs was burned and some part beaten down and spoiled,
> and so drave the rebels out of these holes: besides this they had in

sundry places their great ordnances so set that in certain streets and places none could go but in peril and danger of their shot.

The people of Exeter were brought close to starvation by the siege. It was the new Lord of Tavistock and its estates, Lord John Russell, who was despatched to relieve the city, with an army largely made up of German, Italian and Spanish mercenaries. The farmers, miners and labourers of Devon and Cornwall were no match for such fighters. Russell ordered his troops to slit the throats of 900 rebel prisoners in ten minutes, after one battle. The foreign mercenaries, many of whom were Roman Catholics, were appalled. The city was eventually relieved, and Russell's troops hunted the rebels from battlefield to battlefield. Contemporary historians describe 700 slaughtered as the army chased the rebels up on to Dartmoor. Gallows all over the county were kept busy that year.

## The Cornworthy Seven

No monastic stone was left unturned by the Dissolution, however poor and unimportant. The estates of Tavistock Abbey may have been worth a thousand pounds when they were seized by the King, but Cornworthy Priory added a mere £69 to Treasury coffers. Nevertheless, it did not escape.

An imposing gatehouse is all that is left of the erstwhile home of the Cornworthy Seven. Its bulk stands in a field of lush green grass, on the outskirts of the village, home to crows that nest in crevices in the stone. This was once the smallest of the three Devon convents, and easy prey for the King's commissioners when they came to seize its land during the Dissolution.

Cornworthy Priory was a retreat, which offered seclusion to widows, unmarriageable daughters, and well-to-do ladies who wanted to get away from the stresses of medieval life. Inside its walls, the nuns read, did their embroidery, but unlike their holy brothers, did not produce illuminated manuscripts or copy religious works: writing was not considered a suitable accomplishment for women in these unenlightened times.

Cornworthy Priory was not an enclosed order. The seven Augustinian nuns indulged themselves by visiting friends and relatives, going to market, keeping pet dogs and even having guests! To defray their expenses, the priory took in young women of noble birth and educated them. In 1470 the seven- and ten-year-old daughters of Laurense Knyghte were taken in for 20d. Sometimes the convent acted as a nursing home, agreeing to look after people for the rest of their lives in exchange for a lump sum.

In 1521, the nuns' behaviour had become so scandalous, that the Bishop of Exeter was forced to write to them. He ticked them off for keeping boarders

*All that remains of the westernmost convent in England.*

without a special licence. While this may not seem at odds with their vocation to modern sensibilities, their other misdemeanours certainly seem to have been. The nuns were reprimanded for sleeping in separate rooms, rather than in a communal dormitory; instead of eating together they also ate separately, both contravening the idea of community expected of those taking holy orders. In line with the communal lifestyle adopted by Jesus and his apostles, they were also expected to give up their worldly goods. But the bishop charged them with owning private property. The Cornworthy Seven apparently failed to take their vocation at all seriously, chattering while listening to 'contemplative readings', and failing to say mass together in church. These aristocratic nuns were also fashion-conscious. They wore 'pompous apparel' and walked about indulging in worldly behaviour, although what exactly this meant has not survived in the records.

For all this the Cornworthy Seven got their comeuppance. In Cromwell's master plan for the Dissolution, the smallest religious houses were targeted first. There was no place for former nuns in the new Church of England. Taking their pets and private property, one assumes the Cornworthy Seven high-tailed it back to their families when they were evicted. What happened to them has been lost in the mists of time.

CHAPTER 2

# COWS, CONIES AND COMPOST

It was climate change that drove the subsistence farmers of Grimspound down from Dartmoor. This Bronze Age community left their walled farm enclosure and huts, just as later medieval farmers would abandon their long-houses. Many of Devon's Victorian farm workers left their tied cottages during the great agricultural depressions of the 1840s and 1870s. Some migrated to the towns, while others took ship for pastures new in Canada, New Zealand, Australia and America. In the latter part of the twentieth century, barns were no longer used to take in the harvest, but to take in visitors, as farmers struggled to diversify and maximise their assets.

Devon's farming practices, some regarded by outsiders as quaint even in the eighteenth and nineteenth centuries, disappeared. The Red Rubies, North Devon's famously hardy native breed, had been used as draught oxen for the plough for centuries. But the milk and meat produced had also made them favourites in the colonies. In 1627 a bull and two heifers were exported to the New World, and the first corned beef was produced from Devon cattle by William Pynchon of Massachusetts in the nineteenth century. In the 1800s a herd of Red Rubies was started in Tasmania by William Kent, and their ability to thrive in extremes of climate has led to herds in South Africa, Australia, and Brazil – where there are more pure-bred Devons than in any other country. Exports to Brazil even continued during the Second World War, and one top-class bull was lost when his ship was torpedoed by a German submarine in 1940.

Francis Quartly was one of the Devon farmers who built the fame and reputation of the Red Devons nationally. In 1796 he walked his best cattle from Molland to Bath where they won a silver cup. But the animals were so battered by the long journey that he refused to repeat the experience. The Quartly family built the reputation and pedigree of their herd, between 1703 and 1890, helped by the old Devon legal practice of awarding leases to tenants for three lives or 99 years. The stability of tenure, which this gave Devon tenant farmers, meant they could invest in the future.

The Devon Reds and their counterparts in the South Hams are today a rare sight on the lush Devon pastures, and their meat demands a premium. The red has been replaced by the ubiquitous black and white of the Friesian and other modern favourites. Many farmers have given up cattle altogether, turning to cauliflowers or caravans to provide an income from the land.

## Rabbit Warrening

The Bayeux tapestry depicts the Norman catering corps carrying lop-eared rabbits in a basket as they step on to English shores. Every army must be fed, and the Normans were no exception; they brought vital supplies with them,

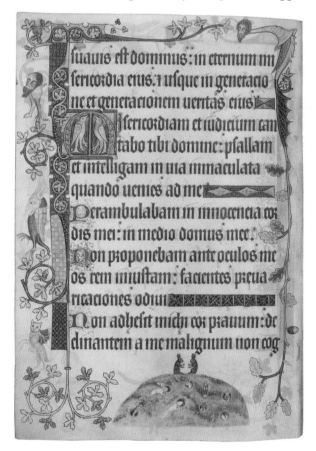

*Fourteenth century boxing rabbits on top of a warren, as depicted in Queen Mary's Psalter.*

and introduced the ancient practice of rabbit warrening to England.

The lowly rabbit was originally an immigrant from Spain. As the Roman Empire covered the continental map with imperial purple, so the conquerors tasted and adopted local delicacies. So by the time of the Norman conquest, rabbits were farmed in France.

The rabbits that feature in the Bayeux tapestry were not the first of their kind to be seen on British soil. Recent archaeological digs have unearthed the butchered bones of rabbits in layers dating from the second or third century AD, during the height of the Roman occupation. These sets of bones have been identified as those of the somewhat smaller Spanish variety: so far there has been no evidence that they were farmed in England at such an early date. That said, it is thought that, prior to the Ice Age, the rabbit was a native.

Most of the earliest documentary references to rabbit farming have a connection with Devon. Islands were a popular location for rabbit warrens in the Middle Ages, as predators were easier to control and the rabbits could not escape. The earliest surviving document records that a rabbit warren on Drake's Island in Plymouth Sound was given to Plympton Priory in 1135. Rabbits were also farmed on Lundy as early as 1183, when the tenant of the time was given permission to take fifty conies a year from the warren: until the eighteenth century a distinction was made between 'rabbits' which were the young, and 'conies' which were the adults. The earliest known warren on Dartmoor is that at Trowlesworthy, which is surrounded by water on three sides, and is almost an island. This is known to have been used until at least 1272.

Henry I, whose reign covered the first three decades of the twelfth century, was the only English-born son of William the Conqueror. He was keen to encourage the growth of rabbit farming, as the beasts were in demand for their fur and meat. He authorised the Abbot of Tavistock to maintain warrens, one of which was in Dolvin Wood, south-east of Tavistock. Within this enclosure, on the slope of Deerpark Hill, was a small house called 'le lodge', in which the warrener would have lived. The vast estates of Tavistock Abbey also included the Scilly Isles, where a satellite community of monks based at the priory on Tresco managed the land. In 1176 letters went back and forth between Tavistock and Tresco in a dispute about rabbits. The constable of the Scilly Isles was under the mistaken impression that he did not have to pay the abbey tax on rabbits taken from the island warren: he was probably being disingenuous, as rabbits were a noted luxury. The Bishop of Exeter had to intervene and threaten excommunication, before the constable relented. Over the sea he travelled, and upriver to Tavistock, to take an oath before the altar of St Rumon, that the abbey would receive all the rabbits due.

These early references reveal what prized beasts rabbits were – after all a threat of excommunication was not made lightly. Rabbit meat featured on all the best menus. In one feast during the reign of William the Conqueror, the King and his retinue consumed a thousand rabbits. In 1240, rabbits were the highlight of Christmas dinner at the court of Henry III. Whereas the common coney later came to be regarded as a meal for poor agricultural labourers, medieval rabbits were a rare and expensive delicacy, which cost four or five times as much as a chicken. In the thirteenth century, a rabbit was worth more than a day's wages. Demand outstripped supply, so it is hardly surprising that medieval monarchs encouraged the spread of warrening.

A fourteenth-century illustration in Queen Mary's Psalter shows two women catching rabbits at a warren. On one side is the wimple-clad ferret handler, pushing the ferret into a burrow entrance. On the other side of the mound, a woman holds a net over the warren exit. It is almost like a posed publicity picture, showing the ladies of the household engaged in an elite sport. For just as water features and decking became fashionable garden accessories in the late twentieth century, so a rabbit warren was the fashionable garden feature for gentry on their estates from the late Middle Ages, and even on into the seventeenth century.

Dartmoor is dotted with what archaeologists refer to as 'pillow mounds', in which rabbits were molly-coddled. These artificial burrows were constructed from a heap of stones and covered with earth. A trench was dug round the mound to improve drainage, as rabbits prefer to live in well-drained grassy heathland and coastal dunes. Excavations of pillow mounds have revealed that inside is a series of rooms, often supported by a network of stones. The loose soil and good drainage encouraged the rabbit population to remain at home rather than roam further afield. The mounds themselves are more reminiscent of a bolster than a pillow: long rectangular lumps, about a metre above ground level, and from 6 to 150 metres long. These warrens were built at 90 degrees to the contours on sloping ground, again to encourage drainage: young rabbits are very prone to drowning.

On Dartmoor, where warrening survived into the early twentieth century, warreners covered the top of the mounds with peat turves cut from the enclosing ditch. The warrens on Dartmoor are often set in fields bounded by stone walls, designed to prevent attack by predators and escape by the rabbits. In the kennel field next door lived the warrener's dogs. Before the era of shotguns the warrener deterred predators with ingenious traps and once these stoats, weasels or foxes were captured, he would release them to be finished off by the waiting dogs.

Rabbits – fed, watered, and protected by man – soon multiplied. In 1555, the Swiss naturalist, Conrad Gesner, wrote: 'There are few countries wherein coneys do not breed, but the most plenty of all is in England'.

These Spanish immigrants adapted to our cooler climate so well that by the end of the seventeenth century it was estimated that a million were kept in England. These were not only the common brown coney, but the more desirable silver-grey; and black, for rabbits were also farmed for their fur. Their skins were a valuable part of English export trade particularly in the sixteenth century.

Warrens grew larger and the animals' diet was supplemented with winter feed of bracken, gorse and turnips.

In one extraordinary case in the Plym Valley, a tin-mining lease for the Bottle Hill Mine stipulated that the miners had to cater for the needs of the rabbits during their exploration. In the same way that road developers have had to incorporate badger tunnels under road developments, the miners had to lay granite slabs across the leat that they constructed for the mine.

It was the agricultural revolution of the eighteenth century that brought a halt to widespread commercial rabbit farming. New technology such as Jethro Tull's famous seed drill and the genetic engineering of sheep and cattle to produce a higher meat yield, meant that landowners had more profitable ways of using marginal land to produce food. By the end of the eighteenth century the number of warrens was in decline. But the high moorland of Dartmoor was not even marginal farmland. Many landowners had imported manure, lime and other soil improvers to turn the thin peaty soil into a fertile loam. A variety of crops had been tried over the years, with little success. Rabbits, on the other hand, were an ideal 'crop'.

A stone post with the date 1807 survives to record part of the boundary of Hentor Warren. Boundaries and warren walls were sometimes built from the remains of hut circles or ancient field boundaries, so are not always easy to differentiate. But all over the moor – if you know where to look – it is possible to find stones with initials carved into them. Documentary or physical evidence of warrening survives at Willing Walls, Trowlesworthy, Ditsworthy, Legistor, Sheepstor, Vighill and Huntingdon Warrens. Largest of all is Headland Warren, an enclosure of 600 acres, near the Warren House Inn. Here rabbits were kept in small fields thickly planted with gorse, which gave the animals shelter above ground without the need to burrow. In severe winters and heavy snow, warreners would supplement the rabbits' diet with hay.

The Georgian travel writer and country parson, Reverend John Swete, was on his way from Chagford in 1797 when he passed another Dartmoor warren:

> On my approach to the turnpike I found myself surrounded by innu-
> merable Rabbits, and recognizing a house or two by the way side dis-
> cover'd that I was at Mead's Warren. To it there was no fence but a
> few stones piled on one another, and ranged in a certain line, evi-
> dently serving to ascertain its limits than to preclude the Rabbits from
> roving: indeed on the dry hill beyond this barrier or boundary they
> appeared to me to be as numerous, as they were within the restricted
> line... Nothing could well be more rugged than this spot.

One of the main tasks of a warrener was to keep down the vermin population.
Foxes were among the predators, but the stoat was the most serious threat.
Remains of many elaborate stone traps have survived. These were set in runs
established by the vermin, and once the prey had triggered a pressure plate,
the slate doors dropped. Drystone walls on the moor sometimes contain the
distinctive grooved stones that formed parts of these traps.

With the wider use of the gun in the eighteenth century, warreners built
themselves vermin houses. Remains of these rudimentary stone hides can be
seen at Trowlesworthy, Legistor and Hentor. From their vantage point
among the rocks, the warreners would pick off stoats and foxes during the
breeding season in late spring. Similarly the warreners built small stone-
lined cool houses covered with turf, which acted as rudimentary fridges.

In a bid to make their businesses more profitable, rabbit keepers looked to
completely artificial farming methods. They dug pits six or seven feet deep, and
reinforced the walls so that rabbits could make burrows in them. These pits were
covered with a lid, made of wood, oiled sailcloth or oilcloth, to keep the rain out,
and to stop the animals from escaping. Lids were lifted during fine weather.

As the industry at home declined, so imports flooded in from the Low
Countries and the new colony of Australia. The first rabbit fur arrived from
Australia in 1869, but soon our colonial cousins were sending carcasses and
eventually tinned rabbit. In 1889 Australia shipped over £350,000 worth of
skins, and this figure had doubled by 1903. The rabbit was no longer a luxury,
and it was the poor who wore rabbit-fur hats.

With these foreign imports came a resurgence of interest in rabbit farming, and a spate of manuals on the subject. Titles such as *Rabbits for Profit*,
and *The Wild Rabbit in a New Aspect*, or *Rabbit Warrens That Pay*, spoke
enthusiastically of the profits that could be made. In 1896 one rabbit devotee,
John Simpson, wrote:

At the most moderate estimate, I am sure that every acre of any moderately good estate, wood or fields, would produce annually at least fifty good rabbits, and leave ample stock.

Mr Morant, author of *Rabbits as Food Supply* and *How to Fold Them In Our Poor Pastures*, was even more enraptured when he wrote in 1884:

A cow consumes daily as much grass as will 150 rabbits. The rabbits will in 12 weeks realise 1s 6d (7½p), £11 5s 0d (£11.25), whereas the produce from a cow will certainly not amount to £6.

It was during this new rush of optimism that Wistman's Wood Warren was set up on Dartmoor in the 1890s. But this optimism was misplaced and mistimed. Warrens were becoming more expensive to run: a warrener had to be employed full time. The wild rabbit population of escapees offered an alternative supply of rabbit meat and fur, without overheads. Parliament had given tenant farmers the right to trap and shoot rabbits on their land, and to sell them for meat in the Ground Game Act of 1880. For the tenant farmer it was a good way to supplement his income. The rabbit warrens were doomed.

However, a few rabbits continued to be kept for meat and fur in the back gardens of homes in Devon. For example the Burgoyne family, who lived in a Victorian house in Veales Road in Kingsbridge, kept both rabbits and hares for meat in the closing years of the nineteenth century.

But it was the virus myxomatosis, which finally killed a farming method that had been practised in Devon for a thousand years. The virus had first been identified in 1896, in laboratory rabbits in Uruguay, where it was found not to be lethal to the indigenous rabbit population. It was hailed as a potential solution to the problem of rabbits which had proliferated in Britain and particularly in Australia, where it led to the rabbit-proof fence that was put up across the continent. After experiments with the virus, an epidemic of myxomatosis spread across Australia in 1950–51. A retired doctor near Paris introduced it to control the rabbits on his estate in the summer of 1952, and within nine months it had arrived in Kent. The rabbit population has never fully recovered and currently stands at about half the 1952 level. Today the practice of rabbit warrening survives in name alone.

## Plague and Progress

The congregation of St Andrews Church, Halberton, settled into their seats as their vicar, Edward Girdlestone, made his way to the pulpit to deliver his weekly sermon. As they had done regularly in this year of our Lord 1866, they had prayed fervently for deliverance from the plague that was sweeping through the country: cholera. There had even been two deaths in the little North Devon port of Appledore, where it had probably been brought in by ship from Bristol. But the farmers in the congregation were also praying for deliverance from an agricultural plague – a plague far worse even than foot- and-mouth disease. This was the deadly cattle plague or rinderpest. Little did they know that their vicar, Edward Girdlestone, was also preoccupied with the bovine plague, but for a very different reason. The words of his sermon would fall on stony ground in Halberton, but would germinate into radical changes that would ultimately alter the lives of agricultural labourers forever.

The heyday of Devon's agriculture had been in the sixteeenth and seventeenth centuries when the small- and medium-sized farms so typical of the county found a ready market for produce in the naval ports. But by the early nineteenth century, when Charles Vancouver published his *General View of the Agriculture of the County of Devon*, Devon's agricultural labourers had acquired something of a reputation.

> The reaping and harvesting of the wheat is attended with so heavy expense, and with practises of so disorderly a nature, as to call for the strongest mark of disapprobation, and their immediate discontinuance, or at least a modification of their pastime after the labours of the day. The wheat being ready to cut down, and amounting to 10 to 20 acres, notice is given in the neighbourhood, that a reaping is to be performed on a particular day, when as the farmer may be more or less liked in the village, on the morning of the day appointed, a gang consisting of an indefinite number of men and women, assemble at the field, and the reaping commences after breakfast, which is seldom over till between eight and nine o'clock. This company is open for additional hands to drop in at any time before the twelfth hour, to partake of the frolic of the day.

What Vancouver omits to tell his readers is that Devon agricultural labourers were customarily paid a chunk of their wages in farm cider. This notoriously strong brew fuelled the 'frolics'.

> By eleven or twelve o'clock the ale or cider has so much warmed

and elevated their spirits, that their noisy jokes and ribaldry are heard to a considerable distance, and often serves to draw auxiliary force within the accustomed time. The dinner consisting of the best meat and vegetables, is carried into the field between twelve and one o'clock: this is distributed with copious draughts of ale and cider; and by two o'clock the pastime of cutting and binding the wheat is resumed, and continued without other interruption than the squabbles of the party, until about five o'clock, when what is called the drinkings are taken into the field.

A picnic in the shade of a tree followed, after which the harvest was completed, and the labourers trooped off to the farmhouse for a harvest supper until the early hours of the morning. Vancouver may have disapproved of what he witnessed, but his description reflects a certain warmth, as he describes the good humour accompanying the highlight of the agricultural year.

Vancouver was writing during the long years of war with France, and the blockade that accompanied it had given farmers a ready market. But with peace came imports of poultry, cheese, butter and corn from Normandy, and small farmers were unable to weather the economic depression that followed. The plight of the farm labourer grew correspondingly worse – so much so that many families from agricultural areas took ship for a new life in the colonies.

When Canon Edward Girdlestone became vicar of Halberton in 1862, he had come from a parish in Lancashire. He was shocked at the poverty of Devon's agricultural labourers by comparison with those in Lancashire, and became their champion. In an article for *Fraser's Magazine* called 'Landowners, Land and Those who Till It', he contended that landowners treated their labourers as slaves.

In their eyes the labourer is a serf, and ought to remain a serf. He must be content with a cottage, in comparison of which a barn or a stable is a palace, wages barely enough when he is at work every day and all day long to keep body and soul together...with nothing in prospect but parish pay and the union.

Canon Girdlestone was vicar of a parish of 8,000 acres, in which there were some sixty farms. He was shocked not only at the living conditions of these farm labourers, but at their pay. Agricultural wages in Devon were lower than anywhere else in the country, standing at seven or eight shillings a week. Girdlestone estimated that a labourer needed a minimum wage of twelve shillings a week.

In May 1865 the entire agricultural community of Britain was paralysed by the news that the dreaded rinderpest had entered the country. This disease, which kills 90 per cent of infected cattle, was unknown in Britain until 1714. When it hit the country again in 1745, the epidemic lasted for ten years. On 25 May 1865, an infected cargo of live animals from Asiatic Russia docked in Hull and was sent by train to the London markets. Within twenty-four hours the symptoms of cattle plague were spotted: high fever, red patches round the eyes, a discharge from the eyes, nose and mouth, frothy saliva, and constipation followed by diarrhoea. Infected animals were dead within six to ten days. By the time the disease was diagnosed, the animals had been sold to farmers all over the country. By August the first case had appeared in Devon and an exclusion zone was in force. Farming areas near ports were particularly vulnerable. In September, a consignment of cattle arrived to provision HMS *Britannia* at Dartmouth, and was found to be infected. One North Devon farmer who bought an infected calf sent it to his brother's farm when symptoms developed. But when the brother tried to get rid of the animal at market, officials became suspicious. Restrictions were placed on the movement of cattle, and inevitably farms began to become overcrowded as farmers were unable to make room for new stock. This is a picture all too familiar from the outbreak of foot-and-mouth disease that devastated Devon in 2001.

It is no wonder therefore that the farmers of Halberton were preoccupied with cattle plague as they sat in church on that Sunday in 1866. The disease had not spread to the parish, but that did not stop Canon Girdlestone from using the bovine plague to grab their attention. The farmers' Sunday reverie was shattered as the vicar told them that cattle plague was a visitation from God, because they treated their farm labourers worse than their cattle. As he lambasted them about pokey, damp cottages and starvation wages, the farmers' fury grew. After the service they decided to desert the Church of England for the Wesleyan Chapel. But when they arrived to worship with the Methodists the following Sunday, the Methodist minister told them to get back to their own church. So the farmers stayed away from church altogether, even withholding their portion of the church maintenance fund. One of the county's newspapers, *Trewman's Flying Post*, described the farmers as 'at daggers drawn'.

Their campaigning vicar was unmoved. In another sermon a few months later, on 18 September 1866, he scoffed at the farmers' retaliation 'on God's minister for some supposed offence':

...because taking Holy Scripture for his guide, he boldly denounced the sin, which of all others seems to have most natural connexion [sic] with a Cattle Plague: a determined resistance to any improvement in the position of the labourer and his family.

Girdlestone had the sermon printed and sent round to every household in the village so they could read the logic of his arguments.

It requires but a small knowledge of the elements of political economy to be aware that the better paid, clothed, housed, educated, and generally tended the labourer is, the more both physically and morally, he is valuable to his employer. He is stronger, healthier, more intelligent, honest, industrious, provident, thriving, independent, in a word, in all respects a better and more useful servant. The horse, the cow, the sheep, nay, every kind of brute, it is well known, amply repays the care which is taken of them. Ten thousand times more does the human servant. And while neglect of the beast which perish is comparatively a small sin, neglect of the being who is destined to live forever, and for whom Christ died is a sin for which no one surely, with his eyes open, would wish to be responsible.

Girdlestone and his family were ostracised by landowners and farmers, and he was the subject of anonymous poison-pen letters in the local papers. Taking up his own pen, the vicar began campaigning through the letter pages of *The Times*. In October 1866 he wrote:

In one family, the man – a young strong, industrious fellow – has 8s. a week if the weather be fine, from 1s.11d. is deducted for rent. So that he brings home never more than 6s.1d. for food, clothing, and fuel for his family, consisting of a wife, three young children, and a fourth on the way. This is not by any means an uncommon case. In many instances deduction is made not only for rent but for grist (corn that is ground for flour) at the farmer's price, so that the labourer sometimes does not carry home more than 3s.6d. a week in coin. I know of two strong lads in one family, aged respectively 16 and 14, who receive from the farmer who employs them, the one 3s.9d., the other 2s.6d a week; and the farmer, reckoning these miserable earnings of the two lads together with the father's wages, stated in a public paper that he gave his labourers 14s a week. In some cases the labourers are not allowed to keep pigs, lest they should steal food for them from their masters, which I verily believe they are far too honest under any circumstances to do.

Agricultural work was tough, physical labour with the attendant risk of injury. There was, of course, no sick pay or disability benefit, and few Devon farmers helped in the event of sickness or accident. Canon Girdlestone quoted an example in the same letter to *The Times*:

> A shepherd near me broke his ribs in his master's service. Owing to his being shepherd, he had his house rent-free, in addition to his 8s. wages. But during his illness his rent was stopped out of his son's wages.

Through contacts in his previous parish in Lancashire, Girdlestone started a migration scheme to relocate Devon farm workers to the north, where wages and conditions were far better than they were in Devon. A carter who had relocated to Bolton with his wife and family wrote to the vicar, who appended the letter to one of his own to *The Times*. The carter had been earning 8s. a week, plus a pint and a half of cider in Devon. His wages had risen to 18s. a week in Lancashire:

> We got to Bolton at 11 o'clock quite right, and we have got a comfortable house close to foundry, and we hope out of gratitude to your honour to prove ourselves worthy to fill the situation your honour have been so kind to obtain for us, thinking that the best way to thank your honour. We beg leave to say, from what we have seen of Bolton already, we never wish to see Devonshire more.

By the time he left Halberton in 1872, Girdlestone had been instrumental in organising the migration of 600 farm labourers and their families from Devon to the north-west of England. He was dubbed the Agricultural Workers' Friend, campaigning for the payment of wages in cider or other alcohol to be outlawed. Through his letters to *The Times* he was also the catalyst for the new Agricultural Workers' Union, founded in 1872 by Joseph Arch.

When Edward Girdlestone preached his last Devon sermon in June 1872, he was still campaigning for local farmers to raise labourers' wages. But the farming hierarchy had dug in their heels, knowing that the elderly vicar would not remain in the parish forever. His last service was attended by a journalist from *Trewman's Flying Post* who reported the Canon's jokey final comment to his detractors:

There were in the neighbourhood a few farmers and gentlemen, and he might, he thought, add, a few magistrates, who if they could get hold of the bell ropes, would ring a merry peal on the bells at his departure.

Girdlestone carried on campaigning from his new parish in Gloucestershire, where he died twelve years later. The Halberton farmers, meanwhile, were forced to increase wages by 50 per cent, thanks to the farm labourers' new trade union. By 1880 the village school had doubled in size: farm labourers could now afford an education for their children.

## Lime

Shimmering plumes of heat rose from granite buildings all over Devon for hundreds of years. To one anonymous homeless man in Barnstaple town centre in 1840, the lure of such warmth was too much to resist. Hungry and destitute he snuggled up to the heat thrown out by the lime kiln in the town square. As the vagrant grew drowsy, and slipped into unconsciousness, he was unaware that he would not see the dawn. In the morning, as the people of Barnstaple bustled about their early morning business, a foreign and unsettling odour hung in the air: the smell of roasted human flesh.

Romantic ruins on estuaries and rivers are all that remain of the hundreds of lime kilns that helped improve the county's acid soils. For hundreds of years cargoes of limestone were brought upriver and deposited on the shore. This was the raw material for one of the most dangerous industries of the region's past. County roads were jammed with carts and packhorses taking lime inland. The slow march of Exeter's limestone wagons forced the city fathers to take a radical step. Traffic jams plagued the area near the city's old North Gate, while as many as twenty pairs of horse-drawn carts negotiated the Pit – a steep decline and incline – as they travelled to and from the lime-kilns in St Leonards. In 1834, the city splashed out £3,500 on the Iron Bridge, which crossed the Pit.

Devon gent, Tristram Risdon, was impressed by the end result of this agricultural improvement, which he noted in his survey of the county at the end of the sixteenth century:

Of late, a new invention has sprung up, and been practised, by burning lyme, and incorporating it for a season with earth, and then spread upon the arable land, hath produced a plentiful increase of all sorts of grain amongst us, where formerly such never grew in any living man's memory.

There's no record of the discovery of the benefits of lime, but as the population increased after Risdon's time, so did the supply of food. The industry was considered so important that wagons carrying lime were exempt from tolls.

By 1829, when the Reverend Thomas Moore published his *History of Devonshire from The Earliest Period to the Present*, lime kilns had popped up on every creek and inlet:

> So extensive is the use of lime as a manure in Devonshire, that not only are prodigious quantities raised from limestone and marble rock in various parts of the county, but there are at least twenty kilns between Weare Giffard and the mouth of Bideford harbour, for the purpose of importing lime from Wales, and three or four scattered round the bay. There is indeed scarcely an inlet or creek, either on the northern or southern coast of the county that is not supplied with a lime kiln; and when the stone is not found in the vicinity, vessels are employed to convey it from the lime rock districts. The immense quarries at Oreston near Plymouth and the adjacent ports, supply the kilns on the whole range of the Tamar,

*Exeter's iron bridge, built to ease traffic congestion caused by limestone wagons.*

Tavy and St Germains rivers, as well as some other districts. The beautiful cliffs at Berryhead in Torbay, and at Babbicombe, furnish those on the Teign, the Exe, and the adjoining coast.

Nearly the whole of the south-western portion of Devon abounds with lime works. Those of Chudleigh, especially, and its vicinity are numerous, and the rocks have long been celebrated, not only for their beauty but the excellence of the lime which they supply, which is remarkable for its extreme whiteness. In the centre, and towards the northern districts of the county, little lime-rock is found; and the quarries in that direction produce a darker kind of lime, which is not so adapted to every kind of soil. The principal of these quarries are at Drewsteignton and South Tawton and the large excavations near the present limeworks of the latter place show that works of this kind have been carried on there for a great length of time.

In line with the 'romantic' ideas of his age, Moore was concerned by the destruction of the countryside for profit:

The artist and man of taste may possibly turn from works of this kind with something like disgust, lamenting that the ruthless hand of commerce is permitted, with provoking concern, to demolish by piece-meal the grand and magnificent ornaments of the coast, and that the owners of these splendid scenes, with the sordid love of gain absorbing all other considerations, are literally retailing the picturesque and beautiful by weight and measure; whilst he for needs of industry and productive labour will observe only in such operations a rich increase of agricultural produce, and consequently a great benefit.

But the destruction of Devon's natural beauty was not the only criticism levelled at this industrial process. There was conflict in the maritime fraternity, regarding the boats carrying limestone up the Taw and Torridge estuaries in North Devon, as outlined in this complaint from the man working as a Bristol Channel pilot:

The promiscuous deposit of limestone imported from Wales which is dropped in the most reckless way along the foreshores of both rivers [Taw and Torridge] and projects into the navigable channels... these...have been the cause of many accidents.

Lime was also used to make building mortar, as limewash for walls, and for

*Not a castle but a lime kiln, high above the shore at Sidmouth.*

sealing the glass in leaded lights.

Cornish parson, Richard Polwhele, visited the lime quarries at Bishop's Nympton in the late eighteenth century. What he saw was an eyesore, which the locals had nicknamed the Burning Mountains. He described the sight in his *History of Devonshire*:

> A few years since, when I visited this neighbourhood, there were two heaps of rubbish thrown up to a great height from one of the lime-quarries, that were then actually burning, and had been burning for more than a year before I visited this spot. The larger heap covered more than an acre of ground, and the other nearly the same space. The heaps, I was told, were not visibly reduced. The farmers had used the white ashes on these heaps for manure; and this dressing, I was told, had produced a rapid vegetation, fertilizing the ground far more than common lime would.

Lime was normally burnt in kilns, built into steep banks on the riverside, and the ruins of these bottle-shaped hearths still line creeks and inlets. The Reverend Swete kept a detailed account, illustrated by watercolours, of his journeys throughout Devon in 1797. Unfortunately the curious lime kiln which he passed on the western side of the bridge at Aveton Gifford, has not survived:

> To this bridge the tide reaches, flowing from the mouth of the River

about four miles and bringing with it small barges, used in the conveyance of Lime stone. A kiln for calcining this Marble rises close upon the hither extremity of the bridge and that it might appear ornamental from a Villa a little below, hath been decorated at its angles by four turrets: the converting [of] Houses of a plain simple construction into Castles with terrific battlements, and lime kilns in a marsh into Priories or Abbies is not a difficult matter, but doth it not convey to the Spectator a depravation [sic] of taste? – where there is no consistency there can be no true taste! And there is little if any here I think must strike one at the first glance: for it will be hardly possible for a Person to conceive that the one had ever been a 'place of defence' or the other appointed to Religious Uses – But of this Gentleman, the constructor of these edifices, cannot be allowed any pretensions to Architectural taste, he will yet be entitled to the approbation of the community for the considerable improvements he hath made in the Agricultural line: I learnt that Mr Savery the Proprietor who is an atorney at Modbury, had (since his purchase of the estate, not many years since) trebled its worth – and this He hath chiefly effected by raising embankments so as to preclude all incroachment [sic] of the tide, over his marshes – it matters little what the taste of such a Man is: his deserts are of higher import, and his name ought to be enrolled among those, who have by their merits obtained the commendation of their country.

Mr Savery's community spirit saved him from the worst lashings of the vicar's tongue! While the crenellated lime kiln at Aveton Gifford may not have survived, a similarly fanciful kiln has survived on the Torridge river close to the stone bridge at Weare Giffard. This collection of kilns, which looks like some medieval fortification, has given its name to the hamlet next door, Annery Kilns. The remains of some eight ovens are still visible, as is the ramp up which the limestone was brought from barges on the river.

Another eighteenth-century writer, William Marshall, who was so often scathing of things Devonian, was almost complimentary when he commented in his book *The Rural Economy of the West of England* that Devon's lime kilns were:

Large and of expensive construction; some of them costing not less than thirty or forty pounds each. But their duration is in proportion: one which has been built thirty years is still firm and sound on the outside. The walls are of extraordinary thickness; wide enough on the

*Part of the complex of furnaces built to burn lime at Annery Kilns. Wagons brought lime from the river up the ramp to the right.*

top, for horses to pass round the kiln and deliver the stone. The body or inside of the Devonshire kiln is not well formed. The sides are too straight; the cavity is not sufficiently egg-shaped – is too conical – too narrow in the middle, the contents, of course, hard – do not settle down freely and evenly – as they do in a well shaped kiln.

On the North Devon coast at Appledore, records show that it was women who unloaded limestone from the boats. Their wages were so low and the conditions so harsh that in 1843 they went on strike for higher wages, and won. But the job of unloading limestone was a doddle compared with that of the furnace workers. Surprisingly records show that a few of these were also women.

Limestone was broken into lumps half the size of a brick and fed in through an opening in the top, until there was a ten-inch layer. A five-inch layer of coal formed the next layer and so on until the kiln was filled. A brushwood fire was built in the hearth, which widened out underneath, and the fire was lit. As the coal and lime layers caught fire, reaching a temperature of 1,100°C, carbon-monoxide fumes engulfed the furnace worker. Nowadays this gas is often associated with student flats equipped with poorly ventilated gas fires. The effects were the same: inhalation of the fumes led to drowsiness, paralysis and eventual suffocation.

These kilns would stay lit for months on end, and they posed a hazard to the unwary. The unfortunate tramp whose roasted body was discovered at the kiln in Barnstaple's town square was just one of the recorded casualties. In another

*Remains of a lime kiln converted into an ice cream parlour.*

incident two boys were burnt to death at a lime kiln near Chittlehampton.

Aside from the dangers of the furnace itself, the lime burner had to rake out the highly volatile end product, quicklime, before sprinkling it with water to produce slaked lime. Every two tons of limestone produced one ton of quicklime, which was added to the soil at three tons per acre. William Marshall watched farm labourers as they spread lime on raised ridges in the fields. Each worker began:

> ...at one end of the ridge; and with a hack or single-handed mattack, hacks down the heap; mixing the whole intimately, by beating it with the side of the hack; raising it up again with the point; and again hitting it sideways, with a flight and dexterity to be acquired only by practice. When the two ingredients are sufficiently blended, the compost is thrown back with a shovel, and formed into a roof-like heap; still continuing to burst any lumps the hack has missed, with the back of the shovel, and to mingle the parts as evenly as possible.

The last recorded use of a lime kiln was in the 1960s, but as the industry waned the coastal extraction points for the lime were simply abandoned and the lime kilns gradually fell into disuse. Despite, or perhaps because, of their location, some lime kilns have been converted for new use; for example, a kiln on the banks of the ria near Kingsbridge, has been converted into a house.

# CHAPTER 3

# SEA CHANGES

In 1588 the ships of the Spanish Armada, harried less by Sir Francis Drake and rather more by dreadful weather, were scattered along the English coast. The hospital ship *San Pedro* was among them, coming to a dreadful end on the rocks close to the Shippen, the lump of rock behind the coastguard cottages where locals kept allotments, in Hope Cove. No contemporary accounts describe the wreck and its survivors, but the *San Pedro* may have left an extraordinary legacy. Parson Richard Polwhele travelled through Devon at the end of the eighteenth century, recording both the commonplace and the unusual. He was not averse to sampling local dishes, and at Slapton Sands, just along the coast from Hope Cove, he tried cuttlefish, or as it was known locally 'codell':

> They are about a foot long, and four or five inches broad; their skin is white and looks like the sinews of veal boiled, and is speckled with small purple spots. This skin wraps up the body in the form of a conical bag, having a couple of fins of a thin flimsy substance, beginning from the back and spreading out when they swim. When the skin is taken off and the body cut open, it forms a triangular piece of white nervous flesh, like the white leather in veal, and when fried tastes well enough, but sweet, very much like the razor fish.

Such a culinary experience has not survived into the twenty-first century. But this taste for cuttlefish, a member of the squid and octopus family whose hood is supported by the dried bone familiar to beachcombers, is believed to be a legacy of shipwrecked foreign sailors. Over the centuries hundreds of men have staggered ashore from wrecks, introducing coastal villages to foreign delicacies. Cuttlefish is eaten in the Spanish coastal region of Galicia, so the origin of Polwhele's culinary experience may well date back to the Spanish Armada of 1588.

## Pilchards

Long before the era of sandcastles, sun cream and surfboards, seasonal visitors filled the pockets of coastal Devonians. Cars, canoes and caravans are signs of the modern migration of money from afar. Sun glints on windscreens; the sea glitters with thrashing bodies; and the sound of laughter ripples across the beaches. Hundreds of years ago the picture was not so dissimilar, but the visitors came by sea. From the hewer's hut high on the cliff, a cry would go out. Other voices in the village took up the cry as the sea glittered with the gleaming bodies of pilchards. This plentiful supply of fish was the bounty on which fortunes could be made. Men, women and children would run to the beach from houses, pubs and barns, grabbing nets and oars as they went and several boats would be launched into the surf. Rowing or sailing out to the shoal, each boat encircled the fish with a seine-net, 500 yards long.

The Reverend Edmund Butcher described in detail just such a scene and its aftermath in his charmingly titled 1820 publication, *The Beauties of Sidmouth Displayed: being a descriptive sketch of the situation, salubrity and picturesque scenery*:

> The boat having carried out the net to a certain distance, greater or less as circumstances may require, the seine is shot from the boat, which, as it moves on, forms a circle, being supported by a vast number of corks affixed, at equal distances, to the outside ropes of the net. From each end of the seine, when the semi-circle is completed, are cords extending to the beach, and which are held by persons stationed to haul or pull in the seine, when completely cast into the sea: these individuals form two rows, which gradually close as the net approaches the shore.
>
> The produce of each haul is divided in the following manner: the owner of the seine and boat is entitled to one half of the fish caught; and also to an equal share of the remainder with the rest of the crew, between whom the other half is divided share and share alike. When women [...] take a part of the adventure, the supposed superiority of strength in the male quite superseded that politeness which, in some other departments of society, pays a compliment to female assistance; for the lady gets only half as much as the gentleman.
>
> Whether fish are taken or not, the labour is not over when the seine is pulled in. It is necessary that the net should be carefully

overhauled, that is, spread regularly out upon the shingles for drying; as, when it is first taken out of the sea, it is left in large hillocks,
in which situation it would rot and not dry. This overhauling, after
an unsuccessful shoot, is a very flat business – nearly an hour of toil
is added, after the several labourers have found that there is not a
fish a-piece to repay them for their time and exertions.

Pilchards were and are a delicacy. Great shoals appeared regularly off the
South Devon coast from the fourteenth century until the early part of the
nineteenth century. As lovers of warm water, they were drawn to Devon in
years when temperatures soared.

Over 400 years ago, five men from the hamlet of Hope Cove in the South
Hams had a bumper catch. One day in 1583, they made a haul of 90,000,
which they landed at the eponymous Pilchard Cove. A survey in 1566
revealed that there were eighty-four seine-nets in South Devon, of which the
largest number, eleven, were in Salcombe. Seining, from the French word for
a drawstring purse, was still in use in the town in the 1970s, although by then
the pilchards were long gone, and it was used to catch mackerel or whiting.
In the 1950s and 1960s, the special cotton pilchard nets still hung in the old
lifeboat station in Inner Hope.

A few miles west, a hewer's hut on the ridge of Burgh Island, and the
island's fourteenth-century pub, The Pilchard Inn, serve as reminders of the
fortunes that were made. Pilchard shoals were still appearing in Bigbury Bay
in the 1840s. Writer Daniel Defoe left an eyewitness account of the hiatus
caused by the arrival of a pilchard shoal. This one was driven into Dartmouth
in 1724 by a school of porpoises and Defoe had persuaded a local merchant
to take him out on a sightseeing trip to view the open sea:

> Coming back with the tide of flood, I observ'd some small fish to
> skip, and play upon the surface of the water, upon which I ask'd my
> friend what fish they were; immediately one of the rowers or sea-
> men starts up in the boat, and throwing his arms abroad, as if he
> had been bewitch'd, cryes out as loud as he could baul, 'a scool, a
> scool'. The word was taken to the shore as hastily as it would have
> been on land if he had cry'd fire; and by that time we reached the
> keys, the tide was all in a kind of an uproar.
>
> The matter was, that a great shoal or as they call it a scool of
> pilchards came swimming with the tide of flood directly out of the
> sea into the harbour. My friend whose boat we were in, told me this

*Villagers at Beesands hauling in a catch with a seine-net in the early twentieth century.*

was a surprize which he would have been very glad of, if he could but have had a day or two's warning, for he might have taken 200 tun of them, and the like was the case of other merchants in town; for in short, no body was ready for them, except a small fishing boat, or two; one of which went out into the middle of the harbour, and at two or three hawls, took about forty thousand of them.

This bumper catch could quickly transform into a heap of rotting fish in those days before refrigeration. Pilchards and herrings were salted for winter, and in recent memory some cottages still had an earthernware salt crock outside the front door. The fish were also exported from Dartmouth and Plymouth to the Mediterranean, as well as to towns and cities inland. Daniel Defoe sampled some pilchards only hours after they were landed:

We sent our servant to the key [sic] to buy some, who for a half-penny, brought us seventeen, and if he would have taken them, might have had as many more for the same money; with these we went to dinner; the cook at the inn broil'd them for us, which is their way of dressing them with pepper and salt, which cost us about a farthing; so the two of us, and a servant din'd, and at a tavern too, for three farthings, dressing and all...and very well too.

However, this was not a crop to be relied on: pilchard shoals failed to appear for years on end. Seventy years after Defoe recorded euphoria in Dartmouth, Parson Richard Polwhele toured the county, and found an altogether different picture, which he recorded in his *History of Devonshire*, published in 1797:

> Pilchards with which many parts of the coast of Devon excessively abounded formerly, have no [sic] almost left it. That house upon Slapton Sands, now called the Cellars, was built purposely for curing pilchards. There prevails a report well authenticated, that at certain times this fish was taken in such immense quantities, that for want of being able to dispose of them in good season, a considerable tract of ground was manured with them.

The pilchard industry in Plymouth is known to have been important as early as 1378, and by the early seventeenth century the town's fishing fleet was said to number between 100 and 200 boats. But during the sixteenth century, the pilchard catch was a hot topic in the town and provoked a dispute, which led to intervention by none other than William Cecil, the Virgin Queen's righthand man.

Fish was an important part of the diet in the Tudor period. An act of Parliament in the reign of Edward VI had decreed that fish was to be eaten on Fridays and Saturdays. William Cecil, who first became Secretary of State in 1559, was instrumental in extending this to include Wednesdays. His aim was political. The fishing fleet was regarded as a training ground for the navy and the industry brought employment to the coastal population – all of which was necessary for the defence of the realm. This was quite aside from the economic benefits. However, Cecil discovered that the number of boats fishing from Plymouth was declining and tried to stimulate the industry by restricting imports.

This was an era of change in the fishing industry itself. Seine-netting was becoming more popular, which meant that fewer fishermen were needed to net the catch. Much of the pilchard catch was being cured for the export market, packed into hogsheads and pressed down with weights, rather than smoked individually. This was done in fish cellars, owned and run by the merchants. It was merchants, and particularly the Cornish merchants, who were the troublemakers.

Instead of the Plymouth fleet landing the catch at the town quay, merchants would encourage them to unload at their cellars at the mouth of the Sound. Cellars had been built at Cawsands and Rame, on the Cornish shore of the Sound. For the average Plymothian, for whom pilchards were a cheap and nutritious meal, this meant a shortage of fish, and what was available was sold at inflated prices.

It was Plymouth's strategic importance as a naval base, the key to maritime power in the west, which led Cecil to intervene; trade in the town had to be healthy to maintain this growing naval base. In 1578, the smaller fishermen and the people of Devon and Cornwall, asked for the help of the Queen. The 'greedy merchants', they complained, were artificially inflating the price of fish, and giving the fishermen low prices for their catch. The dispute rumbled on. In 1581, Plymouth's mayor, the adventurer Sir Francis Drake, and the town council, imposed fines on people in town who were colluding with the merchants, by supplying them with fish. Women in the town were particularly implicated.

The resolution of this conflict of interest between the merchants and the people of Plymouth became paramount as England engaged in conflict with Spain. It was the view of Cecil and the Privy Council that the commercial interest of the fishermen should be sacrificed for the national good. The merchants were instructed not to build any more fish cellars, and ordered in 1588 to bring two thirds of the catch to Plymouth. Pilchard exports were banned, except to friendly foreign powers.

In a sense the dispute resolved itself. The two sides would never agree, but when Plymouth asked for financial help to strengthen its fortifications, the Queen helped them out. She gave them an annuity from the customs duties gathered in Devon and Cornwall, as well as duty imposed on every hogshead of pilchards that was exported. It was now in Plymouth's interests to encourage the merchants curing the pilchard catch in their cellars at the mouth of the bay.

One day in 1870 an extraordinary scene took place in Brixham's Fish Market. A crowd of some 200 people was celebrating. Raising their teacups they toasted the health of Lord Churston; they had won a great victory. This was neither the relief of some far-flung city in the British Empire, nor were Brixham residents on the side of the Kaiser in the Franco-Prussian War, this was a victory in the war of the sexes. The grand tea party in the Brixham Fish Market soon got rather wild, as the fisherwomen of the town let their hair down. As the local newspaper put it: 'Some of the elder fisherwomen going

*Brixham Fish Market in the nineteenth century.*

through the old country dances with marvelous grace and elasticity.'

Their champion, Lord Churston, had led the Brixham fisherwomen to victory in a battle to retain a right, which their sex had enjoyed for generations, of selling fish in the market. The men went to the fishing grounds, hauled in the catch, brought it back to the quayside and unloaded it. But it was the women who had traditionally sold the fish, and a group of men had decided, foolishly, to challenge their monopoly. The men's logic was faultless: if the women could do it, so could they. But officials had informed the men that they could not sell fish without an auctioneer's licence. The men were furious. If they had to buy a licence so should the women. Lord Churston took the case up on the women's behalf, and won.

Brixham had the largest fishing fleet in the country in 1850, with 130 fishing smacks. Since the middle of the eighteenth century the Brixham fleet had been supplying fish to London. In 1800 innovative fishermen from the little town had invented a new method of fishing, by trawling a net from the ship. This was a new and far more efficient fishing method, soon copied by other Devon fishing fleets. But in *The Housekeeper's Guide to the Fish-Market*, published in 1843, the author J.C. Bellamy took a gloomy view of this new technique:

Trawling is the main feature of the Devon fishery, while seining and driving are the characteristics of the Cornish. The Hake is, in Devon, principally taken by the Trawl, but in Cornwall, it is captured by the hook and line. The supply of fish brought to Plymouth market is mainly the produce of trawling, but, it is deeply to be regretted that this species of fishing should be conducted by men of such reckless proceeding. Vast quantities of *fish in their worst conditions*, great numbers, especially Hakes, Congers, and Flat-fish, *laden with spawn,* and still larger quantity of *young fish,* particularly the Gurnards, Pouting, Haddock, Breams, &c. are continually abstracted from their element to do only temporory [sic] negative good to the community, not to speak of the great proportion *consigned to the manure heap,* while the stock itself is thus materially injured. The common produce of the trawl in winter, consists of Gurnards, Mary-soles, Plaice, Thickbacks, Soles, Whiffs, Brills, Hakes, Rays of several kinds, Poutings, Whitings, Scads, Dorees, &c.; all taken in 30 or 35 fathoms.

It would be a very important improvement in economy, could measures be taken to compel the Trawlers to fish in smaller companies at a time, and in turn, and thus to give a more regular, and less redundant supply to the fish-market.

Prescient words indeed, but trawling did bring prosperity. The greatest delicacies caught by Devon boats, such as turbot, sole, sturgeon and salmon, were sent by coach to Bristol, Bath, and even London. Trawlers sometimes delivered their catch to other Channel ports such as Portsmouth and even to the Channel Islands. France was another ready market, particularly for hake, skate, pilchards, herrings, and mackerel.

With the advent of the railway, fish was sent regularly to Billingsgate Market in London. The fishing fleet in Exmouth in the late-nineteenth century was sending to London up to forty tons of herrings a day in the herring season – February and March. But herring shoals, like their pilchard cousins, can be unpredictable. Faced with empty nets time after time, the Exmouth fishermen eventually had to sell up.

By 1900 about a thousand men and boys were employed in the largest fishing fleet on the South Coast at Brixham. The Brixham fleet also braved the waters of the North Sea in the hunt for rich shoals. So many of the men fished off the north-east coast that many eventually settled in Grimsby. In 1883 a fleet of twenty-five trawlers set off for the rich fishing grounds of the

North Sea, where they spent the next three or four months. With them went a floating church on board the *Jeffrey Drew* – these were devout men, who never fished on the Sabbath. Catches were transferred to steamships, which took the catch to market while the fleet remained at sea.

Keeping the catch fresh was a priority and from the middle of the nineteenth century enterprising individuals imported ice that had been hacked out of frozen lakes in Norway. Great slabs of ice were packed in straw and loaded into the holds of fast brigs for the journey back to their home ports. James Bigwood went a step further, building an ice factory at Kings Quay in Brixham in 1900. Water was taken from a reservoir and frozen in a refrigeration unit powered by steam: the steam engine was later replaced with a diesel unit.

### The Cod Squad

Sitting as it does on the upper reaches of the Dart, Newton Abbott hardly seems a likely centre of the cod-fishing industry. Yet, in the eighteenth century, fish were accepted as currency by Newton Abbot shopkeepers. The legacy of the deep-water fishing fleets can still be found in names such as Newfoundland Way. Hundreds of teenaged boys from the town and its rural hinterland went off to seek their fortune in the Newfoundland fisheries. For this was the town where men signed on to the boats which set off for the cod banks in summer, returning months later laden with fish. In fact, Newton Abbot and its environs supplied more men to the trade than any other place in Devon.

This was the age of exploration, and as men sailed further and further west, they found their journey impeded by vast, dense shoals of cod. Italian navigator Giovanni Caboto, known in the English-speaking world as John Cabot, sailed from Bristol in the *Matthew* and discovered the Newfoundland fishing banks, 2,000 miles across the Atlantic. Soon entrepreneurs from across the county were getting in on the action in an effort to make their fortunes: among the first Devon ships were the *Guilford* and the *Samson*, which sailed from Plymouth in 1527 to exploit this huge natural resource, and a small mill a few miles from Newton Abbott produced the specialist hooks and knives for the entire Newfoundland Fishery. Yorkshire metal workers forged their own versions up in Sheffield, complete with a forged maker's mark, but they were caught and sued in court by the Devonians.

Those who survived this dangerous voyage would sometimes settle down for a season on land, returning with a cargo of cod. Other ships would also call at the banks, taking the cod to be sold on the continent. The vital and fortune-changing links with the New World had thus been established – a factor that continued to affect the course of Devon's history for several centuries to come.

The cod was dried on wooden hurdles on the Newfoundland shore, before being packed in casks. On the west coast of Norway this technique of drying fish can still be seen, but the Devonians had learnt it from the Newfoundland natives. Before consumption, the fish had to be soaked to eliminate most of the salt. The result was a gelatinous lump, known in Newton Abbott as 'old toe rag'.

At the height of the Newfoundland trade, in 1635, there were 10,000 Devonian men employed in the industry. Many of those who left the shores of Devon failed to return, preferring to settle in Newfoundland. Some men took their wives and girlfriends, others embarked on bigamous marriages.

The great expansion of the Newfoundland fleet took place between 1580 and the mid-seventeenth century, also a period when piracy flourished. As their ships sailed back towards the mouth of the English Channel, crews knew that pirates would be lurking off the coast of Spain. An Exeter sailor, Joseph Pitt, wrote an account of his capture by Algerians. In the early morning light of 11 September 1679, a sail was spotted by one of the crew on the *Speedwell*:

> About Mid-day, being almost overtaken by them (the Enemy being but a mile distance from us) our Master said, it will be in vain for us to make our Flight any longer, seeing it will be but an hour or two e'er we shall be taken, and then, probably, fare the worse if we continue our flight. I may leave any Person to judge what an heartless Condition we were in; but yet still we could not forbear kenning the Ship, that unwelcome, Object, which, Devil-like, was eager in the Pursuit of us. All hope now failing, there being no place for Refuge, we haled up our Sails, and waited for them. As soon as the Pirate came up with us, the Captain being a Dutch Renegado, and able to speak English, bid us hoist out our Boat.

Crews were small on these Newfoundland fishing boats, and there were four men capable of doing the job – Pitt himself had been scalded, and another man had been washed overboard in a storm a few days earlier.

> And therefore, before we could make half ready to hoist out our Boat, they came a-board us in their own. I being but young the Enemy seem'd to me as monstrous ravenous Creatures.

*Brixham was home to the largest Devon fishing fleet in the nineteenth century.*

The terror of young Joseph Pitt is palpable – he was only fifteen years old. Like many other Devon seamen he and the rest of the crew were sold as slaves. But we have Pitt's account of this extraordinary incident, because unlike many others, he escaped fifteen years later and made his way home. There are accounts of others who were ransomed by their captors.

Cod was not the only intensely lucrative commodity to be had in the competitive seas of the North Atlantic. The Globe Hotel at Topsham was the place where men signed on for the whaling ships in the mid-eighteenth century. Crews faced the threat of pirates as well as the notoriously dangerous hunt for the whale, which was killed for its oil and meat. The British Government offered a bounty to encourage ships to sail for Arctic waters off Greenland in a bid to challenge the dominance of the Dutch whaling fleet, such was the potential income from winning this monopoly. When these cash incentives were at their highest in 1754, The Exeter Whale Fishery Company was formed. Although the Exeter company dropped out of the trade in 1787, the Dutch fleet was eventually successfully ousted by the British.

## Seaton Salt

Devon baronet Sir John Churchill spent the first decade of the eighteenth century galloping around the continent fighting the French. His family lived near Axminster, and the War of Spanish Succession, during which he was to crush the enemies of Britain, was to bring him fame, fortune, and a title. But the war which made John Churchill the nation's darling, was probably the reason another Devon landowner revived an ancient industry. France was the principal source of salt, and by 1703 the precious commodity was fetching outrageous prices. Enter stage right Sir John Trevelyan, owner of a small estate at Seaton. As Sir John Churchill fought his way across the continent, Sir John Trevelyan resurrected the salt industry in Seaton, an industry which had been recorded 700 years earlier, in the Domesday Book.

That Norman land survey recorded twenty-two saltpans across Devon, with saltworkers at six other places. The legacy of Devon's salt industry survives in place names around the country, Salcombe, Budleigh Salterton and Saltash among them, and salt-work remains can be traced in earthworks in a field below Seaton Church, and further north on land adjacent to the East Devon District Council Cemetery. It was a profitable and essential industry in the centuries before cans and freezers were invented to preserve food. Such was the value of salt that Roman soldiers received part of their pay in salt: the modern word 'salary' is derived from the Latin word *salarium*, meaning salt. And of course it was a sign of your superior status in medieval society if you sat above the salt. Homer called it 'the divine substance'.

Records show that the monks at Otterton Priory made a good living from salt production, sending it inland to villages along the River Otter by packhorse. In 1145 there is a reference to salt ponds at Seaton and also at Beer. A survey of Sir John Trevelyan's estate made in 1682, reveals that there were three fields called Salterne-way – probably a reference to earlier salt production. A decade later, Celia Fiennes, that intrepid lady who travelled through England on a side-saddle, watched salt production down the coast at Lymington in Hampshire.

> The sea water they draw into trenches and so into severall ponds that are secured in the bottom to retain it and it stands for the sun to exhale the watery fresh part of it. When they think its fit to boyle they draw off the water from the ponds by pipes which convey it into a house full of large square iron and copper pans, they are shallow but they are a yard or two if not more square, these are fixed in rows one by another, it may be twenty on a side, in a house under which is the furnace that burns fiercely to keepe these pans boyling apace and as it candys about the edges or bottom so they shovel it up and fill it in great baskets, and so the thinner part runns through on Moulds they set to catch it which they call Salt Cakes; the rest in the Baskets drye and is very good Salt, and as fast as they shovel out the boyling Salt out of the pans they do replenish it with more of their salt water in their pipes.

Sir John Trevelyan may have visited Lymington to research the salt process, and certainly one of his early salt makers came from a village nearby. Part of Trevelyan's estate was the salt marshes in the Axe estuary, which had silted up over previous centuries. It was here on the western side of the River Axe, between Seaton and Colyford, that he revived the salt industry. It was 1704, the year that the other Devon baronet, Sir John Churchill, was trouncing the French at the Battle of Blenheim.

The French salt, which was so vital, was refined from rock salt. Sea water contains two extra compounds, magnesium sulphate and magnesium chloride. If these are not removed, they leave a bitter taste in the mouth. This makes the end product unsuitable for use in butter, cheese or at the table. More importantly in the pre-freezer era, it made the salt less efficient for curing food. Magnesium sulphate and magnesium chloride slow down the rate at which salt penetrates meat or fish, which means that although the outside layers of food are preserved, the inner flesh goes bad before it can be cured. These factors made the French salt highly desirable, particularly in Devon, as ships fishing off Newfoundland had to preserve the catch for several months before returning home.

When sea water is heated, a scum rises to the surface, which is skimmed off. This contains the least soluble compounds, calcium carbonate and calcium sulphate. Sodium chloride, which is table salt, crystallises next but has to be removed before the crystals of magnesium have been deposited: this happens at roughly the same time which makes it a tricky process.

The exact details of Trevelyan's sea-water salt works have not survived. But some facts are known. Workmen dug rectangular ponds in the marsh, about two to four feet deep, and lined them with clay – an old technique used for making dewponds. These saltpans were extensive, covering up to half an acre. The spoil was used to form a low bank round the perimeter. At high water during spring tides, the sea flooded in across the marshes and was captured in the ponds. Salt-making was seasonal work, done between May and the end of August, to make best use of the warmth of the summer sun, which evaporated the water to make a more concentrated brine.

This brine was siphoned off to a cistern adjacent to the salterns. Sometimes spelt salterne, these were the huts where the brine was boiled, often built of clay with a hole in the roof to let the smoke out. (It is known that in other salt making areas at this point in the process, the brine was poured over salt-rich sand collected from the sea-bed.) It was then boiled hard, in shallow iron pans hung over the fire, until the salt crystallized. Then, just as Celia Fiennes described, the salt crystals were shovelled into baskets and hung to dry.

Sir John Trevelyan's first salt makers at Seaton marshes were a local man Edward Drayton, and David Langar, who was from Milford near Lymington. Both men were described on the lease as maltsters, but two years later the partners were in trouble with the taxman. Salt tax had been introduced in 1698 and stood at 75 per cent; whereas foreign salt remained untaxed! The two men seem to have fallen out with the local Officer of Salt. In a 'humble petition' Edward Drayton told a sorry tale to the salt commissioners in London:

(He) brought it to that Performance that the Duty thereof...rose sometymes to 40 sometymes to 50 and sometimes 60£ a moneth Had the Misfortune of Late to have all his Salt Houses burnt down, his Salt wasted and other goods relating thereunto wasted and consumed. However, your petitioner, finding his saltworks would turn to Account, made a Shift to rebuild his houses and repayre his works with intention to carry on the same and hoped ye Government would...have favoured him therein.

The amount of salt tax they were paying, meant they had a healthy business, despite the fire. And it looks as if the Commissioners came down on their

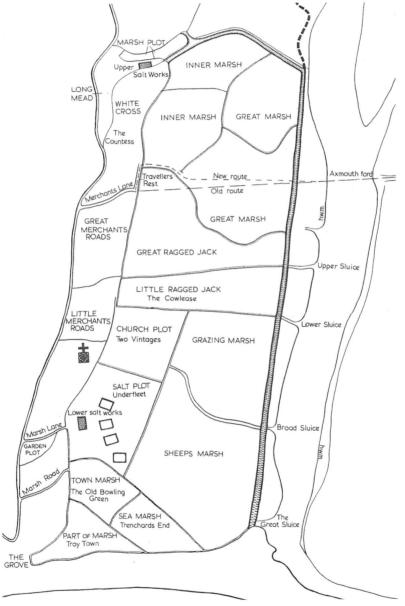

*A sketch map showing the location of the eighteenth-century Seaton salt works.*

side. Their landlord, Sir John Treveleyan, allowed them to extend their enterprise to other parts of the marsh for no extra rent. Things were looking good, so good that in 1716 the Poor Law Guardians attempted to squeeze more money from Drayton and Langar to pay for those in the workhouse. This attempt to raise the Poor Rate twelvefold was successfully contested by Sir John on behalf of the salt makers.

By 1727, when Sir John Trevelyan let the marsh to new tenants, Samuel Pengelly and Edward Benger, there were two salt works on the marsh. But while these salt makers may have been producing a greater volume of salt, the annual rent had halved since the marsh was first leased.

Six years later the lease of the marsh and salt works was up for auction at The New Inn, Seaton. Trevelyan estate records name the two salt works as the Little Saltwork and the Whitecross work, and they were for sale complete with utensils, boiling pans and cisterns. But the bidding did not meet the reserve price, and the estate accepted a lower bid at the end of the year from Joshua Manston. When his lease ran out another auction was held in 1741, but the sale fell through.

Sir John Trevelyan died in 1755, and his son George became the 3rd baronet. A survey in the following year showed the only trade or manufacturing in the parish was fishing.

Events elsewhere probably contributed to the demise of what had seemed such a promising enterprise. In 1670, before Trevelyan was even born, rock salt had been discovered in Cheshire. It was far more economic to refine table salt from rock salt, and the result was of far better quality. When Daniel Defoe visited Bideford in 1724, for his book, *A Tour Through England and Wales*, the salt trade between Cheshire and North Devon was well established.

> The trade of this town being very much in fish, as it is also of all the towns on this coast, I observed here, that several ships were employ'd to go to Leverpool, and up the river Mersey to Warrington, to fetch the rock salt, which is found in that county, which rock salt they bring to Biddiford and Barnstable, and here they dissolve it into brine in the sea water, joyning the strength of the two bodies into one, and then boil it up again into a new salt, as the Dutch do by the French and Portuguese salt: This is justly call'd salt upon salt, and with this they cure their herrings; and as this is a trade which can but of a few years standing, because the rock itself has not been discover'd in England much above twenty years; so the difference in curing the fish has been such, and it has so recommended their

herrings in foreign markets, that the demand for them has considerably increased, and consequently the trade.

The salt works of Devon were abandoned once more.

## Weir Wars

In the spring of 1999 a crew of archaeologists was seen moving in pairs for safety across the sticky estuarine mud of the Taw estuary. Their destination was a series of wooden posts that had been exposed by the tides and weather of previous weeks. Even at low tide these wooden remains were in places only ten centimetres above ground, and many were buried completely. Others were obscured by seaweed and shellfish. But to these trained eyes, what could be discerned was a line of posts, up to a metre apart, right out into the river channel. Led by a marine archaeologist, and often working up to their waists in mud and water, what they brought to light was one of Devon's fish traps or weirs. With it the archaeologists uncovered the story of a dispute between sailors and fishermen, which had rumbled on for centuries.

When Bad King John signed the Magna Carta at Runnymede in 1215, one of the clauses he put his name to was an attempt to settle this dispute, 'All the fish-weirs for the future shall be removed from Thames and Medway and throughout all England, except upon the seashore'.

As a legal document it is poorly worded. Lawyers could have had a field day arguing over the definitions of 'fish-weirs' and 'the seashore'. But the intention must have been to ensure that fish weirs did not hinder river navigation, which is hardly surprising – some of the weirs excavated by archaeologists in North Devon extended hundreds of metres out into the estuary.

Wicker fish traps have been found in Denmark dating from Mesolithic times. These were wicker cones, which ensnared fish as the tide ebbed away. Fish weirs work on much the same principle, and have also been found dating from Saxon and medieval times. Many fish weirs were owned by monasteries, as fish was an important part of the monks' diet. Tristram Risdon gives us a brief description of a weir at Wembury, which once belonged to Plympton Priory; his account in the *Survey of Devon* was written only sixty years after the Dissolution:

> There you may behold a large and profitable pond, strong walled and gated, which at every tide openeth itself, when the tide storeth it with sea-fish, for the provision of the house, the ebb shutting the gate again.

So lucrative was this system of fishing that it led to numerous disputes in relation to rights and profits. One of the first documented weir wars was associated with a weir owned by Tavistock Abbey. On a modern map the names of some of these local weir sites are still recognisable. For example, on the River Tamar, once the best salmon river in England, at Calstock, Weir Head is marked. Further upstream Tavistock Abbey owned another weir at a site now called New Bridge. This was a substantial well-built weir made of oak, known as Gulworthy Weir, and it was here in the sixteenth century that tempers raged when a dispute flared up between local people and the abbey. The locals had grown used to supplementing their income with salmon, lampreys and trout taken from the river. In 1527 the weir was sixteen feet high and they complained that the fish could no longer pass upstream, and that it also interrupted the breeding of salmon. An inquiry into the dispute was held at Tavistock, but on Whit Sunday afternoon a crowd of 200 angry people gathered and lit bonfires on Hingston Down. Fuelled by their resentment, the mob led by one William Harris, descended on the weir, hacking it down before setting fire to it. Meanwhile the abbot had mustered a posse of 160 men from Tavistock. When the posse arrived at the weir the rioters scarpered. Five years later Henry VIII ordered all weirs in estuaries to be destroyed, and on 17 November 1535 all those in Devon

*Archaeologists brave the treacherous mud to excavate and record one of the controversial weirs.*

were reported to be down.

But a technique so ancient and so successful was bound to continue. Certainly Daniel Defoe encountered a type of fish weir when he visited Totnes for his book *A Tour Through England and Wales* in 1724. As a Londoner, he was intrigued by the quaint ways of rural Devonians. What he witnessed was a fish trap that made use of the mill dam by the bridge over the River Dart:

> We had the diversion of seeing them catch fish, with the assistance of a dog. The case is this, on the south side of the river, and on a slip, or narrow cut or channel made on purpose for a mill, there stands a corn-mill, the mill tayl, or floor for the water below the wheels is wharf'd up on either side with stone above high-water mark, and for above 20 or 30 foot below it, on that part of the river towards the sea; at the end of this wharfing is a grating of wood, the cross bars of which stand bearing inward, sharp at the end and pointing inward towards one another, as the wyers of a mouse-trap.
>
> When the tide flows up, the fish can with ease go in between the points of these cross-bars, but the mill being shut down they can go no farther upwards; and when the water ebbs again they are left behind, not being able to pass the points of the grating, as above, outwards; which like a mouse-trap keeps them in, so that they are left at the bottom with about a foot, or a foot and half [of] water. We were carryed hither at low water, where we saw about 50 or 60 small salmon, about 17 to 20 inches long, which the country people call salmon peal, and to catch these, the person who went with us, who was our landlord at a great inn next the bridge, put in a net on a hoop at the end of a pole, the pole going cross the hoop, which we call in this country a shove net: The net being fix'd at one end of the place they put in a dog, who was taught his trade before hand, at the other end of the place, and he drives all the fish into the net, so that only holding the net still in its place, the man took up two or three and thirty salmon peal at the first time.

At the end of the eighteenth century, William Marshall visited the remains of a weir a few hundreds yards below the confluence of the Rivers Tavy and Walkham. He described it in his book, *The Rural Economy of the West of England*, published in 1796, as 'a strong dam or breastwork, ten or twelve feet high, thrown across the river. On the Buckland side was a salmon trap, which was a compartment 12 or 15 feet square'. He goes on:

It is remarkable...with respect to salmon, that although the entrance is by no means so narrow as to prevent even the largest from returning, it is believed that there is no instance of those which have once entered, quitting their confinement, though they may have remained in it several days. A circumstance, perhaps, which can only be accounted for, in the natural propensity or instinct, which directs them against the stream, and will not suffer them to give up any advantage which they may have gained; the ascent into the trap being an effort of difficulty: in this case perhaps too great.

Both Defoe and Marshall were impressed by the devastating efficiency of fish weirs. Eventually this very quality would lead to the end of this ancient fishing technique in Devon.

A further complication and reason for dispute was that mariners on the Taw and Torridge rivers at this time found fish weirs dangerous as they navigated the waters. Not only were the posts of the weirs (identified by archaeologists in 1999 opposite Appledore) once some ten feet high, but also the longest of the two wings of an estuarine weir was built right out into the river channel. In the fish weir quarrel between sailors and fishermen, which began in 1847 and rumbled on for years, one wing was described as 'a mile or better in length'. After complaints from the mariners the Admiralty was called in. The owner of these weirs close to Crow Point was Sir Arthur Chichester. According to one witness to the dispute this controversial clutch of weirs was

*Fish weirs are often found in conjunction with lime kilns: this is Ashford Weir.*

said to be of ancient origin:

> It is an ancient weir. Drake rebuilt it many years since. It was cut
> down at this time by some of the sailors of Appledore and so
> remained for some years. The neck weir was destroyed some thirty
> years since by the people of Appledore.

By the end of 1847 the argument was hotting up, as letters flew back and forth
between London and Devon. This rather curt letter was sent to Chichester's
solicitors by the Admiralty in December that year:

> Sir, Captain Vetch having reported to the Lords of the Admiralty
> that the New or Upper, and the Lower or Crow Weirs, near
> Appledore, are injurious to Navigation, I will thank you to inform
> me whether it be the intention of Sir Arthur Chichester to have
> them removed or to defend legal proceedings in respect of them.

The result of the dispute was a detailed chart of the estuary drawn up by
Lieutenant Alldridge in 1851, with which archaeologists have been able to
pinpoint archaeological remains.

But the weir wars were not over. In 1851, William Trevisick featured in the
pages of the *North Devon Journal* after he maliciously damaged the weir near
Ashford lime kiln. In 1861 the Salmon Fishery Act was passed which restricted

*Crow Point near Appledore, subject of a nineteenth-century legal battle.*

fish traps, yet half a century later, in 1912, a boat was nearly wrecked on the weir near Ashford lime kiln and the Board of Trade was informed.

Although there was a fish weir still in use in Lynmouth in the 1970s, what spelled the end for this ancient fishing method was its very success. The scale of some of those that have been excavated must have enabled them to capture an enormous amount of fish – so fish stocks diminished. Soon salmon on rivers such as the Tamar were to become a scarce resource, reserved for gentlemen and ladies fishing with a rod and line.

## The Hope Cove Crabmen

Thousands of holiday-makers visit the South Hams village of Hope Cove every summer, drawn by its sandy beach and harbour in the lee of the Bolt Tail. Behind the harbour, thatched white cottages cluster round the square of Inner Hope, a short walk from the old lifeboat station. In the summer season leisure boats cover the flat sand behind the sea wall, a wall that is regularly swamped by waves when the weather turns.

Hope Cove, is the most easterly of the villages on the coast of Bigbury Bay, a coast lined with treacherous rocks, the scene of numerous wrecks. Henry Hingston, a local merchant and Quaker, may well have had Hope Cove in mind when in 1703 he wrote a pamphlet attacking local wreckers:

> I have been deeply affected to see and feel how sweet the report of a shipwreck is to the inhabitants...and what running there is on such occasions, all other business thrown aside and away to the wreck... more sweet to hear all are drowned and so a proper wreck, than that any are saved.

Wrecking and smuggling are certainly reputed to have been among the pastimes of the local community. On one occasion, so the story goes, the women of Hope Cove are said to have seduced the excise men while their men folk smuggled in contraband. Its location makes the village an ideal spot to carry on nefarious doings far from prying eyes inland. The Coastguard Service was set up in 1822 specifically to catch smugglers, and by 1841 Hope Cove merited a contingent of nine coastguards stationed in the village. To avoid collusion, these men were always posted away from home, and moved on every few years.

Smuggling and wrecking aside, the staple income of the village came from fishing for crab and lobster. Hardy fishing families lived in the once-basic thatched cottages that are now let to holiday-makers in Inner Hope. From the harbour these men rowed or sailed out into the bay: a Hope

Cove boat was about 18–30 feet long with an open deck and no wheel-house. Each man spent the winter months from December to May, weaving so called 'inkwell' crab pots from willow. The process was intricate and time-consuming, but sociable, as the men sat by the harbour smoking clay pipes and chatting. Young boys would start to learn the rudiments of weaving by making the bottom of the pots, which took less skill. In these winter months, the fishermen would supplement their diet and income by catching rabbits on local farms, and keeping their market gardens up to scratch. Every cottage had a large earthernware crock by the door, where meat and fish was salted down for the winter.

With the spring, the new crab and lobster pots would be taken out to the fishing grounds, whose locations were passed down through the generations. It was an unwritten law that fishermen respected and kept away from the fishing grounds of other villages, but when diesel engines gave boats the potential to fish further afield, this tradition died.

Lobsters and crabs lurk in rocky crevices in deep water. Off Hope Cove, a couple of favourite spots were East and West Rutts, two pinnacles standing in thirty fathoms of water, their seaweed-covered crests only apparent at the lowest spring tides. But other favourites included the wreck of the *Ramillies*. Large rocks were tied into the pots to make them sink and stop them mov-ing, while on the surface the lines were attached to slices of cork. To tempt the catch into the traps they were set with tit-bits regarded as delicacies for crab and lobster: red gurnard, skate back, salted mackerel and salted conger.

Because of the force of the tide, and the weight and depth of the pots, they could only be raised and lowered at 'slack tide'. This varies along the coast; at Hope Cove it is between two and two-and-a-half hours after high water, but at Prawle Point, east along the coast, it is three-and-a-half hours after high water. The fisherman then had until the same point on the rising tide to empty and reset the pots, a period of about three or four hours. During spring tides, water surges in so much faster that pots would sometimes have to be dealt with the following day.

This seasonal round, which had lasted for generations, changed dramat-ically in the 1920s with the advent of the first petrol engines. The potential size of the fishing grounds increased enormously. In the 1950s Hope Cove had a fishing fleet of about fifteen boats, but by the 1980s this had dropped to five, only two of which were based permanently at the cove. Today there are none.

By the 1980s, many of the more 'romantic' but mundane tasks were unnecessary. Plastic and metal pots had replaced wicker; synthetic rope had replaced sisal; and plastic had superseded cork and glass as the material of choice for floats and buoys. So if the materials had made the job less tedious, what happened to the Hope Cove fishermen? The answer lies partly with the Y-chromosome. For centuries the men of the Jarvis, Legassick, Hurrell, and Thornton families had gone into the fishing trade. But as the generation who had fished between the wars died out, only two Jarvis boys took to the sea. The Hurrell brothers chose not to become fishermen, and the other families had produced girls. While there was a tradition of strong women taking to fishing round the coast at Hallsands and Beesands, only one Hope Cove woman took it up: Ellen Partridge. One theory is that this was due to the strong influence of the Methodist Chapel, where many of these families worshipped. Certainly no fishing took place on Sundays, and the fishermen would not even pull their boats off the beach in the event of bad weather, if this meant working on a Sunday.

For centuries the men of Hope Cove had been forced to pull boats off the beach in the event of a strong south-easterly or south-westerly. This was a necessity, thanks to the location of the village and its harbour. Failure to do this would mean fishing boats, and therefore men's livelihoods, were swept away and wrecked on the rocky coast. Before the advent of the internal combustion engine, boats were hauled up the slipway by horsepower. Once the tractor appeared on the scene, one man drove while others steadied the boat. As the size of the fishing fleet dwindled, so the handful of fishermen struggled. It was safe to bring the boats off the beach with three men, but once the number dropped to a pair, the task became too dangerous. The last crabmen to make a living from Hope Cove were Eric and John Jarvis, David Clarke, David Morgan and Ian Pedrick.

*David Clarke, one of the last Hope Cove crabmen, at work in his boat* Hopeful.

# CHAPTER 4

# LABOURS LOST

Ask any visitor to name a product from Devon's industrial past, and a quizzical look will appear. After a moment's thought lace manufacture might be top of the list, as dedicated followers of fashion filled the bellies of thousands of Devon lacemakers for three hundred years.

From its beginnings in the mid-sixteenth century, the lacemakers of Honiton acquired a reputation for producing some of the finest and most expensive lace in England. In 1676 there were 5,299 lacemakers in East Devon, of which one third lived in Honiton. This luxury lace was also pro-duced in other towns such as Sidmouth and Beer but was all sold as Honiton lace. The intricate designs were handmade by outworkers in ultra-fine thread, hence the expense, and then assembled by specialists. Fickle fashion, combined with cheaper machine-made lace, led to its demise, and by 1940 there was not one person making a living from Honiton lacemaking.

Less well known is the demise of North Devon's 1,500 glovemakers who worked in two factories at Torrington and Appledore. Before the advent of the internal combustion engine, when humans beings travelled on foot or by horse, gloves were an essential part of every wardrobe. Sheepskin and fur kept the digits warm as mail coaches thundered along unmade roads. Leather gloves protected the hands of horse men and women across the Empire. And ladies of fashion had gloves of taffeta, lace and silk to comple-ment every outfit. Even in the early 1960s, white gloves were still considered de rigeur for formal occasions.

Leather gloves were the specialty of the Pilton Factory, and manufacture was a lengthy process. Hides arrived already stretched and seasoned, and were sorted as suitable either for men or ladies. Gloves require soft and pliable leather so the skins were soaked in a concoction of cod oil and soap before being put out to dry in the field above the factory, which was still known as 'rack field' in 1971, although it was by that time a market garden. Once they had been dyed in vari-ous shades of brown or grey, the skins were hung from nails and kiln dried.

Hides destined for sheepskin gloves were doused in very hot water when they arrived at the factory before being subjected to the 'egging' process. Millions of eggs were separated, and the yolks broken into a vat of water in which the leather was 'treaded'. What happened to the corresponding number of egg whites is not recorded!

Men perched on high stools evened out the skin surface before the actual glovemaking could begin. The leather passed through a team of thirty pairs of hands skilled in a minute part of the process, beginning with the foreman cutter, and ending with the box makers.

Vaughan's Glove Factory in Torrington once turned out 24,000 pairs of handmade gloves a week, which like those from the factory at Pilton, were

*Wheal Betsy engine house.*

transported all over the world. But as fashion changed this factory, too, was put out of business.

Similarly, detachable collars, cuffs and shirt fronts were also made in North Devon. In 1880, a thousand people were employed at three collar factories in Bideford and another in Appledore. But the post-war depression, coupled with a change to more informal clothing, led once again to closure.

Devon was also a source of raw materials for many heavy industries. The engine house at Wheal Betsy, Mary Tavy is a striking legacy of lead, silver and zinc extraction; iron was mined at Molland, Ashburton, Brent, Combe Martin and Holne; and other minerals exploited include micaceous haematite.

## Tin Tyrants

For 500 years, Dartmoor and four towns on its perimeter were tyrannised by a group of wild men outside the law. The tinners polluted waterways, abused their neighbours and threw opponents into gaol. A neighbourly dispute with a tin miner could leave a gaping hole beneath your house or garden. And thanks to Bad King John these wild tinners had every right to carry on as they did – their rights were enshrined in English law.

Every river and stream on Dartmoor contains alluvial deposits of tin. Like all metals it was a valuable asset to any warrior nation. Combined with copper it could be forged into bronze, the metal of choice before the discovery of iron. It was the presence of tin that turned the eyes of the Roman eagle to these shores. It was the raw material for coins and pewter.

By the reign of the crusading Richard I, the importance of tin as a national asset was fully appreciated. In 1198 Richard passed a charter to ensure that tinning was carried out only under licence. Official scales were installed at Exeter so that the King knew the amount of metal extracted and could make sure that he got his cut.

And it's thanks to these regulations that we know the name of one of these early miners: Roger Rubi. He almost certainly came from Rubbytown three miles from Tavistock on the south-western reaches of the moor and was obviously a man of some standing in the mining community. In 1198 he was appointed to a special jury set up to establish aspects of tin-working practice in the county. At this point in the latter half of the twelfth century, Devon was the largest source of tin in Europe.

In the last months of the twelfth century, Richard I was killed while indulging in his favourite pursuit: he was besieging a castle in France. His brother John, who colluded so unsuccessfully with the Sheriff of Nottingham against the legendary hero Robin Hood, took the throne. And it was John who gave the miners carte blanche. In his charter of 1201 he gave them permission 'to mine for tin and dig turves for smelting tin everywhere in the moors and fiefs of bishops, abbots and counts as they have been accustomed to do'.

In practice, if a miner thought he had discovered tin, he marked his pitch by 'bounding' the four corners with a heap of turves at each corner. Legally he was not obliged to tell the landowner, or to ask for permission, although the landowner had the right to a tenth of the profits, if there were any. Along with these prospecting rights, the tinners were given the right to govern themselves, and to run their own courts of law. This was an extraordinary move. Justice in England at the time was meted out by a plethora of courts, run by the Church and lords of the manor. But the new Stannary Courts were run by the miners themselves and they were tried by a jury of twelve of their peers. The only crimes tin miners could not get away with were murder, manslaughter or what was termed 'mayhem'. The state had created a privileged elite.

Dartmoor's tin republic had its own Stannary Parliament, which had equal status with Parliament at Westminster. It was presided over by the warden, an officer of the Crown. The most famous figure to hold this office of warden was Sir Walter Raleigh, who was instrumental in doubling the wages of tin labourers. The twenty-four members of the Stannary Parliament were elected by a franchise that extended to all tinners except those who were paid wages. This was a far wider electorate than was generally the case in England, before electoral reform in the nineteenth century.

The rights given to the miners offered some men a chance to escape from the rigid society in which they lived. All but the rich were enslaved to a feudal lord. In return for a few strips of land to grow food, peasants were obliged to provide their labour. King John's new rights for tin miners excluded the tinners from any obligation to other lords and masters. So if they fell out with their landlord, or had committed a crime, this offered them the chance to leave the land and make money on the moor.

A century later Edward I exempted tin miners from all local taxes and tolls: a financial privilege that must have acted as an incentive to potential entrepreneurs. What is extraordinary is that it was not until the sixteenth century that the gentry became involved as mine owners. This was truly a way in which an ordinary man could better himself by hard work.

The industry was run by the four Stannary towns: Ashburton, Chagford, Plympton and Tavistock. 'Coinages' were held twice a year, when miners brought their smelted tin into town strapped onto packhorses. Officials weighed and assayed the tin blocks in public, checking the quality by clipping off a small piece. If it was deemed up to standard it was officially stamped. Pewter manufacturers, dealers and merchants travelled to these events from London, Holland and even Italy. Tin was also sent to the four Devon mints at Lydford, Exeter, Barnstaple and Totnes.

The Stannary towns were also the venue for the Stannary Courts, where members of the public could air their grievances against these men who were outside the law. In the late fourteenth century the tinners were obviously getting out of hand and abusing their privileges. In 1376 concerned citizens petitioned Edward III, asking for an inquiry into 'Many Extortions, Oppressions and Grievances practised by the Tinners and Officers of the Stannaries.' The tinners had been taking their prospecting too far. Tin miners are recorded as even digging in churchyards to find tin! The petitioners asked that the miners should not be allowed to dig in 'Pastureland nor among Woods, nor among Houses, nor disturb Waters or any running Waters out of Malice'.

There is also a hint at the amount of local resentment at the abuse of power by the Stannary Courts. According to aggrieved locals, once they were under arrest, instead of punishment the tinners were 'suffered to go at large, from which much Danger has many times happened'.

There is no record of the King's response to these accusations, but the miners do not seem to have moderated their behaviour. Indeed, nearly two centuries later the tinners kidnapped the local MP, Sir Richard Strode, and marched him over the moor to Lydford where they threw him into the castle, built in 1195, which served as the Stannary prison. Strode had dared to accuse the tinners of polluting the River Plym with the waste from their streaming activities. As they sieved through the tin ore further upstream, sand and gravel was washed further down. The Plym had silted up and was becoming unnavigable for shipping. Strode didn't languish long in Lydford Castle which he described as 'One of the most annonyous contagious and detestable places within this realm'.

A century later Richard Foster was imprisoned there. He described how he was kept in pitch darkness, without any form of heating, on a scaffold of a few planks without rails suspended over 'a very loathsome deep hole thirty foot deep and too dirty to be expressed'.

Tristram Risdon, the Devon antiquary, who wrote *A Survey of Devon* between 1605 and 1630, records an incident that shows how busy the Stannary Court at Chagford could be:

Here is holden one of the courts for stannary causes, where, on the sixth of March, 1618, the house in which it was kept, standing on decayed pillars, by reason of a fuller court of resort than ordinary appearing, through the pressure, rent in sunder, and the walls fell in; amongst whom the steward, an honest and discreet gentleman, with nine others, were slain, and many others hurt and wounded.

The heyday of Dartmoor's tin industry had already passed by the time Risdon was writing. Production had peaked at 252 tons in 1524, and the embellishing and building of churches in moorland villages, such as Widecombe, is evidence of the riches that were made. Average production between 1600 and 1650 had dropped to only 25 tons a year. By this time according to Risdon, it was a tough and dangerous occupation for the miner, or 'spadiard', as he calls him:

A spadiard, a daily labourer in tin works, with whom there is no labourer in hardness of life to be compared; for his apparel is coarse, his diet slender, his lodging hard, his drink water, and for lack of a cup, he commonly drinketh out of his spade or shovel, or some such other thing, without curiosity in satisfying nature.

Early miners streamed tin in the same way that gold miners panned gold in

*A watercolour of the Eylesbarrow tin workings showing the water wheel.*

later centuries. Hummocks of tin waste can be found all over the moor, along-side streams. Water was often diverted into channels to help the process. Later miners dug shallow cuttings above the lodes with pickaxes, but experts believe that shaft mining was not used until the eighteenth century. In the seventeenth century T. Westcote described a form of open-cast mining in his book *A View of Devonshire*:

> He spends all day (or the major part thereof) like a mole or earth-worm underground, mining in deep vaults or pits, as though he intended (with noble Sir Francis Drake) to find a way to the antipodes; yea, a nearer, and so to surpass him: for it is somewhat of that profundity, that notwithstanding the country (so they term the earth over their heads) is propped, posted, crossed, traversed, and supported with divers great beams of timber to keep them in security, yet all is sometimes too little; they perish with the fall thereof notwithstanding.

Once the tin was streamed or dug out, it was crushed on a mortar stone, before it was smelted in a furnace. Early tinners performed this process in a type of clay oven, which was heated from below. From about the fourteenth century, furnaces were built in blowing houses, and the bellows to keep the furnace going was powered by water.

Crushed ore and charcoal were layered inside the furnace, and molten tin dripped through on to a mould stone below. The result was tin of extraor-dinary purity. Ruins of these small granite buildings are found near streams all over Dartmoor. These roofless shells would have been thatched: a fire hazard for such an industrial building.

Dartmoor's tin production was in decline until a slight resurgence in the 1820s. Metals were in demand as the industrial revolution advanced. Tin-plating of iron had been developed in South Wales, and created a demand for tin until this too declined at the end of the nineteenth century. But tinners of earlier times had exploited the most accessible tin ore already. Technology had advanced and steam engines could now pump out the water that saturated the moor, plus ore could be taken out by rail. But unless prices were buoyant, little profit could be made. In 1893 Devon mines pro-duced only 52 tons of tin, and this was low-grade, unsmelted tin, which was only 65 per cent metal.

The Birch Tor and Vitifer area had been worked by earlier tinners known as 'the old men', and when miners in the early nineteenth century were sinking a shaft they discovered the remains of an earlier one. An unknown source described this to the Plymouth Institution in 1891:

> The adventurers found, on opening up the ground early in this century, a shaft, sunk by the 'old men' fifteen fathoms (90 feet) deep, which was circular and lined from top to bottom with a stone wall, fairly and neatly put together. This shaft was deepened and worked by the Vitifer Company with great success.

Vitifer Mine employed 100 men in the middle of the nineteenth century, but by this time Dartmoor tin was continually undercut by cheap tin imported from Malaya.

The largest concentration of mines was in the area close to the present Warren House Inn. At Headland Warren on Dartmoor a medieval longhouse is all that remains of the community of tinners that worked the two mines nearby. Men travelled from all over the area to work at the mines until 1914, and some residual tinning continued until the Second World War. The pub, built in about 1845, was noted for brawling tin miners who bunked up in a shed at the mine, only travelling home after the Saturday shift. The Golden Dagger mine was extremely damp, men worked up to their waists in water, and suffered from rheumatism, bronchitis and inflammation of the lungs. At nearby Hexworthy by contrast, it was hot and dry and men had to work in cramped conditions.

Small-scale prospecting near some earlier tin mines took place during the First World War, and the immediate post-war period. Old waste dumps were worked during this time, and later as part of the drive for raw materials during the Second World War.

*Above left: A mould stone at Merrivale and right a typical Dartmoor mortar stone used for crushing tin.*

## Industrial Espionage

Even today the journey from Devon to Norfolk is not to be taken lightly. But when Francis Enchmarch and William Perkins made that cross-country trek in 1752, it was a sign of desperate times. Francis and William were setting off on a mission of industrial espionage: they planned to steal the secrets of their Norwich counterparts in the wool industry, and use them to restore the fortunes of their home town. Such was their desperation to improve the financial position of Tiverton that they were prepared to poach the technology and ideas of their competitors. Their underhand, undercover mission was a success but it nearly cost them their lives.

The two men came from Tiverton, a prosperous town with a population of over 8,000 people, many of them incomers attracted by its prosperity as a centre of the wool trade. Contemporary writers claim that the town buzzed and clacked to the sound of 1,500 looms, with 700 people employed as wool combers. In 1741 the town was hit by an epidemic of 'Spotted Fever', which, according to local historian Martin Dunsford writing fifty years later in his *Historical Memoirs of the Town and Parish of Tiverton*:

> ...depopulated the town so much that grass grew in the streets; distressing scenes of mortality were daily exhibited. In the course of the year, 636 persons, about one in twelve of all the inhabitants of the parish, were buried. Ten or twelve funerals were seen in St Peter's church-yard at one time. The ceremony of tolling the bell was omitted, to prevent a too general alarm.

Foreign affairs were adding to the troubles in Tiverton. Britain was at war with France, but on this occasion she was at war with Spain as well. Bonnie Prince Charlie and his followers were also creating havoc, by trying to invade England to restore a Stuart king to the throne. These distant events combined to dampen the demand for wool and to block trading routes. But Tiverton's wool trade was also threatened by the clothiers of Norwich. Fashions were changing and the East Anglian weavers were producing finer and cheaper woollen cloth. Norwich 'stuffs' had pushed the Devon serges out of the lucrative Spanish export market. Cloth exports from Norwich to Spain were worth £31,000 in 1711, but only a decade later had risen to £112,000. The same thing happened to the Dutch trade – and the German trade was about to go the same way. The Norwich weavers were putting their Tiverton brothers out of work.

Local worthies had tried to lighten the lot of the poor by setting up

*A nineteenth-century lithograph of Tiverton, showing the distinctive outline of Heathcoats Mill.*

factories in the workhouse. Looms were often set up in workhouses, and workhouse overseers tended to be recorded as manufacturers of cloth. Excavations in Barnstaple on the site of the old workhouse uncovered postholes which archaeologists believe to be the site of looms worked by the inmates. The scheme in Tiverton's workhouse was doomed to failure, as Dunsford recorded in his book:

> So many losses were sustained by waste, keeping the manufactured goods on hand, without an opportunity of proper sale etc, that the materials were ordered to be sold, to the best advantage possible, proportionate dividends be made to the creditors, and the trade abolished.

Hunger and anger stalked the streets of Tiverton. In 1749, several merchants began to import Irish worsted to be woven into a type of cloth known as 'duroys'. This threatened to put the wool combers, who prepared the raw material, out of work. They took industrial action. Martin Dunsford records how:

> They immediately returned all their work to their several masters,

took away the pads out of the comb-shops, and declared they never would comb again 'till the Irish worsted was thrown quite out. A special meeting was likewise had of all the members of their club (union), wherein it was determined, to subsist themselves out of their common club stock, 'till the weavers should starve or the merchants and serge makers comply.

But the strike fund soon began to run out, without any sign of a compromise. As stalemate continued, the strikers even made death threats to the merchants, and threatened to burn down their houses. The army was called in, but resentment continued to simmer beneath the surface. Dunsford records that it culminated in the Battle of Fore Street:

One day, the wool-combers being assembled in full club at their house, the Half Moon, in the Fore Street, and unluckily a body of weavers passing by, hard words arose and some blows were exchanged; the shops were soon shut, and a dreadful battle ensued, with stones, clubs, glass bottles, bats etc, in which many were severely wounded on both sides.

The mayor called in the troops and read the riot act. But the militant wool combers were unwilling to compromise. They demanded that the merchants stop importing the controversial Irish yarn. Dunsford claims that, eventually, hundreds of them left town, travelling the country as jobbing wool combers.

Against this background of unemployment and unrest, clothier Francis Enchmarch formed a daring plan: to steal the new techniques of the Norwich weavers and set up in competition to them. In 1752, he and weaver William Perkins set off on their undercover mission to Norwich. Unfortunately no record of the details of their mission appears to have survived, but they would hardly have blended in with the populace of the Norfolk city: their accents alone would have marked them out as strangers. According to Dunsford they stayed there 'a considerable time' in order to understand the intricacies of the Norwich trade. At some point, their presence aroused suspicion. They had no visible means of support; they had been asking too many questions; taking too close an interest in the Norwich weavers:

About the time they had effected their purpose, the manufacturers of Norwich suspected their design; and it was with great difficulty and hazard that they escaped from the city. Had they fallen into the hands of their pursuers, it probably would have cost them their lives.

No doubt when the two men returned they were regarded as heroes, and a few years later Francis Enchmarch became mayor. Production began. Tiverton was soon producing the cloth for which Norwich was famous: camblets, 'tarborates', damasks, plain and figured barragons, lutestrings, calimancoes, 'tarbines', brocade damasks, cambletees, 'dominies', figured druggets, 'draft twisted druggets'. The drying racks of the town's cloth trade sparkled with colour: scarlet, purple, crimson, yellow, blue and green. Men, women and children now had jobs and, as Dunsford shows, things were looking up for the town:

> Several houses in Bampton Street were converted into general workshops, where seventy or eighty people were daily employed, and about as many without doors (as outworkers) in different parts of the town, which greatly enlivened the inhabitants, by the hopes of establishing a new trade which was likely to raise the town of Tiverton to as high a state of splendor and importance, as at any past period of time.

Although at first it was a great success and employed several hundred people, the business collapsed suddenly in 1761 (exactly why this happened is unclear). Once again many wool workers in Tiverton found themselves unemployed and by 1770 the town's population had fallen by 1,800 compared with 1730, and between 1720 and 1780 the town's poor rates had more than doubled. Martin Dunsford recorded the impact of the interminable wars with France:

> The perpetual wars however in which the nation has been plunged have now completed the downfall of the manufacture, excepting such a portion of it as is required to supply our own East India possessions, and some small demand for Home trade.

Tiverton was just one of the towns on the Devon–Somerset border whose economy was based on wool. Wool had become the boom commodity throughout the Middle Ages. In its wake it brought fabulous wealth to landowners and, in particular to the Church. It filled the treasury with revenue as Richard the Lionheart galloped overseas to spend vast sums in the battle against Muslim expansionism, known as the Crusades. Wool money helped to finance the navy, which mustered in Plymouth Sound to sail against the Spanish Armada. Wool literally helped to defend the city of Exeter during the Civil War, as its citizens barricaded the city with bales of wool. Devonian heroes such as Drake and Raleigh made fortunes from the wool trade, while county gentleman used their wool profits to finance almshouses, so that even the poor could benefit. Wool brought hundreds of years of prosperity to Devon, and left a legacy in many towns and villages.

Sheep are still a feature of the Dartmoor scenery, ambling across roads in their unhurried fashion. This moorland provides ideal fodder, as sheep are prone to diseases brought on by over-lush grazing.

It was the Cistercian monks who took over Buckfast Abbey in 1148 and first latched on to the profit to be made from the moorland, which formed a substantial part of their estates. The Devon Cistercians were soon exporting the valuable raw material. Towards the end of the reign of Good Queen Bess, Hooker wrote his *Synopsis Chorographical of Devon* (1599), which described the extent of the woollen trade:

> There is no market nor village nor scarse any privat mannes house where in theise clothes be not made, or that there is not spinninge and cordinge for the same: as the daylye travellers can so witness it for wheresoever any man doth travell you shall fynde at the hall dore as they do name the foredore of the house he shall I saye fynde the wiffe theire children and their servantes at the turne spynninge or at their cardes cardinge and by which comoditie the common people do lyve.

Whole families combed, spun and wove the cloth. It was washed, cleaned and finished in water-driven tucking mills, and these woollen mills hummed in every town: Barnstaple, Tiverton, Cullompton, Crediton, Axminster, Honiton, Ashburton, Totnes, and Chudleigh, to name but a few. The wool industry even had its own currency, trading tokens that could be used locally, until such practice was abolished by Charles II.

As there were vast fortunes to be made from wool, entire communities grew dependent on the trade. In 1810 the editor of Tristram Risdon's *Survey of Devon* wrote:

> The returns of the town of Tiverton alone, were estimated in the year 1612 at the sum of £300,000 a year, and in a brief granted by

King James after the great fire there, it is set forth that 'Their great trade kept always in work 8000 persons, men, women and children.'

But in the days of thatch and wooden-framed buildings, this prosperity was precarious. The fire of 1612 to which he refers destroyed 600 houses. Wool and wooden looms were highly flammable, so conflagrations were a common occurrence:

On a Monday, their market day, in April AD 1598, it was fired about one of the clock the same day, to the great terror and amazement of all the people, which began in the west part of the town beyond the river, the wind being so vehement and high, as the like seldom hath been seen; and it was carried by force thereof with such violence, that the whole town, within little more than an hour, was consumed; the people in the meantime so amazed, that they knew not what to do. Many were burned; namely, one Hartnoll, a blind man, lying in his bed, was carried to the market place for his safety, and yet there burnt; also one Laund, and his wife, shifting for themselves, were found, arm in arm, burnt in the street; sundry others, some in their shops, some in their bakehouses. There were six hundred houses burnt, with great wealth in them, the church, chief place, with two alms houses only saved, one of them being in the middle of the flame; which being re-edified about fourteen years after the first fire, on the fifth of August was a second time consumed by a like terrible flame, the church manor house, and alms houses again freed.

Despite the disaster, and the yarn, cloth and weaving looms that were lost in this fire, the town was rebuilt. But after another fire in 1731, an act of Parliament was passed so that lead and slate roofs were substituted for thatch.

Blundell's School, untouched in these fires, is one example of the philanthropy indulged in by those who made a fortune while the Devon wool industry was at its height.

The school house there built, is a goodly ornament to the place, which was the bounty of Peter Blundon, a wealthy clothier and native of the place; in whose memory a yearly feast is holden on St Peter's Day, with sufficient allowance thereunto appointed.

*Endowed with wool profits, Blundell's School in the nineteenth century.*

Chudleigh was another great wool town, which was hit by a disastrous fire three-quarters of a century later. It left over 1,500 people homeless and without food. What followed was a relief effort on an extraordinary scale:

> The inhabitants were without provisions of any kind, from Friday morning, till Saturday, when a wagon loaded with bread and beer, arrived from Exeter. On the following day, provisions ready dressed, were sent from the neighbouring towns; Lord Clifford, who resides at Ugbrooke, about a mile distant, threw open his house for the sufferers, and ordered several sheep to be dressed for those who could not leave the ruins. A number of tents were sent from Exeter, as a temporary covering for those who were obliged to lie in the fields. Subscriptions were opened in London, and in all the towns in the counties of Devon and Cornwall, for the relief of the sufferers, and the sum of £21,000 and upwards was collected. The total loss sustained by the fire, has been estimated at £60,000. The town is now nearly rebuilt.

What gave Devon the edge against competitors was its established trade links with continental Europe, access to a plentiful supply of wool, and water power. The county's streams and rivers washed the cloth and powered the mills. Each town was famed for its special type of cloth. Tostocks from Tavistock; bays and frizados from Barnstaple and Torrington; and Tiverton,

Ottery and Crediton produced kersey – a finely spun cloth with a market stretching as far as Turkey and the Levant or eastern Mediterranean. Honiton became prosperous after pioneering the weaving of serges, a coarse cloth, which was also produced in Tiverton, Exeter, Tavistock and Totnes. In the closing years of the seventeenth century the serge trade on the Devon–Somerset border brought enormous wealth to the county. But it was just as important to the national exchequer. Between 1688 and 1715 Devon exports were the most important sector of the English wool textile trade. Out of total exports of £3 million, it was worth £850,000.

In the reign of the Merry Monarch, Charles II, a law was passed that made it compulsory for the population to be buried in a wool shroud. This was enacted so that more cotton rags were available to the paper industry. Parish priests had to record whether burials complied with this law, and those whose families could afford it, paid a fee to be exempt.

Seventeenth-century Exeter was a busy manufacturing town, its streets filled with the chatter of foreign merchants, their ships loading and unloading at the wharves. On the site of the cathedral cloisters, destroyed by their rampaging soldiers during the Civil War, Parliamentarians built a serge market. Celia Fiennes visited the city in the latter part of the seventeenth century, when the woollen industry in the area was at its height. She was impressed by the part it played in the economy of the city and surrounding countryside, as she wrote in her book *Through England on a Side Saddle in the Time of William and Mary*:

> There is an incredible amount of serges made and sold in the town...the large Market House set on stone pillars which runs a great length on which they lay their packs of serges, just by it is a walk with pillars which is for the yarn; the whole town and country is employed for at least twenty miles round in spinning, weaving, dressing and scouting, fulling and drying of the serges, it turns the most money in a week of anything in England, one week with another there is £10,000 paid in ready money, sometimes £15,000, the weavers bring in their serges and must have their money which they employ to provide the yarn to go to work again.

Exeter's narrow streets were crowded with packhorses and their excrement. Smells of the farmyard mingled with the distinctive aroma of damp wool as weavers arrived with the finished product to deposit at the fulling mills, then departed with yarn back to their cottages to weave into more cloth. This

*Signs of prosperity in Exeter which was the mecca for wool traders.*
*A merchant's house above and below Tuckers Hall.*

newly woven cloth was in demand for a reason long forgotten today, but for this description left by Celia Fiennes:

> But first they will clean and scour their rooms with them – which by the way gives no pleasing perfume to a room, the oil and grease, and I should think it would rather foul a room than cleanse it because of the oil – but I perceive it otherwise esteemed by them, which will send to their acquaintances that are tuckers the days the serges come in for a rowle to clean their house.

The feminine sensibilities of Miss Fiennes may have been aroused by the prospect of fouling a room with the perfume of oily rolls of cloth. But she is sanguine about the smell, which must have accompanied the fulling process, whose principal agent was stale urine, known euphemistically as a 'domestic wash'.

The use of urine as a cleansing agent, thanks to its high ammonia content, has been recognised since at least Roman times. Receptacles known as fulliones, stood on street corners in ancient Rome, as both a public service and a convenient method of recycling. Recognised as a useful by-product of boozing, collectors would tour pubs with a 'piss-pot', which was passed round, so that gentlemen could relieve themselves.

During local elections in 1765, the wool combers and weavers of Tiverton even used urine as a political tool. The wool unions were supporters of Charles Baring, an Exeter merchant. They tried to stop urine collectors from selling this essential substance to one of Baring's opponents, Mr Webber, who was the town's mayor. 'There was a constant and almost universal cry about the town many days – "Baring for ever. No piss for Webber"', according to local historian Martin Dunsford, who left an outline of this extraordinary dispute in his book *Historical Memoirs of the Town and Parish of Tiverton* writing fifty years later. The boycott was successful – such a vital part did urine play in the preparation of the wool bales. Celia Fiennes left a description of this particular industrial process:

> Then they lay them to soak in urine then they soap them and so put them into fulling mills and so work them in the mills dry until they are thick enough, then they turn water into them and so scour them; the mill does draw out and gather in the serges, it's a pretty diversion to see it, a sort of huge notched timbers like great teeth...

Huge dripping wads of serge were carried out to fields all round Exeter, and other wool centres. The wool legacy survives in place names such as Rack School in Exeter, and Rack Park in Kingsbridge and the phrase 'on tenterhooks' also survives from this drying process. Celia Fiennes continues:

> When they are thus scoured they dry them in racks strained out, which are as thick set one by another as will permit the dresser to pass between, and huge large fields occupied this way almost all round the town which is on the river side; then when dry they burl them picking out all knots.

Burling irons were like giant tweezers, used to pick off imperfections before the nap was raised with teazels, and the cloth was finished.

> Then fold them with a paper between every fold and so set them on an iron plate and screw down the press on them, which has another iron plate on the top under which is the furnace of fire of coals, this is the hot press; then they fold them exceeding exact and then press them in a cold press.

Devon principally exported white or undyed cloth. The dyers were highly skilled, the secret recipes of each colour contained in a notebook, which they would take with them to another employer, and on their death were passed down through the family. Woad, with which the ancient Britons were said to have painted themselves in readiness for battle, was used for blue and shades of black. As the American colonies opened up, so cochineal arrived to give bright red; brazilwood and peach wood yielded brown; and the dense inner bark of *Maclura tinctoria*, was the source of fustic, a yellow dye. Celia Fiennes witnessed the process during her journey *Through England on a Side Saddle in the Time of William and Mary*:

> I saw the several vats they were a dying in, of black, yellow, blue and green – which two last colours are dipped in the same vat that which makes it differ is what they were dipped in before which makes either green or blue; they hang the serges on a great beam or great pole on the top of the vat and so keep turning it from one to another, as one turns it off into the vat the other rolls it out of it, so they do it backwards and forwards till its tinged deep enough of the

colour; their furnace that keeps their dyepans boiling is all under the room made of coal fires; two men does continually roll on and off the pieces of serges till dipped enough the length of these pieces are, or should hold out, twenty there was in a room by itself a vat for the scarlet, that being a very chargeable dye no waste must be allowed in that, indeed I think they make as fine a colour as their Bow dyes are in London; these rollers I spoke of, six yards.

During the Napoleonic Wars the market for woollen exports was restricted but Devon's woollen trade found markets further afield as coarse woollen serges were exported to the Chinese market by the East India Company.

*Water-powered no longer, Weare Giffard Mill in its present incarnation.*

But the Chinese, it seems, had an ulterior motive, as recorded in the anonymous preface to Risdon's *Survey of Devon* in 1810:

> It is understood that one of the uses which the Chinese make of these goods is to extract the colour from them, which they apply to the dying of articles in their own manufacture; and that, for this purpose, the Devonshire Serges, are shredded or cut up into small pieces, and rendered useless as a cloth. Such advantages do the possession of the sciences give to a nation, that while chemistry has enabled us to discover and imitate the processes by which the inhabitants of the east fixed the various tints upon their cottons, we oblige them to take our colours in the expensive, and to us profitable form, of an article manufactured of our staple commodity.

Wool brought four centuries of prosperity to Devon but this, inevitably, came to an end. The continual continental wars of the eighteenth century closed trade routes. British ships, many of them from Devon, had held the monopoly on trade with the American colonies until the colonists revolted. By the early 1770s, half of England's trade in textile goods was from Yorkshire. The factories built to house the Yorkshire industry also housed the new technology of the industrial revolution such as the Spinning Jenny. Over the Pennines in Lancashire, mills were starting to produce cheap cotton goods – cotton was becoming a substitute for wool. Between 1760 and 1800 the consumption of raw cotton exploded, rising from £1.2 million to £51.6 million. The northern manufacturing towns also had another advantage: a cheap and ready supply of the one raw material Devon could not offer, coal. Devon could not compete.

As the Devon wool trade declined, county woollen mills were given a new lease of life. Loughborough industrialist John Heathcoat set up his lace factory in Tiverton in 1816, employing 1,500 people. Driven south by the militant actions of the Luddites who smashed his machinery, Heathcoat brought a new era of prosperity to the town, although the mill that he converted was burnt down in 1936.

In a reversal of the normal history of water mills, the former woollen mill at Weare Giffard was converted into a state of the art flour mill in the late nineteenth century. Keeping apace with the relentless march of progress, not only was it fitted with the most up-to-date machinery, the workplace was lit by electric light. And its pioneering owner, Thomas Fry, installed the latest gadget of his day, the telephone. No longer powered by water, despite its proximity to the powerful waters of the River Torridge, it has now been converted into private housing. In the interim it served as the village community centre with a dance hall and skittle alley.

## King Copper

The Tamar River is the natural boundary between Cornwall and Devon. From its source on the western edge of Dartmoor it meanders through wooded countryside and farmland. Supplies came up this river to serve the wealthy abbeys at Buckland and Tavistock. In the nineteenth century the Dukes of Bedford sailed upriver to visit the family holiday home on their Devon estate. Where the abbots of Tavistock had once enjoyed a good day's hunting on Morwell Down, the Dukes took their guests shooting in the woods. Visitors marvelled at Morwell Rock, a great granite cliff rising above the river, topped with woodland. This Arcadian scene was described by Parson Richard Polwhele in his *History of Devonshire*, published in the late eighteenth century:

> We suddenly emerge from a gloomy path, upon a rock called Morwell rock, projecting almost perpendicularly over the Tamar, and exhibiting at once so romantic a scene, as in the opinion of good travelled judges is not to be equalled even in Europe. The scene is tremendous, and yet beautiful – several hundred yards under our feet.

When Queen Victoria came to visit the 7th Duke of Bedford in 1856, the royal barge passed through a forest of masts, as ships queued to dock at the busy industrial port. Morwellham Quay, which had served abbots and dukes, now served King Copper. Half the world's supply of copper was shipped from this Devon village, but in the twentieth century it was abandoned, its industrial legacy lost.

It was the opening of the Wheal Friendship copper mines, a few miles away on the western edge of Dartmoor, which triggered the boom years at Morwellham. The mine opened in 1797, and was the most productive among the clutch of mines in the Tavistock area. The market town, which had built up around a community of Benedictine monks, became a frontier town where miners drank away their wages. Rachel Evans described the mine, which she recommended as a 'visit of interest' in a guidebook of excursions from *Tavistock, Home Scenes*, published in 1846:

> Can any scene be more desolate than the one now presented? The frowning and arid waste of Black-down is broken by immense heaps of refuse thrown up from the depths below. A few bare

unsheltered cots of the miners only serve to exhibit still more plainly the dreary aspect of the spot. We descend into the deep excavation which marks the site of the mine. All the business above ground is here industriously proceeding.

The mighty steam engine with its steel works as bright as any drawing-room grate, is for ever raising and depressing its heavy arms, one bearing a ponderous weight of stones, the other drawing from below the superfluous water, which would otherwise fill up the recesses of the mine. This place was honoured some short time since by a visit from many of the Literati who attended the British association at Plymouth... The mine that day presented great interest to those who love to look upon the great and learned of the earth. Here might be seen a set of engineers admiring the workmanship of the above-mentioned steam engine, or peering into an immense iron cylinder, which was lying on the ground prepared to be used as one of the boilers. Now they marched towards the largest water wheel in the kingdom, which is 150 feet in circumference, 50 feet in diameter, and 11 feet across the hoop, turns the works, and assists in drawing the ore from the mine. A shed protects the wheel from the storms of winter, or other injury: within its gloomy shades I have stood with awe and delight, watching the solemn progress of the gigantic machine, and admiring the small rainbows formed by streams of sunshine gilding the falling water which in its rapid course throws a perpetual shower around. A group of mineralogists stood among the busy sifters and cleaners of the ore (women and boys who perform this lighter work), seeking to discover some specimen which might prove of value to their far-off collection. Some of the most adventurous spirits descended the deepest shaft of the mine (which is 200 fathoms below the surface of the earth), in workman's attire. One fastidious beau was hesitating as to the best mode of carrying the candle which he was to take with him to the depths below. 'Us carries un 'tween our teeth, or sticks un in our hair,' observed a wag among the Cornishmen hard by 'Then I must decline any such proceeding,' said the horrified gentleman as he stalked with disgust away; while the rest proceeded, holding their light in one hand, and grasping the slippery ladder by which they went down, with the other. A shout from the counting-house, where numbers of their brethren were dining, announced some time after, the moment of their emerging from the pit...

These mines made vast profits for investors; copper was one of the key elements of the industrial revolution sweeping Britain at this time. Steam engines had shifted the pace of manufacturing up a gear, and as an excellent conductor of heat, copper was the material of choice for many components. With the great railway expansion that took place throughout Britain in the 1840s and 1850s, copper was in demand for locomotive fireboxes. Copper wire was also used in the thousands of miles of cable, flashing messages on the new telegraph system.

Although copper ore was mined on Dartmoor, it was smelted down to the magic metal in the furnaces of South Wales. As Dartmoor terrain does not lend itself to easy road building, so the ore was brought downstream on the River Tavy, but to reach the River Tamar from Tavistock for the onward journey, the ore had to be taken by packhorse. The roads were not surfaced, the journey was slow, and a backlog of ore lay at the mines awaiting removal.

The Tamar offered a cheap and convenient mode of transport out to sea via Morwellham Quay, but between Tavistock and the port lay the granite hump of Morwell Down. At the turn of the eighteenth century, canals were the motorways of Britain, and it says something about the hubris of the age, that a rock one-and-a-half miles thick was not allowed to stand in the path of profit. Mining engineer John Taylor was twenty-four years old when he began the canal in 1803. Beginning close to the Abbey Bridge in Tavistock, it drops four feet over its four-and-a-half-mile length. Of that, one-and-a-half miles were cut through Morwell Down. Dynamite was not available at this time, and its cruder precursor produced sulphurous clouds. The canal was dug out by hand by teams of men and women, some of whom were in their fifties. Problems were legion. The rock was much harder than Taylor had anticipated, water threatened to flood the tunnel, and costs almost doubled. That said, even while the canal was still under construction, contemporaries were impressed by its scale and the ingenuity of its engineer. Seven years after construction started, the editor of Tristram Risdon's *Survey of Devon* wrote of the 'Tavistock Canal':

> From the nature of its formation it will require considerable time to
> execute, as a tunnel nearly two miles in length, is cutting through a
> hill, the strata of which consists of slate and granite rock. Three
> objects are proposed to be attained by this spirited undertaking:
> first, to form a navigation which may convey, from the shipping in
> the river Tamar, limestone and culm for general use; coals and iron
> to the mine, smelting works, and iron works in the neighbourhood;

and carry down to the river, the products of the country, chiefly consisting of copper ores, slate, pig lead, and manufactured iron.

In planning this extraordinary tunnel through Morwell Down, Taylor was aware that there might be further copper lodes in the vicinity of the tunnel itself, as Risdon's editor reveals:

> The second, and perhaps principal inducement with the proprietors for undertaking the tunnel, is the discovery of copper and tin lodes in the hill through which it is cut. The third purpose for which this canal is designed is, as a grand watercourse, by which an abundant stream is conveyed, and applied with considerable falls, to engines of great magnitude, which work the mines on its line; and will, besides render its banks in all probability one of the most eligible situations in England for manufactories requiring extensive powers of machinery.
>
> More than half the tunnel is already cut through, and in doing this some lodes have been discovered, from which copper and tin ores are now raising. The level is 140 yards beneath the surface of the hill, and the ores and waste are brought out at the ends of the tunnel in boats. Shafts, at certain distances, are sinking from the top of the hill to meet the tunnel as it proceeds, and the water is pumped out of these, by rods which are in motion throughout a length of a mile and three quarters; which motion is given them by an immense waterwheel, 40 feet in diameter, working at the foot of the hill... The rubble boated out of the tunnel has been applied to form a vast embankment, over which the canal is carried across a valley, at the height of near 50 feet above the surface of the River Lamborn, which flows through an aqueduct [sic] arch in its centre. The canal will enter the navigable part of the river Tamar, at Morwelham quay, where ships of considerable burthen discharge their cargoes; the boats will ascend to the end of the tunnel by inclined planes, or locks, as may be deemed most expedient when the time comes for their execution.

The canal emerged 240 feet above the river, so from here trucks were lowered down the incline to waiting vessels at the quay.

The village at Morwellham Quay was a pretty spot built on the flat fertile land by the river: a handful of cottages, a pub which dated back to the fifteenth century, water meadows and banks of strawberries. But in November 1844, a new copper seam was discovered beneath a wood owned by the Duke of Bedford, and the village of Morwellham Quay was transformed. Rachel Evans' guidebook to the area was published two years after the new copper mine was discovered. She and a group of friends made an excursion to the village:

> We cannot say much for the picturesque aspect of our resting place. Morwellham is only a quay for the landing of the goods of a Company who have them conveyed to Tavistock by means of the before mentioned canal. But it presents a scene of busy industry, with its unloading barges, and shouting sailors, and hammering workmen, and train of wagons ascending or descending an inclined plane, which conducts to the canal in the wood above. A quantity of ore is here shipped off to distant smelting-houses.

The new mine, Devon Great Consols, was the richest copper mine in Europe and counted among its investors the mother of William Morris. Vast fortunes were made: £1 shares soared to hundreds of times their original value. In 1856, twelve years after the mine had opened, copper ore production reached its peak. The copper lode was over thirty feet thick, and there were forty miles of underground levels. On the surface, the muddy scar across the landscape covered 140 acres.

Writer Anthony Trollope visited in 1858, and described it in his novel *The Three Clerks*:

> It was an ugly uninviting place to look at, with but few visible signs of wealth. The earth which had been burrowed out by these human rabbits...lay around in ungainly heaps; dirt and slush, and pools of water confined by muddy dams abounded on every side; muddy men with muddy carts and muddy horses, slowly crawled hither and thither... On the ground around was no vegetation; nothing green met the eye, some few stunted bushes appeared here and there, nearly smothered by heaped up mud, but they had about them none of the attractiveness of foliage. The whole scene though consisting of earth alone, was unearthly, and looked as though the devil had walked over the place with hot hoofs, and then raked it with a huge rake.

Many miners and their families lived at Morwellham Quay and walked to

*Huge trunks of Baltic pine hold up the roof of Devon Great Consols, a rich deep lode of copper.*

work at the mines two or three miles away. Copper mine agent John Phillips, was living at Ding Dong Cottage with his wife and seven children in 1851. Groundbreaking legislation in 1842 had banned children under the age of ten from working underground in the mines. But childhood is a modern concept so at the ages of eleven and twelve, William Phillips and his brother Francis were already copper miners, while their nine-year-old brother James was an errand boy at the mine, which employed 217 boys. Tallow candles, made of animal fat, were stuck to their caps with a lump of mud, to throw light on the rock face. These candles were notoriously smoky, irritating the eyes. In his novel, Trollope described the descent into the mine, which William and Francis would have made daily:

> He was invited to get into a rough square bucket, in which there was just room for himself and another to stand; he was specially

cautioned to keep his head straight, and his hands and elbows from protruding, and then the windlass began to turn...

Miners descended to the third level in this series of buckets, but the lower workings were reached by ladders in narrow shafts. The journey terrified Trollope's clerk Mr Neverbend:

> It seemed to him as though nothing but a spider could creep down that perpendicular abyss. And then a sound, slow, sharp, and continuous, as of drops falling through infinite space on to deep water came upon his ear; and he saw that the sides of the abyss were covered with slime; and the damp air made him cough...and he was perspiring with a cold, clammy sweat.

The young Phillips boys would have worked twelve-hour shifts in such conditions. Miners worked in pairs, one holding the drill to the rock face, while the other hammered it in. Victorian journalist Friedrich Engels reported that once they had walked home, children often fell asleep too exhausted to eat or even wash off the mud from the mines. Life expectancy was short; forty was considered an advanced age; and it was not uncommon for women to outlive as many as three husbands.

Women were also employed in the copper industry. The bal-maidens, wearing their distinctive bonnets, smashed the rock with hammers once it was mined, splitting out the lumps of ore ready to be smelted. There were 168 girls employed at the mine, which was the largest employer in the Tavistock area. In the boom years, Devon Great Consols employed 1,200 people, and workers walked in from outlying villages such as Gunnislake and Calstock.

The huge quantities of ore taken from the mine had to be transported to Morwellham Quay, for shipping to the smelting works in South Wales. The Tavistock Canal had been built to serve the Wheal Friendship Mine, but Devon Great Consols was five miles north of Morwellham, at Blanchdown, accessible only by road. As miners churned out huge quantities of ore at the mine, the only way to transport it from there to ships waiting at the quay was by packhorse. With limited capacity, bad roads, and steep hills, the poor packhorse could not keep up with output from the mine and production had to be restricted.

Turning once again to cutting-edge technology, a new railway was built in 1858 from the mine at Blanchdown to the edge of Morwell Rocks. From here, ore trucks were winched down a 1:3 incline by a stationary engine,

*Morwellham Quay in its heyday, showing the overground rail system and huge pile of copper ore waiting to be shipped out.*

emerging from a tunnel directly into the village to run on rails to the quay-side. Industrial accidents were common. One man was killed when he took a forbidden short cut across the incline and was cut in half by a cable. A quay labourer was crushed when part of the dock collapsed on top of him.

Bargemen, coopers, shipwrights, blacksmiths and engine drivers, were all part of this noisy industrial scene. After work the men could slake their thirst at the Ship Inn with beer brewed by the 84-year-old malster Laurence Gulley. Behind the pub was a communal bread oven (an invention revived all over England during the Second World War). The workers paid medical insurance, which entitled them to sickness benefit while they were off work, and covered doctors' fees. Children too young to work went to school in the village, where there was a choir and brass band, and a shop run by the Martin family.

The heyday of Morwellham Quay lasted only fifteen years, but during those years ships could be seen queuing in the lower reaches of the Tamar. Vessels of up to 200 tons sailed up from the mouth of the river until it narrowed. From there, teams of men hauled the ships up to the quayside. Manpower was later replaced by steam power, with a tug on standby to pull the ships upstream and manoeuvre them to the dock. Imported timber was

*The lost village of Newquay showing the pub and cottages.*

landed from Canada and the Baltic to be sent on to the mines for the massive pit props required to shore up the tunnels. Numerous quay labourers unloaded the ships, a job which took two days, reloading with gleaming piles of copper ore.

By 1859 output from the mines was so large that the quay had become too small. Docks at the villages of Newquay and Gawton, just downstream, were already shipping the excess with which Morwellham was unable to cope. The pretty cottages and gardens alongside the river at Morwellham were demolished. Where the water meadows and orchards once stood, a massive new wharf was excavated from the river mud. The new quay was paved with tiles and regularly swept to prevent the copper ore becoming contaminated.

Francis Duke of Bedford, on whose land the village and mines stood, had made a vast fortune. Prompted by a cholera outbreak he demolished the overcrowded and unsanitary tenements of Tavistock, built new rows of model workers' cottages and an imposing town square. He also built twenty cottages behind the existing village at Morwellham Quay, to house some of the workers who had flocked to this industrial boom village. But King Copper was soon to be deposed.

As the seam of copper at Devon Great Consols began to run out, mining companies turned to the element found in massive quantities in association with it: arsenic. During the early years of the copper boom deposits of arsenic pyrites had been dumped as spoil or left in situ. By the 1860s the industrial properties of arsenic were being recognised. Thought of today as

*With the copper boom over, Morwellham's village shop advertises tea and hot water for tourists just before the First World War.*

a poison, it also made an effective insecticide used in sheep dip, and was later used to combat the cotton boll weevil, which devastated the plantations in the American South. But arsenic was also used to harden more malleable metals such as copper, and was used in paints and dying processes. By 1867 the mine began to concentrate on arsenic production, and huge arsenic roasting ovens and flues were built. By 1880 the mine was producing half the world's supply of arsenic, and these ovens and flues covered eight acres. The end product, a white powder, was stored in barrels made by the local cooper and shipped from the quay. This arsenic powder was 99.5 per cent pure and a sixth of a teaspoonful was enough to kill a man. The powder refined from this one Devon mine was enough to kill half the world's population! Arsenic production kept the mine going for a further thirty years, but copper production had almost stopped. By the end of the nineteenth century, foreign competition from the Far East and Bolivia rendered Devon copper production uneconomic, and Devon Great Consols mine finally closed in 1901.

Villagers from Morwellham Quay were forced to move to find work. As mining skills were transferable, many travelled to the booming mines of

*Morwellham in 1930, the dock is silted up and the rails which carried the ore
trucks have long since been dismantled.*

South Wales, or to the collieries of England's north-east. Others emigrated to
the United States, New Zealand and Australia.

In 1903 the scrap was removed from the docks at Morwellham, expanded
only half a century earlier. Downstream the village of Newquay suffered a
similar fate: its ruined cottages were used as a training ground for the fire
service and little is visible today. Those who remained in Morwellham found
work in agriculture, or eked a living from the tourists steaming up from
Plymouth to view Morwell Rocks. The Ship Inn did good business, building
an extension where visitors could eat their famous roast beef and drink the
local beer. Granite bollards remained to enable pleasure steamers to moor
up, but the paved copper floor laid so carefully half a century earlier was torn
up to be re-laid as paths to the cottages. In 1969 water bailiff Jack Adams was
the sole inhabitant of the row of cottages by the quay that had been at the
centre of the world's copper industry. Grass, sycamore saplings and wild flowers soon obscured the old quay. Morwellham became once again a tranquil
spot, no longer reliant on the mines, until a charitable trust restored parts of
the village, which now operates as an industrial museum.

## Quarry for a King

One day in 1903, a quarryman carved his initials 'W.S.' into the granite wall of Foggintor Quarry. Perhaps it was a slack day: the working life of the quarry was, after all, almost at an end. This graffiti may have been the work of seventeen-year-old William Stephens, one of sixty-six people recorded on the 1901 census return for Foggintor village. Three years later, the Dartmoor quarry, which had supplied sparkling granite to the capital of the British Empire, closed. A few families continued to live in the tiny cottages close by, but the shortage of work and the harshness of weather, have left the village abandoned and in ruins. Today, low cottage outlines stand a few inches proud of the turf: unglazed windows, and one teetering wall survive.

Imposing granite cliffs still rise high above the floor of Foggintor Quarry. Water has pooled in the centre. Within and around the site, great blocks of granite lie where they fell over a century ago, the marks of the masons' tools still visible. Spoil heaps of granite chippings have acquired a blanket of grass, lichen and mosses. The quiet of the moorland is disturbed only by the song of skylarks and low-flying aircraft.

Looking at the waste on the quarry floor today, some fragments show three-inch deep holes bored by drills, set five inches apart. These were filled with explosives to split them section by section from the rock face. Clouds of granite dust covered the quarry and the workforce. Ears rang with the sounds of chiselling, chipping and blasting, as well as the creaking of the seven cranes as they swung the granite blocks overhead. In 1846, Rachel Evans recorded her impressions in her book *Home Scenes*:

> The quarries to which we now turn our attention are hidden from view, until the spectator is close upon them. At one moment he looks over the dreary moor without observing another human being, in another an immense excavation presents itself studded with workmen, as busily employed as bees in the hive; some are boring holes in the flinty rock, others are filling the cavities with powder, some are chipping the rude blocks into shape; others are lifting their ponderous weight by cranes and levers; horses, carts and railroad waggons are in constant employment to convey away the heavy masses of stone (some 20 feet in length) which have been made available in the principal works of the metropolis; the Post Office, London Bridge, and the Houses of Parliament have been constructed by this strong material.

*This part of Foggintor Quarry is now flooded, but 300 men once worked here.*

It was this great building programme in distant London, which kept Foggintor Quarry in business. Locals had no need to quarry for stone as Dartmoor is littered with chunks of granite. Over millennia the moor's inhabitants have built their homes with the material at hand. Abandoned Neolithic hut circles were plundered to build the farms, outbuildings and churches of the Middle Ages. As these were abandoned in turn, the stone was reused for more modern buildings. In the days before planning law, it was not uncommon for moor men to enclose a plot of land and build a small cottage. Tradition allowed that if smoke was rising from the chimney within a day, the builder had the right to both the cottage and land.

It was in the early nineteenth century that Dartmoor's quarrying industry took off. As with so many other industries, the impetus for its growth came from war. Britain had been fighting the French for eighteen years. English coastal defences had been strengthened and the defensive Martello towers had sprung up along the South Coast. In 1812 work began on a breakwater to improve the anchorage in Plymouth Sound: naturally it was constructed from Dartmoor granite.

The government was faced with a growing number of French prisoners of war. At first the men were housed in 'hulks', derelict ships condemned by the Royal Navy. Conditions were appalling, and the hulks anchored in English ports represented a security risk. The government decided to build a prison in the middle of Dartmoor, from which escape would be nigh on impossible. The imposing granite prison at Princetown was built between 1806 and 1809, and at its height housed 6,000 prisoners of war. Although Napoleon was finally defeated at the Battle of Waterloo in 1815, with victory came recession. In these immediate post-war years, workers in industrial towns rioted, and there was a growing agitation for workers' rights.

In Devon, the closure of Dartmoor Prison in 1816 was an economic disaster for the inhabitants of Princetown. But their MP, Thomas Tyrwhitt, proposed a railway line linking Plymouth to Princetown. This was intended to boost the moorland economy by exporting peat and granite, while bringing in lime and sand to improve the soil for agriculture. Having served its purpose for a number of years, by 1957 the railway line was defunct and regarded as an eyesore so was dismantled by British Rail.

Nelson's victory over the French navy at Trafalgar in 1805 had signalled the beginning of British naval supremacy in Europe, but it took another fifteen years for this to permeate the nation, so that by the 1820s a budding spirit of prosperity and confidence was spreading across England.

Quarrying began at Foggintor in 1820 just in time for a post-war building boom that began to sweep the country. In the same year George IV succeeded to the throne with grand designs for his capital city. London was at the centre of a nascent British Empire, spreading red tentacles across India, Australia, Canada, and numerous outposts in between. The previous king, George III, had acquired Buckingham House in 1761, and in 1826 his son George IV began remodelling it in line with the mood of the times. With the man who's been dubbed the Prince of Pleasure at the helm of such a project, it inevitably went wildly over budget, at the taxpayer's expense. The sparkling granite of the new Buckingham Palace, was quarried from Foggintor, and brought down from Dartmoor by the new railway.

This Dartmoor granite appears grey from a distance, but close up it glints with quartz highlights on a surface mottled with graphite grey and coffee cream. Granite is a hard, resistant rock, with widely spaced horizontal and vertical joints, which make it easy to split into rectangular slabs. Its inherent strength makes it ideal material for the construction of imposing public buildings.

A granite-paved track still runs from King Tor halt on the railway line,

*The road to Foggintor, the monolithic ruin to the left is thought to be the manager's house. On the other side of the road is the quarry itself.*

to the village and quarry at Foggintor. Down this road the granite slabs were carried by horse-drawn wagon for transportation by rail. Slabs were loaded on to the trains from a massive stone 'table'.

From the old railway line, the road runs up to the village between the quarry itself to the east, and an enormous spoil heap to the west. Quarry workers lived in stone cottages to the north, south and even on top of this 'big tip'. Its size is unsurprising. When chipping out such huge blocks, 90 per cent of the granite that is quarried is regarded as waste.

On the first census return of 1841, only two houses are recorded at Foggintor. These had been built without permission from the landowner. Most workmen would have walked from Princetown and nearby hamlets. Some of them are said to have set up home in the vast buildings of Dartmoor Prison, which did not house convicts for the next thirty years.

George Giles was steward to the local landowner. He described the busy quarry and the village, which was starting to spring up next to it, in a letter dated September 1841:

A great number of men at work...about three hundred...and much expensive powerful and well-contrived machinery erected...also a

*Ruined cottages, with the waste heap topped by more ruins in the background.*

long building supported on tall granite posts...wherein I found about twenty Smiths busily at work...a comfortable two-stalled stable is attached at one end of this building. Not far from this is another similarly constructed...used as a workshop for Carpenters and Turners; a wing attached to this building serves as an office and store house for Tools and Materials. In addition to this a most substantially built Cottage with stone walls and Verandah and thatched Roof. At a short distance I saw another Cottage on a smaller scale, which I understood had been erected by one of the workmen of the name of William Williams for his own residence, and a large piece of ground enclosed by a hedge (the extent approaching to nearly an acre) and cropped with potatoes which looked in a thriving and healthy condition. In another part I found a number of men engaged in facing up with a stone wall of considerable thickness and strength a heap of Rubbish brought out of the Quarry on the summit of which I was told an extensive shed was to be erected under the Roof of which the Stone Masons may work in all weathers...a range of cottages was in contemplation of being built for accommodating the workmen.

When the census enumerator visited in 1851, wagoners, labourers, carpenters and blacksmiths are all shown as living on site. Like most Victorian workers' cottages, the houses were either one-up one-down or two-up two-down. One cottage, simply identified as 'Foggintor Granite Works', housed the Cole family with five children, plus seven lodgers who must have slept in rows, separated by inches rather than feet. Five of these stonemasons had left families behind in Cornwall. Quarry manager Robert Uren was another Cornishman who brought his expertise from further west on the granite backbone, which runs through the West Country. The ruins of his substantial house are on flat land with the 'big tip' looming above it to the north. Chickens pecked about on the waste heap, fruit and vegetables were grown in the gardens, and peat for the hearth was dug from the moor.

With such cramped conditions, children spent much of their time outside, living the idyllic childhood of modern myth. Older children were soon put to work to contribute to the family income. Eleven-year-old Henry Williams is recorded as a 'learning stonemason' in 1851. Fifty years later, conditions were little improved. The Hext family, with nine children between the ages of one and sixteen, lived in a four-roomed cottage, which also accommodated Granny.

In 1895 J.L.W. Page described conditions in the area in his book, *An Exploration of Dartmoor*:

> The hamlet...consists of a few scattered cottages...somewhat poverty-stricken in appearance. The whitewashed walls are low and sturdy, as walls on Dartmoor must needs be, the ragged thatch is often held in place by ropes of straw or hemp, and not unfrequently [sic] weighted with stone as well. Ideas of cleanliness do not prevail among these cottars, and the space round the door would, were it not for the strong Moor breeze, be redolent of ancient vegetable and soapsuds. But look at the children. Unkempt, unwashed, their hair bleached by the sun, they are as rosy specimens of humanity as you will see between John O'Groats and Land's End. Sumptuous fare is not theirs; bacon and cabbage, I fancy, form the staple of their rough-and-ready dinner, but Dartmoor air does the rest. Go where you will on these highlands, you will find the rising generation the same generally dirty, mostly hatless, but pallid never.

In the 1861 census a schoolmaster was living in the village, so Foggintor children did have access to an education during their early years, but it was not compulsory until the 1870 Education Act. In fact a purpose-built village school was not operating until 1915, by which time the quarry had closed.

Foggintor School closed in 1936, and the site lies under the modern Four Winds car park. The final burst of glory for Foggintor Quarry was to supply stone for the widening of London Bridge in 1902 so that it could accommodate the capital's increasing traffic.

Once again, as happened with so many West Country industries, the economic pressures of a wider competitive market took their toll so that by Michaelmas 1906 Foggintor Quarry was closed and a way of life – both for the quarry workers and their families – was lost forever. Cut-price Scandinavian granite was being imported at a price the Dartmoor quarry simply could not match. William Stephens and his workmates were left unemployed. They would almost certainly have found work at nearby Haytor Quarry, until the increasing use of concrete in the 1920s made many quarries uneconomic.

**Paper Fit for a King**
It is January 1962. Harold MacMillan is Prime Minister; a popular beat combo in Liverpool is starting to make headlines; Nazi Adolf Eichmann has been sentenced to death by a court in Israel. The front page of the *Totnes Times* this week is preoccupied with the unaccustomed blizzards and below-freezing temperatures that have smothered Devon. After a week of ice and heavy snow, the thaw begins, and in a hamlet near the River Dart the last sheet of handmade paper is left to dry. It is Friday, 5 January, and 130 years of papermaking have come to an end.

The wafer-like layers of a wasp's nest first gave man the idea of making paper from wood pulp. Boring holes into trees, wasps moisten the pulp to build their complex structures. Although this observation was made in 1719, it was not pioneered for commercial use until the second half of the nineteenth century. Until then paper was made by recycling cotton and linen rags. More than fifty paper mills are known to have operated in Devon over the last three centuries, but to the connoisseur, it was the paper made at Tuckenhay Mill, near Totnes, which set the benchmark for high-quality handmade paper. And its most famous customer was the stamp-collecting George V.

King George had a vast stamp collection which he kept in his study at Buckingham Palace, recording new acquisitions in his diary. During the grim years of the First World War he purchased one stamp for £30,000. After examining them with a magnifying glass, he attached them to loose-leaf pages made at Tuckenhay Mill. Those albums now line the shelves of the Royal Archives at Windsor Castle. But the royal connection does not end there. As the nation mourned his son, George VI, in 1952, the mourning stationery was printed on

*Today Tuckenhay Mill looks little different from the image on this Christmas card.*

paper produced at Tuckenhay. The paper manufactured by Millbourn and Co. at Tuckenhay was prized by artists and in the early-twentieth century papermakers there also literally made money: the paper used to print bank notes for Siam, Jamaica, the Seychelles and Cyprus, was all made by hand at this mill.

Tuckenhay Mill was powered by the waters of the Harbourne river, just above the confluence with its larger and more famous cousin, the Dart. The Harbourne already powered several other mills further upstream at Harbertonford and Bow. It cuts through a steep valley, running from north to south towards the Dart, and Tuckenhay Mill can still be seen ranged along its east bank. By dint of a series of ponds, pipes and leats, the river powered seven water wheels, the gentle hum of their motion breaking the quiet of the valley.

Water was a vital component in the paper trade. The mill needed a sufficient volume of water in the driest season, without flooding in the wettest. Flooding was always a hazard in paper mills, as it could damage both raw and finished materials. Water used in the process had to be clear and preferably hard, to give the paper the finest texture. Water flowing through marshy ground, or water which was likely to become muddied by rain, had to be avoided. In long, wide, sluggish rivers, particularly in low-lying land, the water was likely to be too discoloured, or too impure to be used in papermaking, because of the clay content. This problem could be overcome if there were freshwater springs near the site, as at Tuckenhay. In 1810, the editor of Risdon's *Survey of Devon*, commented that:

...paper mills are to be found occasionally in Devon, though not so
generally as might be expected from the purity of the water, which
is so grand a requisite in this elegant manufacture.

Demand for paper had increased during the eighteenth century, as daily
newspapers were established. Education was also spreading through the
Church, and there was a resultant rise in the demand for books. The era of
mass communication was dawning and the spreading of ideas was becoming
easier and faster through improved technology.

Tuckenhay Mill began life as a fulling mill, but the woollen industry sank
into decline during the Napoleonic Wars, as the export market vanished.
Gone too was the supply of imported French paper: for it was the French
who were the master papermakers, and many of the terms used in papermaking come from the French. In 1820 there were forty-one mills making
paper in Devon, as opposed to twenty-nine in 1800. So in 1829 it was a logical
move to convert Tuckenhay Mill to papermaking.

In the same way that wool had been brought upriver and unloaded at the
wharf by the Maltsters Arms, so shiploads of rags arrived, to be taken by
horse and cart along the single-track lanes to the mill.

The paper trade was dogged by shortages of this raw material, but
Devon papermakers had a ready supply from ports which supplied waste
materials from the shipping industry – rotting hammocks, awnings, and
scraps of hemp rope. Sailcloth was used for legal paper, one of Tuckenhay's
products. However, when steamships began to take over from sailing ships
and chains also replaced hemp rope, this led to a shortage of maritime waste.
Yet papermaking did not rely solely on maritime waste, it also used old
clothes, the domestic supply of which had to be supplemented by rags from
the continent, because the English were said to be so fond of washing. In
1800, a Dutch commentator complained that England did not 'furnish such
considerable quantities of rags as might be expected from the number of
inhabitants and their superior cleanliness in linen'.

Many of these rags were linen underclothes, which brought with them
the risk of disease, particularly smallpox, which is highly contagious.
Underwear could easily have been in contact with the pustules that accom-
pany smallpox. Despite the population increase during the nineteenth century,
paper mills appealed regularly for rags through local newspapers. In 1860,
an advertisement appeared in the *Totnes Times*, encouraging householders
to keep and sort scraps of material into rag bags. Dressmakers were even
asked to save and recycle odd scraps of cotton thread. This was not just a

*Workers at Tuckenhay paper mill at the end of the nineteenth century. The papermakers are in the front row with the curious hats.*

local shortage caused by the thrifty Devon population; *The Times* offered a £1,000 reward to the person who could suggest a reliable alternative to rags.

At Tuckenhay Mill, it was the women and children who sorted the rags into piles of linen or cotton, removing buttons and other fastenings before shredding. Shredding machinery was cast iron with fearsome teeth, in an era before proper rules and regulations on health and safety existed. Rags had to be shredded into uniformly small pieces, about three inches square, dusted and boiled, before they were steeped in bleach. The bleach, or caustic soda, in turn had to be removed, as any residue left in the pulp would make the end product smell and turn a sickly green. After bleaching and washing, the 'half stuff', as it was known, was beaten into a pulp, which was then known as 'stuff'. Beating softened and frayed the fibres, so that they would mesh together into sheets of paper.

A strict hierarchy existed in the paper trade. At its zenith were the ten papermakers, who had served a seven-year apprenticeship and were often the sons of papermakers. At Tuckenhay, the papermakers lived in tied cottages at Orchard Terrace, a short hop from the mill, across the bridge on the river bank. Most precious to these men was the recipe book, in which they carried the secrets of the trade, handed down from generation to generation. A Colour Book from Tuckenhay Mill survives in the archives at Totnes Museum, but even with the formulae to hand only a papermaker could make sense of the instructions. On 10 November 1939, is recorded the recipe for cornflower blue thin card, known as Millbourn Blue Wove Vellum La Post 40, handmade for the firm of Begg, Kennedy, Elder. On the opposing page is a sample of the finished paper, and a sample after drying. The difference is marked even to an untrained eye.

On page 84, in the same neat handwriting, is an order for a rather special customer, made in March 1950:

For H.M. The King
Millbourn C. Wove Imperial 90
Weight at vat 80th 480
Rags 1/2 NWC 1/2 outshots
Colour no colour no blue (natural rag)
1/2 ts alum 1/2 ts soap

The result was off-white writing paper. But on many of the off-white papers is written meticulously 'too bright' or some other comment. The difference is indiscernible to all but the trained eye. Upon the skilled hands and eyes of these papermakers, rested the responsibility of creating the highest possible quality of paper. They worked in a high-ceilinged vat room, dipping a wooden-framed sieve into a vat of pulp. This rag pulp was mixed with spring water piped from further up the valley, its purity vital to the process and the ulti-mate quality of the end product. This mould was lowered in vertically, and brought out horizontally with pulp attached to the sieve (see picture on p104). It was a papermaker's fear that he would lose 'the shake', the technique by which he dislodged just the right amount of excess pulp and water.

Once the sheets of paper were lifted out, the 'couchers' sandwiched them between sheets of thick woollen felt, building a giant sandwich some eighteen inches high. Even the type or colour of felt was marked in the recipe book. Once the water was pressed out of them, the sheets were pressed again between sheets of zinc, to remove any marks.

In order that paper would take ink, it had to be 'sized' in gelatine, made from animal skins. This was another highly skilled job, where the temperature of the gelatinous mix affected the colour, and the recipe varied according to the quality of rags. The process varied according to the type of paper required, and the high-quality drawing paper for which Tuckenhay Mill was famous was sized in winter. The papermaker's recipe book reveals that sometimes even the felts themselves were sized: 'Too much soap and alum made blisters in paper – sized felts as well as paper, paper quite hard sized'. A batch of sta-tionery for The British Museum had to be re-sized because it was 'too light'.

*A papermaker demonstrates 'the shake', a vital skill for making handmade paper.*

Among the ancillary staff at the mill were the 'beater men' who made up the pulp, the 'felt boys', and the 'dryers' who hung the sheets in a room with slatted wooden bars allowing the air to circulate between them. Originally paper was dried over ropes made from cow hair, chosen because it would not stain the paper. Drying paper sheets took three to five days, before it was left to mature and was reasonably flat. Every particular of the drying process was noted down, as any change could make a difference when making paper by hand. In a trial in October 1941, the resultant paper was noted as, 'For collo-type work, good smooth surface. Extra pressure on drying rolls. 2 days impress. Rolled and re rolled'.

Paper for bank notes was finished off by adding a chemical that helped to prevent forgery. An advertising flyer, produced by the mill during the Depression of the 1930s, shows how specialised Millbourn's products were:

> Made solely by skilled hand labour, and specially suitable for hard
> wear and tear for ledgers in constant use... Carefully sized to resist
> the strongest inks, and to bear erasure. Ideal for use with fountain
> pens... A quality very easy to write upon, due to uniform finish, and
> absence of hairs on the surface.

BEST HAND-MADE WRITINGS.
DRAWING AND LEDGER PAPERS.
LOANS AND COLOURED LOANS.

# Millbourn's
## BRITISH

BANK NOTES-CHEQUE PAPERS,
OLD STYLE HAND-MADE PRINTINGS,
DECKLE EDGE NOTE AND  ·   ·
ENVELOPE PAPERS.

## HAND MADE
## PAPERS.

A. MILLBOURN & CO, L.ᵀᴰ   LONDON OFFICE,
TUCKENHAY MILLS,   30, LUDGATE HILL.

*A trade flyer for Millbourn's, produced during the uncertain years of the Depression.*

The heaviest weight of paper was called Double Elephant, weighing in at 120 pounds. Parchment had historically been made from animal skins, but at Tuckenhay, so the flyer boasted:

> Vellum Parchment made by hand from specially prepared Extra strong rags, to ensure the greatest possible strength as a substitute for Parchment skins and Japanese vellum. Sized to stand Heavy Writing and Erasure. Free from greasiness and ideal for Writing and Ruling.

Among Millbourn's customers were law firms, for whom the mill produced legal parchment, ideal for long-running disputes in chancery. Its merits included 'Extreme Strength and Durability, Impervious to Mildew, Dampness and the ravages of Time'.

The Report of Commissioners on the Employment of Children and Young Persons in 1843 and 1865, identified paper mills generally as good workplaces, with airy and spacious buildings. Children were said, by Victorian standards, to be healthier and better clothed than those in other industries. But rag shredding was dusty work, causing or aggravating respiratory diseases such as asthma, bronchitis and tuberculosis. The rag boiler houses were hot and steamy, causing rheumatism, and bending and stooping over the vats lifting the pulp, must have left papermakers with permanent backache.

The 100-strong workforce was drawn from neighbouring villages, mostly Cornworthy and Ashprington, and on a dark winter's morning the lanes would be full of bobbing lanterns as the workers walked to work. The 1861 census returns for Devon list 815 paper workers in the county. Inside, the mill was lit by gas lamps, until it began to generate and use its own electricity in the early twentieth century. A bell, still attached to the end wall of the building, signalled the start and end of the working day, timed by the clock on the distinctive square tower. The clock tower was added in 1889, when the mill was extended and altered. The clock had come from the parish church in nearby Totnes. It was Henry Symons who made these alterations. Symons was a distinctive figure around the village of Tuckenhay, which he appeared to regard as his feudal domain, which in a sense it was. He even 'inspected' the cottage gardens with a critical eye. But as well as tinkering with the building, he introduced drastic changes to the workforce. Three years after the alterations were complete, he decided to run the mill without properly trained paper workers. Not surprisingly, this inflamed the Original Society of Papermakers, the industry's trade union, which took industrial action. But Symons was no Rupert Murdoch, and his attempt to take on the union was a disaster. He was forced to recruit skilled men to replace those he had sacked. They came from all over the country: the Elstone and Godwin families arrived from North Wales; the Smiths from Wookey Hole; the Lovelands from Kent; and the Lynns from Carshalton. It was these families who saw the boom years at Tuckenhay Mill. After the First World War, there were eight vats working to produce paper, and the mill began producing paper for bank notes.

During the Great Depression of the 1930s, Tuckenhay managed to keep going, but many mills were forced out of work. The Original Society of Papermakers felt the trade was threatened:

A large proportion of present day apprentices are non-papermakers' sons, and as such have not grown up with the traditions of the Trade, which has done so much in the past to produce good Craftsmen. It was the pride of many papermakers' sons to be able to make and couch paper, which he had heard so much talk about, but this is not the case with the present generation.

Although the union was bemoaning this loss of skills and tradition, it was battling against the tide. In 1947 the union itself was wound up. But at the mill in this little Devon hamlet, the ideals and traditions it represented continued. They set up their own union, operating under the same principles and rules, with a benevolent fund and pension scheme.

By 1962 Tuckenhay was one of only four mills in the entire country producing paper made by hand, although machine-made paper was made alongside it from the 1950s. Ignominiously, in its final years, the mill produced paper pulp for foreign markets. In August 1970, Millbourn's went into voluntary receivership. The closure was the front-page story in the *Totnes Times*. According to the report, forty men were told they had lost their jobs as they finished their shifts. Some of these semi-skilled workers had difficulties finding other work, because they lived in 'inaccessible places': villages such as Tuckenhay, Dittisham and Blackawton, within walking distance of the mill. The tied cottages were sold, and twenty-three adults and eleven children were made homeless. Some 130 years of papermaking by hand had come to an end.

After eight years of dereliction, the mill was bought by Peter Wheeler, a surveyor who had developed Camden Lock in London. The vast stone buildings were converted into holiday accommodation, and once again the rumble of a water wheel filled the quiet valley, providing electricity to power the complex and feed into the national grid. But the thud of a water turbine jarred the ears of visitors holidaying in the quiet valley, and it was disconnected. Today an outdoor swimming-pool lies in the spot where a reservoir once collected water from the river, in order to build up the pressure to power the mill; arched windows still bring light into the former vat room, where visitors play badminton; and families sleep in the old drying lofts, where the last sheet of handmade paper once lay on a winter's day in 1962.

### A Little Piece of Home

Sixteen-year-old Robert Guy sailed from Barnstaple to the New World in 1619. We do not know exactly what he took with him, except hope and dreams of a new life. But among the goods that also travelled to the colonies from his native North Devon were items of pottery – pieces of which have been discovered in the earliest Virginian settlements. When Robert Guy landed, the Virginia Company undertook to provide him with clothes, weapons, agricultural tools and household goods, and enough food and drink to see him through his first year. He was also given fifty acres of land, corn and cattle, and was entitled to half the profits from his plot.

Robert was one of seventy 'young single men brought up to husbandry' on that voyage. In other words he came from a poor rural parish, where the population increases at the beginning of the seventeenth century had led to a shortage of jobs and low wages.

Robert Guy sailed in the *Swan*, a ship of a hundred tons owned by merchant John Delbridge. Those who sailed in one of his ships were fortunate as the vessels were well provisioned. This meant that when these young men arrived in the New World their chances of survival were good. On the long journey across the Atlantic, many would-be settlers succumbed to disease brought on by the cramped conditions on board. But Delbridge had a good record: not one of the men who sailed on the *Swan*, died en route. A London ship that sailed on the same voyage with two hundred people lost sixteen before it landed.

But what awaited these early settlers was far from the Promised Land of which they had hoped. Of the 4,000 people sent from North Devon between 1618 and 1621, over 3,000 died almost at once. We know that Robert Guy survived for at least six years, and probably longer: he is recorded as living on Hogs Island in a document of 1625. Once he had established himself, it is likely that he would have given pride of place in his house to a little piece of home: excavations by archaeologists in these early settlements have produced shards of pottery made in the North Devon towns of Bideford and Barnstaple. What John Delbridge and his fellow North Devon merchants had established was a new trade route, and a ready export market for a local commodity.

Another of those who made the voyage from Barnstaple was William Harwood, who became governor of one of the first plantations in Virginia. This plantation, Martin's Hundred, was established in 1618, covering an area of 20,000 acres, a quarter of a mile up the James River. This area just inland from Chesapeake Bay suffers from severe storms, when rainwater would have gushed down the ravines edging the little settlement.

Although the land had been 'granted' to the Virginia Company, it was actually the territory of the Algonquin or Powhatan tribe, whose legendary princess, Pocahontas, married John Rolfe. For eight years after this marriage in 1614, relations between settlers and Indians were peaceful. Colonists cleared the heavily forested land, put up wooden houses, and cultivated fields to grow tobacco. Tobacco was the route to riches. Originally smoked for medicinal purposes, it was beginning to be used recreationally in seventeenth-century England. A colonist could make more money in one year in Virginia than he could if he worked for several years in England. But the consequences of growing a cash crop have become all too familiar (and are still apparent in modern Africa). Many starved. One of the unfortunate twenty-three who died over the winter, Richard Frethorne, had complained in a letter to his parents in England of a shortage of food and other supplies:

> I have nothing at all, no not a shirt to my backe, but two Ragges nor no Clothes, but one poore suite, nor but one pair of shooes, but one paire of stockins, but one Capp... I am not halfe a quarter so strong as I was in England, and all is for want of victualls, for I do protest unto you, that I have eaten more in one day at home then I have allowed me here for a Weeke.

Starvation was not the only adversity faced by the new colonists. The other threat was the locals. The founders of Martin's Hundred had started with idealistic ideas of assimilation. Powhatan children were to be offered an education in the settlement, where they would be taught the English religion and social customs. Families of colonists were to take in local children, and in exchange send colonists to live with tribal families.

When Opecanecough became their new chief, the Powhatan tribe decided they had endured these foreigners for long enough, and vowed to throw them out for good. In the uprising of 1622, settlers were attacked. Contemporary accounts tell us that many Native Indians were having breakfast with the settlers in their houses on the morning of 22 March. This was a common occurrence. But on this spring morning, the visitors suddenly snatched up the colonists' own tools and weapons and set about them. These were the very metal tools and weapons that had helped to cement the relationship. Excavations have uncovered graves that bear out the accounts left by survivors, including the remains of a scalped older woman.

Martin's Hundred suffered particularly badly; nearly eighty people were killed or abducted, and forty graves have been found in Wolstenholme Town, which was at the centre of the parish. The survivors fled upriver to Jamestown. When they returned all that remained were two houses and 'a piece of the church'.

Governor William Harwood, appears to have been absent when the Indians attacked. But in a 'muster' of 1624 to establish the defence potential of the settlement, in his household were four adult males and an arsenal of military hardware including twenty-three swords, suits of armour and chain mail, and ammunition. This was the armour familiar in portraits of Drake and other men of the era, too cumbersome to be worn as the settlers went about daily life. In the interim about fifty settlers had returned to Martin's Hundred but by the time a census was taken of the whole colony in February

1625, nearly half the fifty returnees had died of disease and only twenty-seven people inhabited Martin's Hundred. The six households counted at Martin's Hundred on 4 February appeared to be well provisioned, according to the census.

In this 1625 census, there were six households in Martin's Hundred – mostly single men, and only two children. Fewer than 3 per cent of colonists in Virginia in this period had brought their wives. Women were outnumbered three to one in Martin's Hundred and four to one in the colony as a whole.

At least three people in Martin's Hundred owned boats and regularly travelled upriver to Jamestown. It was here that the earliest North Devon pottery found in Virginia was excavated. These finds date from the 1630s, leading experts to believe that by that time the trade was well established. John Delbridge, who gets much of the credit for establishing this transatlantic supply line, was an MP, three times mayor of Barnstaple, with business interests in Bermuda as well as North America. Early planters who settled on riverbanks acted as middlemen, running stores, selling the limited range of goods that was shipped to the colony. The first known cargo of North Devon pottery to Virginia is recorded in the Barnstaple port books of 1635, but shipments were probably included in vessels to provide basic equipment to the settlers.

By the end of the century, trade was expanding as the neighbouring state of Maryland provided a ready market for North Devon pottery for the expanding dairy industry. The potteries even exported ready-made pottery ovens to the colonies.

Barnstaple and Bideford had developed into pottery towns during the Middle Ages. The raw material for the earthenware was on the doorstep at Fremington, where the clay was clean and free from stones.

By the time settlers were heading for the New World, the Barnstaple potters had set up shop in the grounds of the old Norman castle. The castle was already a ruin, and the land around it had become the castle green. It was in this area at the confluence of the Rivers Yeo and Tavy that potter Peter Takell worked. He is thought to have been the earliest tobacco pipe-maker in the town, and churned out hundreds of pipes, usually to pay off his debts. Near neighbours were John Coulscott and George Beare. Excavations in Bear Street, under the car park built to serve Barnstaple Library, revealed the base of a seventeenth-century pottery kiln belonging to the Beare family. Made of brick with a tile base, it is the shape of an elongated bagatelle board. It is divided by a wall down the centre, on one side of which was the fire and on the other the area where pots were placed for firing. Archaeologists lifted the kiln, and it has been re-laid as part of the display in Barnstaple Museum.

*The Universal British Directory* of 1792 records female potters among the traders: Margaret Besley was a potter in Barnstaple and Mary Carder operated in Bideford.

A Bideford historian, John Watkins, writing in 1792, considered the pottery trade was a way to get rich quick. There was obviously some rivalry between the potters of the two towns, and his view is heavily biased towards his home town:

> The earthenware made here is generally supposed to be superior to any other of the kind, and this is accounted for from the peculiar excellence of the gravel which this river affords in binding the clay. That this is the true reason, seems clear, from the fact that though the potteries at Barnstaple make use of the same sort of clay, yet their earthenware is not held in such esteem at Bristol etc as that of Bideford.

These potteries were producing earthenware bowls, such as pipkins and porringers; pitchers, tankards and chamber pots; baking trays, storage jars and even flat irons. The style was rustic, often decorated with ships, fish,

*The Beare family kilm, the lowest section was lifted by archaeologists and rebuilt in Barnstaple Museum.*

cockerels and flowers. The potters also produced floor tiles, which are to be found in churches in the area round the pottery towns. Sgraffito ware was popular. This was pottery with an ochre-coloured background, on which a dark pattern was made by scratching through a white slip into the clay. It was then fired with a lead glaze.

Throughout the seventeenth century the pottery export trade grew. Ireland and Wales had been early customers, particularly for butter dishes and other products for dairying. Cargoes went out to Barbados and other Caribbean islands, and British ships had a monopoly on trade with the American colonies until the American War of Independence. In 1806 records show that a third of the ships leaving Bideford with a cargo carried North Devon pottery. More pottery was shipped in summer, as production slowed in winter because the industry was highly dependant on the weather. Working hours were shorter in winter, as there were fewer hours of daylight. Between November and February, frost could damage the pots, and it was more difficult to dry the end product.

Wasteland between the houses in these pottery towns was piled up with wooden faggots, used to fuel the kilns. Fires were a constant hazard.

The eighteenth century saw the gradual demise of North Devon pottery, and the rise of the Staffordshire potteries. In the 1790s, William Marshall came to Bideford for his book on the economy of the south-west of England. His snobbery is evident: 'The pottery, for which only, I believe, this Town is celebrated: chiefly or wholly, the coarser kinds of earthernware'.

The increasingly affluent did not want coarse earthernware – they wanted fine china, such as that produced by Josiah Wedgwood, and for a short period by William Cookworthy at the Plymouth China Works. Ironically the white ball clay found at Peters Marland, was exported to the pottery towns of the Midlands.

The potters of North Devon owed much of their export trade to their location. But as foreign trade increased, ships became larger, and could not berth in such shallow waters. The last traditional pottery in Bideford, at East the Water, closed down in 1916, due to lack of demand.

### Plymouth China

Fine porcelain was the ultimate sign of upward mobility in the eighteenth century. The sitting rooms of the aristocracy were adorned with china cabinets, displaying these symbols of their wealth. Trade with the East had introduced the British to translucent oriental china, and to that other Chinese commodity – tea – the drink of choice at many fashionable parties. The first

*William Cookworthy's house in Notte Street, demolished in the 1970s.*

Chinese tea sets to arrive in Britain were considered so fragile that a little milk was poured in first to prevent breakages. So began the ritual that has become synonymous with the English.

Those lower down the social scale, the country gentry and prosperous farmers, drank tea, when they could obtain it, from pewter mugs. But at a cost. These metallic mugs conducted heat, and tea drinking was accompanied by burnt lips and fingers. The alternative was earthernware, but both these were out of date. The fashionable home demanded porcelain, and as prosperity grew during the first half of the century, so public demand grew for the ultimate in consumer goods.

At the dawn of the century, the secret of porcelain manufacture remained just that, an oriental secret. The first European manufacturer to crack the formula was in the German town of Meissen in 1709, closely followed by the French potters of Sevres. The great names of English pottery manufacture were producing beautiful china, but it lacked the transparency and hardness of true porcelain. The porcelain recipe was the ultimate industrial secret, and it was discovered by a weaver's son from Kingsbridge, and first produced in Plymouth.

William Cookworthy had an unpromising start to life. As the eldest of seven children, at the age of fourteen, he was expected to support the rest of the family when his father died. But Cookworthy had all the qualities of a budding entrepreneur. When the impoverished but clever teenager caught the eye of a London chemist, and was offered an apprenticeship, he walked the 200 miles from his home to the capital, to save the coach fare. During his six-year apprenticeship, William taught himself French, Latin and Greek, and impressed his employer with his intelligence and integrity. So much so, that in 1726 he returned to Devon as a partner in a new Plymouth firm of wholesale chemists and druggists, Bevan and Cookworthy. Here William made and sold what we would call today herbal remedies, with an alarming proportion of lead and mercury among the otherwise plant-based ingredients. On his death his notebook contained formulae for 180 medicinal preparations, which he supplied to doctors and apothecaries in Devon, Somerset and Cornwall.

William was a Quaker, and despite his humble origins, knew all the literati and great names of his age. John Smeaton stayed with him at his home in Notte Street near Sutton Pool, during the construction of his Eddystone Lighthouse. Dr Johnson was another member of Cookworthy's circle. The writer was privy to a private demonstration by Cookworthy of the use of dowsing rods to detect metals. Cookworthy's scientific background in mineralogy and chemistry did not prevent him from having an open mind about the less explicable. Dowsing or divining rods were widely used to prospect for metallic lodes.

As a Plymouth-based chemist, the navy was naturally among Cookworthy's customers. The night before the *Endeavour* departed for Cook's first voyage of discovery in the Pacific, her officers spent their last evening ashore at Cookworthy's home. Captain James Cook was leading an expedition for the Royal Society to observe the transit of Venus across the sun. It was this three-year voyage of discovery that was to establish his reputation as a great navigator. But he also built up a reputation, during his career, for looking after his crew: only one man was lost in three voyages, lasting a total of nine years. They sailed through some of what are still regarded as the most testing waters on earth: round the Cape of Good Hope, to the shores of the Antarctic, to the Bering Strait, and across the sparsely populated expanse of the Pacific. William Cookworthy must get some of the credit for the stamina and health of Captain Cook's crew. He was the manufacturer of protein-rich 'stock cubes' that accompanied Cook on these voyages. Although the recipe for this portable soup had been invented by a Mrs Dubois, it was Cookworthy who held the contract to manufacture it for the naval bases in Plymouth and Portsmouth. It was made from offal, including animal hides, which would have ensured a high gelatine content, making it easy to store and transport.

These long voyages of discovery presented another health problem – maintaining a supply of drinking water. Cookworthy worked out in detail how a ship's cooking boiler could be easily converted to distil sea water, and his experiments on this survive in his notebook, stored at Plymouth City Archives. Of course the other health benefit, was that by boiling the water it was also sterilised.

Despite being notoriously absent-minded, Cookworthy was a dedicated, practical and precise scientist. His marriage to Sarah Berry, a fellow Quaker from Taunton, had been happy but short. Her death, only ten years after the wedding, left William with five small girls to bring up, including infant twins. But he could escape from his unhappiness into his laboratory.

Quite what turned Cookworthy's brilliant brain to the conundrum of porcelain manufacture is a mystery, although it was no doubt one of the subjects discussed among his acquaintances. With his background in mineralogy and chemistry, and his laboratory experiments, it would seem natural that he might have ruminated on the solution to this, the industrial secret of the age. The two basic ingredients had been revealed by a French missionary in a letter from China in 1712. It was the precise proportions, and the manufacturing method, which continued to elude the West.

The first record of Cookworthy's interest in porcelain appears in a letter to a friend written in 1745, when he describes examining samples of china clay, discovered in Virginia. But importing raw materials from the New World did not make economic sense, yet at the time there was no known source closer to home. Shortly afterwards, during a visit to Cornwall, Cookworthy discovered there was china clay, also known as kaolin, almost

*Cookworthy's china factory in the High Street.*

on his doorstep. In association with this kaolin, was the other vital ingredient, petuntse, a type of granite, also known as moor stone.

Cookworthy spent the next twenty years trying to perfect the process, building a tall kiln six feet in diameter, in which he fired his experiments. Not only did he have to crack the secret of the exact quantities of china clay and petuntse in the mix, but also the best temperature and duration of the firing. Gradually he discovered that it was the kaolin that gave china its distinctive whiteness, while the addition of petuntse gave the china its transparency. A glaze with these homogenous materials, fired at very high temperatures, resulted in porcelain. But the coal, which was able to heat the kiln to the desired high temperature, was liable to smoke and spoil the product, so he rejected it for wood. Despite the fact that he was not a potter, in 1768 he took out patent number 898 for the sole rights to make and sell, as the patent outlined, 'A kind of Porcellain newly Invented by me, compos'd of Moor Stone or Growan and Grown Clay'.

The glazing process he had developed was far superior to that used in the great pottery towns, and a subject of envy. For a brief two years, Plymouth China was manufactured at a factory near his home at Sutton Pool. It was an ideal location close to the quay where china clay and petuntse were delivered, and the finished goods could be exported. His wood-fired kilns turned out mugs, sauceboats, dinner plates and of course 'compleat sets of Tea China'. Cookworthy employed about fifty people, and used his house in nearby Notte Street as a shop and showroom. William Burt measured its success in his *Review of the Mercantile Trading and Manufacturing State* published in 1816:

> There was such a demand at home and abroad, particularly in America, for its articles which consisted of enameled blue and white china, of all descriptions both ornamental and useful, that they could hardly be made fast enough.

But Cookworthy was no businessman, nor was his partner, the youthful Richard Champion. With the centre of the pottery trade up in the West Midlands, the firm had trouble attracting skilled labour, and Cookworthy was forced to take a turn at decorating the china himself. Firewood was increasingly expensive, and after two years the factory relocated to Bristol, still under the name Plymouth China. The city was a gateway to trade with the rest of Britain and the world, and the huge quantities of wood required for the kilns were more readily available. Despite this, Plymouth China closed in 1778, when Richard Champion was declared bankrupt. True porcelain would never be manufactured in England again. William Cookworthy died two years later in September 1780 and crowds lined the streets between his Plymouth home and the Quaker meeting house where his funeral was held.

Wedgwood speedily negotiated to buy the patent from Champion, but the Staffordshire potters adapted the recipe, using kaolin and petuntse in a mix with 50 per cent calcined bone, to manufacture bone china. This hybrid porcelain did not need to be fired at such high temperatures for such lengthy periods, thereby saving fuel.

*One of the few pieces of Plymouth China to survive.*

# CHAPTER 5

# ONE FOOT IN SEA, ONE FOOT ON SHORE

Nowhere in Devon is far from the sea; at its broadest the county is just over seventy miles from coast to coast. For centuries the sea and the rivers that feed into it provided the most obvious form of transport for goods and people. Those venturing into the hinterland enter sunken lanes, which meander round fields and woodland, making navigation difficult. Rain slices horizontally through the trees, then finds the path of least resistance, running in torrents down the road.

Ferries have been an essential part of Devon's transport infrastructure, connecting the banks of rivers and estuaries. A ferry between Starcross and Exmouth existed from the twelfth century, and even took coaches until the nineteenth century. Water was considered such a superior mode of travel that in the canal age plans were made to link the Bristol Channel with the English Channel. This Grand Western Canal was to run between Taunton and Topsham, but costs mounted and the project was never completed.

County topography has always made communication difficult, and even the modern marvel of digital broadcasting struggles in such a landscape.

## Coast Trade

If you stood on a Devon cliff a century ago, the chances are that you would have seen a small ship 'butting' through the waves. The verb, which John Masefield used in his poem 'Cargoes', was chosen with care. Masefield, who was a former merchant seaman himself, has left us one of the very few descriptions of a coaster, the humble sister to the glamorous tea clippers and liners that sailed the world's oceans. Coasters carried utilitarian cargoes of coal, iron ore and the mass-produced industrial goods in demand in Victorian England. Their trade routes did not have romantic destinations such as the Azores, Valparaíso or Las Palmas. Instead they travelled between Poole and

Liverpool, Glasgow and Plymouth, London and Swansea. These little boats were the worker bees of the industrial revolution. Coasters were an integral part of Devon life for hundreds of years. Now the wharves lie rotting, warehouses have become luxury apartments, and yards which built and maintained the ships are closed. The small ships that hug the Devon coast today are there for pleasure rather than profit.

The wharf which gave its name to the seaside resort of Torquay is long gone. From the foundation of Torre Abbey in 1196, goods unavailable locally would have been landed here to serve the religious community. But it is not until the fourteenth century that we have any records to give an idea of the extent of coastal shipping around Devon.

When Geoffrey Chaucer penned his portrait of a 'shipman', he is thought to have based this sun-tanned mariner on John Hawley, who, like many of his Dartmouth contemporaries, combined his role as merchant and ship owner with that of part-time pirate. Whether or not Chaucer's description was really based on Hawley, Dartmouth was an obvious home port for this medieval sailor. Documents from Chaucer's time record Dartmouth ships and their crews docking in ports all over the West Country, but they also show up in Chester, Wales, Southampton, Portsmouth, East Sussex, Kent and even Kingston-upon-Hull. Foreign imports were landed at major ports such as Exeter, and re-exported to a network of smaller coastal towns. In late fourteenth-century Exeter, 75 per cent of port traffic was coastal ships, carrying cargoes of building stone and roofing slates, coal, corn and fish.

In the fourteenth century we know that Adam Ganne from Teignmouth carried straw to the tiny North Devon port of Appledore in his ship *Nau Dieu*. Just down the coast, on the lower reaches of the Rivers Taw and Yeo, the town of Barnstaple was at the centre of the busy trade up and down the Bristol Channel in the 1390s. This medieval trade was carried in flat-bottomed ships known as 'cogs' and 'ballingers'.

Dartmouth enjoyed its heyday as a port during the sixteenth century. Dartmoor tin was shipped out to Southampton and London, while on the return journey ships from London carried soap, dyes, hops, pitch, tar and cordage for shipbuilding and maintenance.

In 1570 officials recorded the names of sailors and ships that could be available in the event of war. Devon could offer 1,250 men, plus a further 311 who were at sea when the tally was made. Of these, 415 lived within easy reach of Dartmouth, whereas Plymouth (still in its infancy as a major port) and its neighbouring communities could offer fewer than half that number.

Some of those men recorded on the muster would have been relatively unskilled deckhands, whose main jobs were in agriculture. But the town of Bideford, built along the banks of the River Torridge set up a school specifically to help equip the town's children for the trade. In 1625 a teacher was appointed for:

> ...instructing and teaching the children and 'prentices of the inhabitants especially in the art of Arithmetic, [it is] very fit and necessary to teach this in our town...being a town of navigation.

Even though the coastal trade, by its nature sailed along the coast, good navigation was essential. Navigation in the open waters of the Atlantic or the English Channel does not require the same detailed knowledge of the reefs and rocks which lie submerged off the Devon coast waiting to wreck the unwary. This was a trade in which thousands of seamen served, and hundreds lost their lives. To navigate the coast, sailors used 'sea marks', which despite the name were in fact landmarks. These might be chapels or cliff-top beacons, but to the coastal trade they were as good as signposts. They were so vital that in 1566, in the reign of Good Queen Bess, it was a criminal offence to remove them. The penalty was to be outlawed or fined £100. The legislation stated:

> Forasmuch as by the destroying and taking away of certain steeples, woods and other marks standing upon the main shores adjoining to the sea coasts of the realm of England and Wales being as beacons and marks of ancient time accustomed for seafaring men, divers ships have by the lack of such marks of late years been miscarried, perished and lost in the sea.

The coastal trade brought jobs in numerous ports large and small; it brought contact welcome and unwelcome with strangers; and those on land willingly put their own lives at risk to help those in danger on the sea. The crew of the Salcombe Lifeboat in South Hams lost thirteen of her fifteen-man crew when she went to the rescue of the Plymouth schooner *Western Lass* in October 1916. But there were other occasions when the heroes were not members of the rescue services.

In 1891, Devonians emerged from the warmth of an unusually mild, dry February, to find primroses flowering on the steep banks of the lanes. It appeared that spring had arrived. But on Sunday, 8 March, a cold wind blew from the north-east. Next day the wind dropped. The air was still and the temperature fell below freezing. By mid-morning that stillness was disturbed by a south-easterly that rapidly rose to hurricane force. On the tail of the gale, came the Great Blizzard of 1891.

Snow in Devon is a rarity today. The great cliffs of snow that blocked streets and lanes, and barricaded windows up to the first floor on that occasion has never been matched. Wooden fences and telegraph poles snapped under the weight, but the effect the blizzard had at sea was even more devastating.

The three-masted schooner *Lunesdale* was not a Devon ship. She was bound for Runcorn in Cheshire with a cargo of ground chalk, used for cleaning metal plate and whitewashing houses. When the storm hit, the schooner was passing the Isle of Wight, but she was running blind before the wind when she hit the South Devon coast. Even the Start Point lighthouse would have been invisible and inaudible in such a gale.

Crew and captain were clinging to the rigging when she struck the coast to the south of Beesands. Sharp eyes on shore had called out the coastguards, but the roads between the coastguard station at Prawle and Beesands were impassable with snow. Fisherman John Roper braved the fierce seas on the little shingle beach, and threw a lead-weighted line to the ship. Drawing in the line and the rope attached, the captain fastened it to a lifebuoy. But the seas were so rough that it was swept away. As his crew was picked off by the waves, the captain leapt from the rigging and was hauled in by rescuers up to their waists in water. The *Lunesdale* was one of five ships wrecked off Start Point alone that night.

Coastal shipping records are full of tragedies. The *Princess Charlotte* was built in Dartmouth in 1819, and worked the coastal trade for nearly half a century. En route from Port Talbot to Plymouth with a cargo of coal, she foundered off Land's End in a Force 9 gale on 5 January 1867 with the loss of the entire crew. Many ships simply vanished at sea with no firm knowledge of where they went down. In 1863, the Brixham-built *Helen* sailed from South Wales to Penzance with coal in her hold, and went missing. Another Brixham boat, the *Elizabeth*, sailed from Teignmouth in 1868 bound for Runcorn with a cargo of clay; she never arrived. These ships lost at sea were in themselves a hazard. On 25 February 1907, the *Esmerelda* was lost on a voyage from Glasgow to Plymouth. As she beat her way down the Irish Sea, the *Esmerelda* struck floating wreckage ten miles south-west of Kish Lighthouse, but her crew was saved.

Shipmasters had to keep accounts for the owners. Ownership was divided into a complicated system of sixty-four shares, which often included the captain. Other investors might include the widows of sea captains, local businessmen and shipbuilders. Captain Robert Wren, master of the *Sally*, kept meticulous accounts in the closing years of the eighteenth century. He was originally engaged in the transatlantic trade, sailing from Bideford to Canada, Newfoundland and New Orleans. But with the outbreak of the American War of Independence in 1776, the dangers of American privateers in wartime was probably the reason he turned to the coastal trade – insurance premiums were commensurate with the dangers. The transatlantic trade required a much larger crew, and he records that several men jumped ship when they reached their destination. In contrast, coastal shipping required a crew of just five or six men.

Wren's accounts of a voyage between London and Milford Haven reveal the essentials for such a trip. Provisions included beer, beef, bread, potatoes, lard, butter, cheese, sugar and veal, which were supplemented by 'fish bought in Channell'. Before they left port he paid for repairs to the 'tops' and 'gallant', presumably damaged on the last voyage, or perhaps through normal wear and tear. His route took the *Sally* round the Lizard and Land's End, before heading up to South Wales. In these notorious waters running repairs had to be made on board to keep the ship seaworthy. Putting into port wasted time, and would bump up costs with pilot fees and port taxes. So the ship carried nails,

*The Old Customs House (centre of picture) at Bayard's Cove, Dartmouth, used until the latter half of the twentieth century.*

sail needles and thread, a barrel of tar, scrubbing brushes and buckets.

In port Captain Wren paid casual labourers for 'getting things on board', paid for ale for boatmen and carters, as well as pilotage and customs duty. In a series of voyages carrying culm (low-grade coal) to and from Dartmouth, he paid an extra tax, mayoral dues, which amounted to a quarter of the customs duty. These mayoral dues are not recorded at any of the other ports of call.

The crew's diet varied according to what was seasonally available. So when they loaded at Dartmouth in early June 1776, the provisions list included beans, cabbage, calves head meal, 'a pigg', fowls, and '3 tun herrings'.

Once Captain Wren had arrived in port and unloaded, he had to negotiate the next cargo. This was not always plain sailing as his accounts show. In September 1776, among the captain's normal expenses for board and lodging, is included hire of a horse and travel to London 'to endeavour getting employ for the ship in which I did not succeed'.

Dirty and unassuming they may have been, but coasters were vital to the industrial revolution: they were an essential part of the distribution network even after the arrival of the railways.

The Welsh Fleet, as it became known, operated on the route between Devon and South Wales. When the great copper mines near Tavistock opened, copper ore was taken to the nearest port on the River Tamar for export. Unlike tin, copper could not be smelted easily in situ, and was sent

*Ships queuing in the River Tamar to be taken by steam tug to the copper port of Morwellham Quay.*

to the smelters in South Wales. To make the journey profitable, each coaster needed a return cargo, and South Wales had plentiful supplies of one thing that Devon lacked – coal. As Devon miners dug ever deeper for copper, so coal-powered beam engines were needed to pump out the water found at such depths. Shipowners and masters found a profitable two-way trade.

Copper is not an easy substance to transport. Access to the holds of these coastal sailing ships was through a hatch, and cargoes had to be loaded manually, rather than by mechanical means. Ores of different qualities had to be kept separate in the hold, usually with a sail or sand. It was soon observed that the iron bolts, which held ships' timbers together, were corroded by copper ore stored below the waterline. This is thought to be the reason many ships were lost in good weather. Ships which could access ports such as Neath and Morwellham, had to be under 150 tons with a shallow draught, and even after the advent of engines, were often sailing ships. Carrying deadweight copper ore in the hold, made a ship unstable in storms, obviously more prevalent in winter, and one leg of the voyage would be against the wind.

Knowing the dangers of winter voyages, some masters and owners preferred to lay up boats during the winter months, but of course had to cope with the resultant loss of profit. Certainly ordinary seamen would not have been able to consider such a long period without wages. Inevitably quays became congested in winter, and Devon Great Consols Mine is known to have restricted output at certain periods for this reason.

The Rivers Torridge and Taw were the last places in the British Isles where the wooden coastal sailing ships, which had once been such a common sight, survived. Here black-hulled schooners and ketches, with patched sails in grey and brown, still operated into the early twentieth century. William

*William Slade making a sennet mat, part of the equipment of traditional sailing ships.*

Slade was one of the last masters and owners of these romantic vessels. He was born in Appledore in 1892, in those days a seafaring village whose ships and seamen had a reputation in complete contrast to its size. Every man, woman, and child in this tiny port grew up with the smell of tarred rigging in their nostrils. Above the village was a signal tower, built in 1841 for William Yeo, owner of the Richmond Dock, to give him advance warning of his ships passing over the Bideford Bar (it was demolished in 1952). This is the bar of shallow sand across the channel where the Torridge and Taw rivers join to meet the sea. The bar makes entry into Appledore port hazardous, and leaving the port doubly so. In his autobiography William Slade recalled:

> It was a fine sight to see forests of masts and sails going over the bar after Christmas. Sometimes up to 100 little vessels in one tide would leave the port. In calms a coil of ratline would be used to tow the ship. This would be made fast on the bowsprit end and the other end on the after thwart of the boat with a bowline. Two men would be in the boat with oars the length of the boat and according to the direction you wanted to pull the ship the bowline would slide from one side to the other, so that the boat would go from one bow of the ship to the other without easing on the oars. This would give the ship just enough movement to steer, but it was hard work especially when one of the boatmen was only a boy.

To supplement their wages, Appledore sailors joined the Royal Naval Reserve training battery near the village. They fitted their RNR duties in between voyages, or when the weather was bad. Slade continued:

> Many times as a youngster I have seen a crowd of sailors on Appledore Quay early in the morning, watching the bar and the weather. If they couldn't get over the bar, they would hastily put on their naval uniform and be off to the Battery at West Appledore. The men from Braunton would come from Crow and back in the evening, walking from the sandhills home. Those who manned the bigger ships going further away would arrange to spend Christmas at Appledore, as they would nearly always have a month in which to do their drill. As they were paid wages by the trip (or voyage), the owners had to agree.

As an Appledore lad of only a year old, William was taken to sea by his mother. She had sailed with her father and brothers on the family cargo smack, and knew the coastal trade, handling the wheel as well as any man. After leaving school at the age of twelve, William discovered that he suffered badly from seasickness, but he still spent the rest of his life in the coastal trade.

Although his family were shipowners, and his father was a ship's master, William started his life at sea, as generations of seafarers before him, as a cabin boy. On his father's ketch *Ulelia*, he had to cook, scrub, mend the sails, and join the rest of the crew loading and unloading the cargo. Little concession was made for his age:

> Life in those early days was certainly no bed of roses. When at sea I was often miserably seasick and as Father never felt seasick in his life he felt no sympathy for me and perhaps it was just as well. When we got in harbour, the cargo had to be winched out and I had to do my full share. In addition, when the others had their rest between meals, there was always something for me to do. The daily routine was: get up 6am, light the fire and get breakfast going, then on the winch. If there was a minute to spare, run into the galley, see to the fire etc; 8am take the breakfast down for the crew. After breakfast, the others had a rest, but not the boy: he washed up dishes and cleared away the mess, hurriedly got the dinner going and then the shouting commenced. 'Come on, slowcoach, it's time to start work. They are waiting for you.' At dinner time the same again. After tea the crew had their freedom, but the boy still had a lot to do. The stove had to be cleaned out, the fire laid-in ready for the morning and the potatoes had to be peeled for dinner the next day. It was always 9pm before the boy finished work and after a wash it was time to go to bed. How I longed to be promoted to ordinary seaman!

Working hours were long, and easily prolonged by bad weather. In fog all hands had to keep watch for reefs, landmarks and other ships. Rudimentary oil lamps were carried, but many ships were run down and sunk by another vessel in such conditions. Cargoes were not only landed at harbours and wharves, but on beaches. Beaching the ship on shore, the cargo would be unloaded into carts while the tide ebbed, then anchored when the tide came in. Working with the tides in this way, the crew would work for several days to unload, snatching a few hours sleep while the tide was high.

Ships averaged about 100 tons during the nineteenth century, with each being crewed by a team of five or six men. Voyages usually lasted about nineteen days in normal weather conditions, including days in port for loading and unloading. But ships could be held up in port by contrary winds and bad weather, for as long as three months.

Steamships were not used in the south-west coastal trade until the second half of the nineteenth century. Profits were maximised by small crews, and the wind was, of course, free. Steamships required a crew of ten, and although not so prone to the exigencies of contrary winds, required fuel. To make a profit, a steamship had to make a fast turnaround once it reached port, a task made difficult by the fact that many of these ports were tidal. Sailing ships were still a common sight in the coastal trade at the end of the nineteenth century and even into the twentieth.

William Slade was in his late twenties when he witnessed the progression from sail to steam. His ship still carried sail, but he had installed an auxiliary engine after the First World War. As master he was also engineer:

Whilst in harbour there was always plenty to do in the engine room besides having to work the cargoes in and out. The accommodation aft was crude and living conditions miserable, because half the cabin was taken for engine room space and the smell of diesel oil was everywhere. There was no sleep at sea because of the excessive vibration and noise. Often the top of the flimsy deck house leaked

*The busy port of Bideford in the heyday of the coastal trade.*

like a colander, in fact, for twenty years I hardly knew what it was like to have a dry bed to sleep in when away from home. To me it was my living, and I did what I could to make it successful, but only I know how miserable I often felt during the time at sea and how I fought against the desire to lay windbound as often as I could.

Here then is a picture which tallies rather better with John Masefield's 'dirty little coasters'. But Slade did admit that the additional power provided by the engine brought compensations – a shorter working day and a diet that was not restricted to salted beef and fish.

Britain's coastal waters were used as the 'test track' for many cutting-edge technologies in the nineteenth century. The steam engine was in use commercially at sea, seventeen years before it hit the headlines during the 1829 Rainhill Locomotive Trials won by Stephenson's Rocket. Many of the innovations in ship design and shipbuilding were also tested in the coastal fleet. Paddle steamers were the first iron ships – the *Aaron Manby* built in 1821 is thought to have been the first. *The Rainbow*, another paddle steamer, was the fastest ship of its day in 1837. Paddle power was superseded by propeller power, and it was the SS *Archimedes*, launched in 1838, which served as the working prototype on coastal routes. Technology for improving ship stability, navigation, steam turbines, and high-pressure boilers were all tested on coasters.

The building of the iron railroads did not kill the coastal trade, but rather, augmented it. There is even evidence that rail and shipping bosses collaborated to agree freight rates. It was eventually the lorry that killed the golden age of sail and steam, taking coastal freight on to the roads.

### Winstanley's Whimsy

Henry Winstanley was a practical joker, a showman, and creator of two 'theme parks'. But he was also responsible for one of the most daring building projects of the seventeenth century – the first Eddystone Lighthouse.

It was built on one of three reefs running roughly parallel to each other. These rocks stand ten miles from Rame Head, thirteen miles south-west of Plymouth, guarding the entrance to Plymouth Sound. Novelist Daniel Defoe wrote a vivid description in his book entitled *A Tour Through England and Wales*:

In the entrance to this bay, lyes a large and most dangerous rock, which at high-water is cover'd, but at low-tide lyes bare, where many a good ship has been lost, even in the view of safety, and many a ship's crew drown'd in the night, before help could be had for them.

Henry Winstanley was born in 1644, in Saffron Walden, Essex, hundreds of miles from Plymouth. Although he was from fairly humble origins, Henry showed an aptitude for drawing and mechanical invention. His first entre-preneurial enterprise was the house he built in Littlebury, which he advertised to the public as Winstanley's Wonders. Visitors paid a shilling apiece to come through the turnstile built into the front fence. It was a house full of practical jokes and tricks, rather like those employed on a ghost train. One of the attractions was a chair on which visitors sat before it suddenly plunged downwards. This was Charles II's Restoration England, where people loved to indulge in frivolity after the stern puritan years of the Commonwealth when theatres were banned.

Close to Winstanley's Essex home, was Audley End, a country seat bought by the Merry Monarch himself, so as to be closer to his mistress Nell Gwyn. Winstanley was making quite a name for himself among the gentry who visited his house of wonders. He also offered his services as a draughts-man, advertising for commissions to make copper plate engravings of 'nobles and gentlemen's houses'. Charles II offered him the job of keeper of works for Audley End.

Winstanley was beginning to make substantial sums of money, and launched his next project at the Hyde Park end of Piccadilly. He designed and built Winstanley's Waterworks, a series of moving tableaux featuring tricks and fantastic effects with fountains and waterspouts. For thirty years people came from all over England to visit the waterworks, at a cost of up to half a crown.

As the fortunes of the Essex eccentric grew, he invested in five ships. When two of his vessels were wrecked on the Eddystone reef within weeks of each other, he made the long journey to Plymouth to investigate. So it was that in 1695 he heard that there had been a proposal to build a lighthouse on these dangerous rocks, which had not been acted upon for over thirty years.

It was in 1664 that two leading Plymouth gentlemen had first made this preposterous suggestion. Sir John Coryton and Henry Brunker proposed the building of a tower, on the Eddystone rock far out at sea. A team of men would live in the edifice and light and re-light candles, whose flames would serve as a warning to ships fighting their way through the dangerous waters into Plymouth Sound. There was no precedent. Medieval lighthouse chapels built on the cliffs, such as those at Braunton and Ilfracombe, had been used to warn sailors that they were approaching land. But good navigation and luck in bad weather were the only factors that prevented ships foundering on reefs out at sea.

Winstanley joined a syndicate of investors, putting in £5,000 of his own money, and began work in the summer of 1696. His first problem was getting there. Winstanley and his workmen had to leave Plymouth at high tide so that the ebb took them clear of the Sound and out into the open Channel. Heading out to the east of the Eddystone rocks, a journey that could take between three to six hours, they hoped to catch the tidal stream flowing west. With luck this would enable them to approach the reef at low water, when the rocks were exposed. After this tricky and lengthy journey, they would have a mere two or three hours in which to do the work, before the sea surged back over the reef.

In his own account, Winstanley outlined the difficulties that had delayed building work:

> Nothing being or could be left there for the first two years but what was most thoroughly affixed to the rock or the work at very extraordinary charge. And though nothing could be attempted to be done but in the summer season, yet the weather then at times would prove so bad that for ten or fourteen days together the sea would be so raging about these rocks – caused by out winds and the running of the ground seas coming from the main ocean – that though the weather should seem to be most calm in other places, yet here it would mount and fly more than two hundred foot. And therefore all our works were constantly buried at those times and exposed to the mercy of the seas and no power was to come near to make good or help anything as I have often experienced with my workmen in a boat in great danger: only having the satisfaction to see my work imperfectly at times as the seas fell from it at a mile or two distance – and this at the prime of the year and no wind or appearance of bad weather.

Winstanley had designed a tower that would have looked at home in any fairground. The tower was composed of pre-fabricated components, fixed to the rock by twelve iron stanchions. By the summer of 1697 the building was beginning to take shape. England was at war with France during the War of the Grand Alliance, so an Admiralty warship loitered nearby, to guard against attack from the French. But on 28 June the ship was called away on

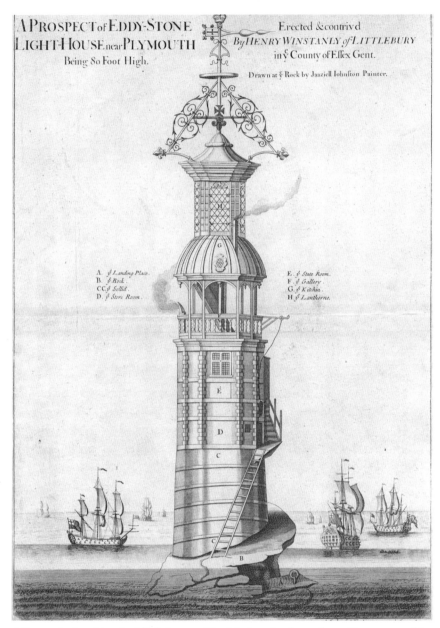

A PROSPECT of EDDY-STONE LIGHT-HOUSE near PLYMOUTH Being 80 Foot High.

Erected & contriv'd By HENRY WINSTANLY of LITTLEBURY in ye County of Essex Gent.

Drawn at ye Rock by Jaaziell Iohnston Painter.

A. ye Landing Place.
B. ye Rock.
CC ye Sollid.
D. ye Store Room.

E. ye State Room.
F. ye Gallery.
G. ye Kitchin.
H. ye Lanthorne.

*Winstanley's whimsical lighthouse. The kitchen is above the gallery, topped by the diamond—paned lantern.*

other duties for a few days. French pirates, either by chance or careful planning, saw a way to make a few 'livres'. Once they were close enough to the reefs, rowing boats were launched. The pirates rushed the workmen, stripped them, and grabbing Winstanley, made a dash back to France.

The pirates must have been delighted with the potential ransom they might expect for this captive gentleman. But once back on French soil they were astonished to find that they had upset the Sun King himself, Louis XIV. Legend has it that instead of showing delight at the capture of such an English asset, Louis was furious and the pirates were punished. Despite the state of war, Louis was aware of the threat posed to French shipping by the Eddystone reefs. Sure enough, Winstanley was back on Eddystone supervising his workmen by 6 July the same year. What is more, Louis had given a personal guarantee for the safety of any workmen building and maintaining the lighthouse.

After his adventures in France, Winstanley carried on with his scheme. Solid foundations twelve feet high and sixteen feet across now stood on the rocks and he and the builders started to camp out on the reef. As he described:

> We ventured to lodge there soon after midsummer for greater dispatch of this work, but the first night the weather came bad and so continued, that it was eleven days before any boat could come near us again, and not being acquainted with the height of the seas rising, we were nearly all the time near drowned with wet and all our provisions in as bad a condition, though we worked night and day as much as possible to make shelter for ourselves. In this storm we lost some of our materials although we did what we could to save them. But the boat then returning we all left the house to be refreshed on shore, and as soon as the weather did permit, we returned again.

By the winter an octagonal lighthouse over forty feet high stood on the reef. Inside was what Winstanley termed in typical showman style, a 'state room'; plus a kitchen and bedrooms; and topping it all was the light. In November 1698 the candles were lit for the first time, as he recorded:

> We put up the light on the 14th of November. Which being so late in the year it was three days before Christmas before we had a relief to get ashore again, and were almost at the last extremity for want of provisions, but by good providence then two boats came with provisions and the family that was to take care of the light, and so ended this year's work.

But Winstanley had underestimated the seas. That winter the light was regularly swamped by waves, and the keepers were terrified by the way the tower shuddered in storms. It was soon discovered that the concrete had failed to set properly. Undaunted, Winstanley drew up plans to strengthen the lighthouse, raising the light itself another forty feet. The joints that tied the base to the rock were encased with bands of iron; the base itself was widened by four feet; and the tower was modified so that it was less top heavy. Winstanley was so proud of his creation that he made a drawing of the lighthouse and sold copies to visitors to his house and waterworks. He even sketched himself fishing from an upper window. The new lantern was eight feet square, and shone with the power of sixty candles. There was also a hanging lantern.

With his extraordinary and eccentric-looking lighthouse complete, Winstanley sailed for terra firma. He had made history. Daniel Defoe gives some idea of contemporary admiration for his achievement:

> The famous Mr Winstanley undertook to build a light-house for the direction of sailors, and with great art, and expedition finish'd it; which work considering its height, the magnitude of its building, and the little hold there was, by which it was possible to fasten it to the rock, stood to admiration, and bore out many a bitter storm. Mr Winstanley often visited, and frequently strengthen'd the building, by new works, and was so confident of its firmness, and stability, that he usually said, he only desir'd to be in it when a storm should happen, for many people had told him, it would certainly fall, if it came to blow a little harder than ordinary.

Henry Winstanley's desire to be in his creation when a storm hit was soon to be fulfilled. Five years after its completion he was in Plymouth to carry out maintenance work. It was November 1703. The gale that hit the country that month came to be known ever after as the Great Storm. Chimney stacks were blown down, hundreds of ships were wrecked and there were reports of men, cattle and even houses torn from the ground by the force of the wind.

There had been two weeks of appalling gales. But on Thursday 25 November there was a lull. Winstanley, who was no seaman, decided to set off for the lighthouse in the early hours of Friday morning. The sea was still quite rough as he left from the steps of the Barbican, but by the afternoon it became ominously calm. Shortly before midnight, the wind veered to the south-west: the Great Storm had arrived. It was at its fiercest between two o'clock and five o'clock on the morning of 27 November. Daniel Defoe visited Plymouth the following year, where he gathered eyewitness accounts:

> This tempest began on the Wednesday before, and blew with such violence and shook the light-house so much, that as they told me there, Mr Winstanley would fain have been on shoar, and made signals for help, but no boats durst go off to him; and to finish the tragedy, on the Friday, Nov.26, when the tempest was so redoubled, that it became a terror to the whole nation; the first sight there seaward, that the people of Plymouth, were presented with in the morning after the storm, was the bare Eddystone, the light-house being gone; in which Mr Winstanley, and all that were with him perish'd, and were never seen or heard of since: But that which was a worse loss still, was, that a few days after a merchant's ship call'd the Winchelsea homeward bound from Virginia, not knowing the Eddystone lighthouse was down; for want of the light that should have been seen run foul of the rock it self, and was lost with all her lading, and most of her men.

Winstanley and his edifice may have been swept away, but he had proved the need for a lighthouse on the reef. The captain of the *Winchelsea* had looked in vain for the light from the Eddystone. He was heading for Plymouth with a cargo of tobacco, and was certain that he was in the vicinity of the notorious rocks when the ship struck. Incredibly two of the crew of the *Winchelsea* managed to get into a boat and made it to land.

Three years later work began to replace the Eddystone light. The new architect was a London silk merchant, John Rudyerd. He was born into a large Cornish family who lived on the wrong side of the law. Little is known about him, but he was the one good apple in a barrel of rotten ones. As a result he was badly treated by the rest of his family and ran away to Plymouth. He found a job as a servant, but was lucky enough to have an employer who recognised his potential, gave him an education, then set him up in business.

One wonders quite what qualified John Rudyerd for the job, but this was before science and engineering were professional occupations, rather than hobbies taken up by gentlemen. The finished product was certainly more recognisable as a lighthouse to modern eyes. It was a conical structure built from granite and oak, and it was to stand guard on the reef for forty-six years. Rudyerd was given two expert consultants to assist him:

*The second Eddystone light designed by John Rudyerd.*

Mr Smith and Mr Northcutt were shipwrights, headhunted from the naval dockyard at Woolwich.

All that remained of Winstanley's lighthouse was an iron chain attached to the rock. Rudyerd attached his tower with thirty-six iron rods slotted into the reef. Ingeniously the slots were filled first with tallow, which melted as the hot iron rods were hammered down into it. To seal the holes, molten pewter was poured into the gaps that were left, melting the remaining tallow and replacing it. Mindful of the kidnapping of Rudyerd's predecessor, the navy assigned four warships to guard the reef, while the work was going on.

Contemporaries voiced their doubts about the ability of this new light-house to withstand the huge seas that swamped the reef. But it was not the sea that led to demise of this second Eddystone light. Poor Henry Hall had already had a traumatic life as one of the first offshore lighthouse keepers. While he was first keeper of Winstanley's lighthouse, his fellow keeper, George Priddy, had died. Unwilling to give his former colleague a burial at sea, and risk accusations of murder, Henry strapped the body to the gallery which surrounded the lantern. As he tended the light every day, Henry was haunted by George's rotting corpse, until a boat arrived to relieve him of the burden. By 1755 Henry Hall was ninety-four years old, and was one of the three keepers on duty when the candles set fire to the lantern.

In the Admiralty archives is the account, given by the lighthouse keepers, of the disastrous fire that took place on 2 December 1755, although some have doubted whether it is entirely truthful. According to the two survivors,

Hall threw buckets of sea water at the fire, while his fellow keepers trailed up and down the stairs, carrying buckets filled from the rocks below. As the fire took hold, the lead cupola over the lantern melted. Hall was throwing yet another bucket of water at the fire above him, when molten lead dripped into his mouth, and down into his stomach. Injured and exhausted, the three men moved from room to room as the flames spread down the tower, until finally they were forced out onto the rock. The fire could be seen from Plymouth, but it was a group of Cawsands fishermen who raised the alarm. Bringing their fishing boat as close as they dared to the terrifying reef, the men launched a rowing boat. It was still unable to land, and they had to resort to hauling the three keepers through the sea. By the time fire-fighting equipment arrived from Plymouth, the lighthouse was a ruin. Henry Hall survived for twelve days, repeatedly telling the doctor he had swallowed molten lead. Reputedly, Dr Spry performed an autopsy on the keeper's corpse, and did indeed find a piece of lead in the pit of his stomach weighing more than seven ounces.

Winstanley and Rudyerd had set such a precedent that the newly formed Trinity House built a light ship to guard the reef until another lighthouse could be built. In 1756, just as Britain became embroiled in the Seven Years War, John Smeaton was recommended by the Royal Society as the architect of the next

*Sailing by John Smeaton's tower, the third Eddystone light.*

137

Eddystone light. Smeaton was a Yorkshireman, who is regarded as the founder of the civil engineering profession in Britain. The lighthouse he designed and built was to become the logo of the Institution of Civil Engineers.

Smeaton had studied mathematical-instrument making and was elected to the Royal Society after presenting scientific papers. He had travelled through what were then called the Low Countries, studying the design and construction of canals, mills and bridges. His first step in the design of this new lighthouse was to study the drawings of his predecessors to work out the strengths and weaknesses of each design. Winstanley's straight-sided tower failed to dissipate the force of the waves, while Rudyerd's wooden construction had proved too vulnerable to fire. Smeaton's design was, he said, based on the structure of an oak tree, and would be made of stone. But he had two strokes of brilliance: he invented a form of quick-drying cement to deal with the wet conditions on the rock (a formula that is still in use today), and he used dovetail joints and marble dowelling to lock each block of stone to its neighbour. As is appropriate to the founder of civil engineering, Smeaton's building techniques became standard practice for the construction of lighthouses. Like Winstanley, Smeaton prefabricated the sections and transported them to the reef. The foundations were laid on 12 June 1757. He chose his labourers, too, employing Cornish tin miners, who were each given a specially struck medal to prove to naval press gangs that they were employed on the Eddystone construction.

The twenty-four candles of the third Eddystone Lighthouse were lit on

*The top section of Smeaton's lighthouse, now a landmark on Plymouth Hoe.*

16 October 1759, just as a storm blew up. But it was not the lighthouse that started to succumb to the force of the sea over a century later. In the 1870s cracks started to appear in the rock beneath its base, and the top section of the tower was dismantled and now stands on Plymouth Hoe; its stump still stands on the reef.

The present lighthouse was built in 1882 and was the first British lighthouse to be automated. It shines with the intensity of 199,000 candles.

## The Long and Winding Road

In 1759 a group of Modbury gentlemen joined the revolution that was sweeping England: they set up a turnpike trust. Tollhouses were built at each end of a stretch of road, and road users charged before travelling on it. This idea had been first mooted in Parliament in 1622, but was slow to catch on. As the amount of traffic increased on the nation's roads, turnpike trusts were springing up all over the country in the early seventeenth century, but Devon lagged fifty years behind. The Modbury gents were not indulging in this new-fangled process for profit; by law all money had to be ploughed back into the repair and maintenance of the road surface. It was a simple and novel idea, but it was one that would not be implemented without some opposition.

The first turnpike trusts in Devon were set up in 1753 in Honiton, Axminster and Exeter. These covered the important main road to London, and other major routes in the area. Tristram Risdon was a native of Devon,

*A tollhouse outside Tavistock.*

*The stone shelter built as the tollhouse to snare local farmers trying to avoid the toll road.*

but even he could find nothing good to say about the county's roads when he complained in his Survey of Devon in the early seventeenth century:

> ...very laborious, rough and unpleasant to strangers travelling those ways, which are cumbersome and uneven, amongst rocks and stones, painful for man and horse; as they can best witness who have made trial thereof.

When the tollhouse near Yealmpton Bridge, on the modern A379 between Modbury and Plymouth, was built the Modbury Turnpike Trust had not calculated on the cunning of local farmers. On the opposite side of the road, at Dunstone Cross, is a small stone shelter. This is believed to be the tollhouse outpost, to catch farmers who were trying to take a rat run round the tollhouse to avoid paying.

County topography has always presented a challenge to road building, particularly in small communities. Modbury was a prosperous little town in the eighteenth century. It sits in a pronounced dip, with a steep hill in and out of town, and the Turnpike Trust decided to take a radical step. Instead of horse-drawn traffic struggling up the incline of Galpin Hill, it built the new toll road in a dogleg. By 1823, the Modbury Trust had extended their toll road all the way to Laira Bridge near Plymouth. But the slow speed of stage-coaches created a bottleneck as the traffic passed along the narrow road through the town, so a bypass was debated as early as 1827. The march of progress could not be slowed, so tossing out the idea of a bypass, they came up with a far cheaper solution: demolition. The Shambles and Round House, both used for generations as the town's markets were simply knocked down.

The great granite lump of Dartmoor, which dominates the centre of the county, presents an even greater challenge to travellers. Once the army began to use the moor as a training ground, they built roads. These cross the remains of the ancient trackways now used only by walkers. Some routes can only be guessed at. The Lych Way once ran from the eastern edge of the moor, via Postbridge to Lydford. This was the route taken to the only burial ground available in the parish. The most conservative estimate makes the last leg of the journey eight hours, even in good weather. As winter claimed more deaths than the rest of the year, these long, cold funeral processions must have had an air of gothic grimness. Fortunately in 1260, Bishop Bronescombe had the good sense to allow burials in the churchyard at Widecombe. A double row of stepping stones across the River Tavy is believed to mark part of the route. This would have allowed the pallbearers to carry a corpse across the river, holding the pall between them.

Throughout Devon the roads were so bad that wheeled transport was unusual until the end of the eighteenth century. Goods travelled up rivers by boat, or into the hinterland via packhorse. When writer Charles Dickens visited Clovelly for an article for the Christmas edition of *All The Year Round* in 1860, the packhorse was still a feature of daily life, as this rather whimsical picture of a bustling scene reveals:

> The old pack-saddle, long laid aside in most parts of England as one of the appendages of its infancy, flourished here intact. Strings of pack-horses and pack donkeys toiled slowly up the staves of the ladders, bearing fish, and coal, and such other cargo as was unshipping at the pier from the dancing fleet of village boats, and from two or three little coasting traders. The staves were musical with the clattering feet of the pack-horses and pack-donkeys, and the voices of the fishermen urging them up, mingled with the voices of the fishermen's wives and their many children.

Imagine that string of packhorses travelling through the under-populated Devon countryside; at risk from robbers on the lonely lanes, the only sound the dull thud of hooves and the tinkle of the bell attached to the leading horse. But anyone who has walked the green lanes of Devon, and in particular the tracks across Dartmoor, can see why the packhorse survived so long in the county. A single horse could negotiate the puddles and rocks of these narrow byways. Tin miners used packhorses, and even pack dogs, to carry tin down from their workings to be assayed and coined at the Stannary Towns. Peat was carried down from Dartmoor in the same way. The packhorse was a vital cog in the county's economy when William Marshall wrote in 1796:

> The furniture of pack horses varies with the load to be carried. Hay, corn, straw, faggots, and other comparatively light articles of burden, are loaded between 'crooks'; formed of willow poles, about the thickness of scythe handles; and seven or eight feet long; bent as ox-bows; but with one end much longer than the other. These are joined in pairs, with slight cross bars, eighteen inches to two feet long; and each horse is furnished with two pairs of these crooks; slung together, so as that the shorter and stronger ends shall lie easy and firmly against the pack saddle; the longer and lighter ends rising, perhaps, fifteen or more inches, above the horse's back, and standing four or five feet from each other. Within, and between, these crooks, the load is piled, and bound fast together, with that simplicity and dispatch, which long practice seldom fails of striking out. Cordwood, large stones, and other heavy articles are carried between 'short crooks'; made of four natural bends or knees; both ends being nearly of the same length; and, in use, the points stand nearly level with the ridge of the pack saddle.
>
> Dung, sand, materials of buildings, roads, &c are carried in pots; or strong coarse panniers; slung together, like the crooks; and as panniers are usually slung; the dung, especially if long and light, being ridged up, over the saddle...
>
> Lime is universally carried in narrow bags; two or three of them being thrown across a pack saddle; which is of wood, and of the ordinary construction.

One man could control a string of up to twenty horses, but compared with the distribution of goods by boat, the packhorse was uneconomic. The average coastal cargo ship in the eighteenth century could carry a load of fifty tons. To move the same tonnage by road required 400 packhorses. Once wheeled transport became more common by the end of the century, it would still take a dozen large wagons, or thirty two-wheeled carts, to carry the same cargo. Horses required daily fodder, in large quantities if they were to climb steep gradients and work harder. Labour costs were higher by road: every cart or wagon required a driver. For the price of ten wagons and forty horses, a merchant could buy two fifty-ton coastal sailing boats, which travelled free, thanks to the wind. Heavily laden horses plodded at a sedate two miles an hour, a total of twenty miles a day, whereas a ship could cover 150 miles in twenty-four hours, although this was often much less in practice. A horse had a working life of five or six years, whereas a ship would last for twenty years or longer, unless it was wrecked – and this was probably the most important factor. Goods that travelled by road might be *delayed* by ice, snow or floods, but were *unlikely* to be lost due to weather. Ships could be delayed in port, and were subject to the extremes of mischievous wind and weather. Cargoes could, and often were, lost at sea. Plodding predictability gave the horse the

Packhorses being loaded at Combe Martin.

advantage, and punctuality was relatively unimportant until the advent of the railways. Arrival and departure times were usually referred to as before, or after, noon.

Farmers and local tradesmen often supplemented their main income by going into business as carriers, and regular carrier services existed in the seventeenth century. In 1722 a wagon service between London and Exeter took only six days. Toll roads speeded up journeys, reducing passengers' travelling times by 60 per cent.

When Tristram Risdon's travelogue of Devon was re-published at the turn of the nineteenth century, the editor was as unimpressed by the roads (despite their improvements) as Risdon had been in 1603:

> The roads of the county cannot now be commended: some of the principal ones are pretty good, but most in the district are bad. It is to be lamented that when improvement began, a better plan had not been adopted; that instead of ascending one steep hill to descend again, more level tracks had not been pursued, which are in most cases to be found, and which frequently the courses of rivers would have pointed out.

He obviously had not travelled through Modbury! Devon was indeed backward in the opinion of Risdon's editor in 1810:

> Specimens of what the roads formerly were are yet visible in many places, and show at once that a passage for wheel carriages was not contemplated in their formation; the carriage of every article by pack horses being the only mode of conveyance almost in the memory of persons now living.

The county's numerous rivers had to be crossed when travelling by road. Across some rivers such as the Avon at Bantham, South Hams, a ferryman – or woman – would row passengers, and their animals, across the water. Towns such as Bideford made a major investment by building bridges. Daniel Defoe visited the 'little white town on the hill' described in his publication *A Tour Through England and Wales* in the 1720s and admired the beautiful but narrow bridge:

> There is indeed, a very fine stone bridge over the river here, but the passage over it is so narrow, and they are so chary of it that few car-

*Laira Bridge over the Plym in 1829. Using a single oar to propel a boat was a common sight in Devon.*

riages go over it; but as the water ebbs quite out of the river every low water, the carts and waggons go over the sand with great ease and safety.

Quite what the carts and wagons did when it was not low water, he does not reveal. The increase in wheeled transport meant that many of these old bridges were demolished, or widened. Road building has always caused heated arguments, and in the eighteenth century road schemes were abandoned because of cost, just as they are today.

Devon's steep gradients were a challenge. On toll roads, extra horses could be added toll-free to pull heavily laden wagons up hill. A few stone posts have survived to mark the point at the top of the hill where this extra horsepower had to be unharnessed. Despite the odds, some Victorian travellers believed they were blessed. G.R. Pulman looked back on the golden days of coaching with rose-tinted spectacles, when he wrote in 1875:

> The country became covered with excellent roads, and the coach-system attained extraordinary perfection. Sixteen four-horse coaches passed daily through Axminster in various directions, but chiefly from Exeter to London, until at length the journey between those places, through Honiton, Bridport, Dorchester, and Salisbury –

some through Chard and Crewkerne, and others through Ilminster and Yeovil – to London, a distance of about one hundred and seventy miles, was regularly performed in sixteen hours. This was effected by means of excellent cattle and short stages. All the 'appointments' were in keeping, from the polished and brass-mounted harness up to the 'swell' coach-man and the scarlet-coated mail-guard, with 'cheery horn' and formidable blunderbus. People now advancing in life cherish 'pleasant memories' of the old coaching-days and the agreeable associations therewith.

Those in the cheap seats on top of the coach, had to hang on as the wheels negotiated the ruts and puddles of Devon's roads. And the basic water-proof clothing of the past was no match for wind, rain, hail and snow. Indoor passengers were closeted in a jolting carriage with poor suspension and, if they were unlucky, had to endure the antisocial behaviour of their fellow passengers. One of Mr Pulman's relations went to some lengths to avoid such inconvenience:

> My relative…was in the habit of occasionally visiting London about the close of the last century, and although he invariably booked himself by the 'flying coach', so as to have protection, if need arose, yet he generally walked the one hundred and fifty miles in preference to the purgatory of being for three days sealed up in the jolting and rumbling machine. His custom was to carry his gun, walk on ahead, shoot by the roadside, and hasten on and have the game cooked by the time the 'flyer' arrived at its halting-place for the night – the passengers sharing the feast, and the whole party spending the evening in accordance with the custom of the time.

The iron railroads arrived late in many parts of Devon. Although the line was completed as far as Exeter in 1844, the branch lines to towns such as Kingsbridge in the south were not built until the first cars were appearing in the county at the very end of Victoria's reign. Known as the Primrose Line, this extension lasted only until the Beeching Axe fell.

Local railway lines in North Devon had an uncertain start. One of the shortest lived was the extension along the coast from Bideford to Appledore and *Westward Ho!*. Tourists had flooded in after Charles Kingsley's eponymous novel was published in 1855, and the branch line was suggested in 1860, after pressure from local businesses. Work began six years later, but the first contractor went bankrupt. Only three months after the death of Queen Victoria in 1901, the line had been completed as far as Northam. Commuters to the collar factory at The Strand, Bideford, packed the carriages during the morning and evening rush hours. By August 1908, when the line to Westward Ho! was complete, passengers were packed into the trains like sardines, and some even had to ride on the steps. Such is the seasonal nature of tourist towns, that the railway company offered 'added value' to passengers. Entertainment was offered in a hall on the 'up' platform, with acts such as the Jolly Dutch Clog Dancers – the hall is now the Buccaneer Pub.

But during the dark months of 1917, as the British Army struggled in the trenches, the line was taken up to be re-laid for the arms industry in Avonmouth, and Pembrey. Locomotives in their stylish green and black livery no longer carried happy holiday-makers and collar-factory workers, but munitions. The line was never rebuilt.

Elsewhere, such was the influence of the expanding railway network on the region that between Black Torrington and Bratton Clovelly a village grew up clustered round Halwill Junction, with which it shares its name. Here the lines of the South Devon Railway, Devon and Cornwall Railway, and the North Cornwall Railway converged. In the 1931 census the population of the junction and neighbouring village of Beaworthy stood at 600. There was accommodation for travellers at The Junction Hotel, a cottage hospital for the sick, a garage, Post Office, bank, police station and a chapel that opened in 1885.

Yet this growth and prosperity was not to last and by the 1960s the North Cornwall line, as well as others in the South West, was earmarked as uneconomic by Dr Beeching. Gerald Smallacombe belonged to the third generation of railwaymen, but also to the last. Both his grandfathers had started work on the railway soon after it opened in 1874, followed in turn by his father and two uncles. Gerald was born in a railway cottage and grew up at Ashbury Station, the first station down the line from Okehampton. He started on the railways in 1952 shortly before his sixteenth birthday and became a cleaner, the lowliest member of the team at Okehampton Station. This was a small depot and soon he became a fireman, a dirty sweaty job, shovelling coal into the firebox. Every fireman was teamed with a driver, and by 1961 Gerald was twenty-three and had graduated to the top job.

It was a busy line and the freight it carried reflected the rural population it served. Cattle specials travelled up in the evenings to Smithfield market. Before the myxomatosis outbreak of the early 1950s, ten to twelve vanloads of rabbits were sent to London every night. Fish travelled up from the port of Padstow, and sacks of bacon came from local slaughterhouses. Trainloads of timber cut from Halwill Forest, particularly during the post-war reconstruction of Britain's cities, all went up the line. Back down the line came cargoes of animal feed and fertiliser; stone for the roads and provisions of every description. The yard at Ashbury Station catered for fourteen lorries. At weekends the platforms echoed with the sound of excited holiday-makers heading for the coast of North Cornwall, the ladies always riding with their backs to the engine to prevent smuts flying into their faces.

One May morning in 1966, driver Gerald Smallacombe got on the footplate of the 4.37 mail train from Okehampton to Bude for the last time. The infamous Dr Beeching's closure of the line, set for October 1966, resulted in the loss of a hundred jobs. When Gerald was forced to leave his job on the railways he went into the business which surplanted the railways: he became a lorry driver.

## The Atmospheric Caper

It is April 1845. Through the doors of the House of Commons walk some of the superstars of the industrial age. They have been summoned to give expert evidence on the latest railway technology; a technology the proponents of which believe will rival and overtake the steam locomotive; a technology that is destined to be used on a line running through South Devon from Exeter to Plymouth. It will soon become known as the Atmospheric Caper.

Some of these engineering luminaries are forgotten now, but among them is George Stephenson. By then in his sixties, he constructed his first locomotive in 1814, and achieved fame when a later prototype, The Rocket, reached a speed of thirty miles an hour in 1829. At his side is his son Robert, aged forty-two, who has followed him into the family business, now managing their locomotive engine factory, in Newcastle-on-Tyne. The Stephensons have described the new technology as 'a lot of humbug'.

Then there is Isambard Kingdom Brunel, whose engineer father had fled the French Revolution. Brunel is an engineering 'wunderkind', appointed engineer to the Great Western Railway when he was only twenty-seven years old. He has also designed the SS *Great Western*, the first steamship built to cross the Atlantic. Brunel is still only thirty-eight, and reputed to need only five hours of sleep a night.

Forgotten now, but another great name is Joseph D'Aguila Samuda, manufacturer of maritime machinery and fittings. He and his late brother Jacob patented the idea which these luminaries have gathered to discuss: the atmospheric railway.

Railway mania was at its height – entrepreneurs and investors were falling over themselves to jump on the bandwagon and capital investment had reached a crescendo. It was this sense of urgency that led Parliament to summon Brunel, Samuda and the Stephensons. Before the House of Commons were several railway bills, which needed to be pushed through to increase the network spreading across the country. The technology of the steam engine had been tested and developed for fifteen years. But there were doubts about its capacity to cope with gradients, and its ability to maintain high speed over long distances. Atmospheric technology, however, was in its infancy. As the Select Committee pointed out:

> If it were practicable to suspend all railway legislation until the result of the Devon and Cornwall, and of the Epsom and Croydon Atmospheric lines were known, it would be perhaps the most cautious and prudent course to wait that result; but such a course, independent of all considerations of expediency, is evidently impracticable.

The first experimental length was built on wasteland near Wormwood Scrubs in 1840, and the system had been tried on the Kingstown and Dalkey line near Dublin. The committee was impressed by the success of the Irish line.

Its proponents believed that what made the atmospheric railway so innovative was that it didn't need to transport its own power source. Without this need to move a cumbersome steam engine along with it, the train was far lighter, cleaner, quieter and safer. The engines that drove it were static, sited at pumping stations at three-mile intervals along the line. These engines drove suction pumps, attached to a length of tube that ran between the rails. Passengers travelled in conventional carriages, but the

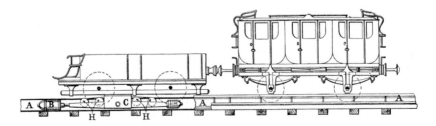

*Engine-less carriages: the mechanics of the atmospheric principle, showing the arm connecting the carriages and the piston.*

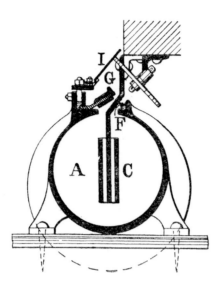

*The troublesome valve and tube within which air pressure built up to propel the carriages.*

leading carriage was attached to this tube by an arm on its underside. The arm, which travelled in a continuous slot in the top of the tube, connected to a piston that fitted snugly within the pipe. To maintain air pressure, the valves were opened and closed by rollers. Weatherproofing was in the form of hinged leather flaps covering the valve. Air, sucked from the section of pipe in front of the train, created a partial vacuum and the greater air pressure in the tube behind the train forced the piston forwards, so moving the carriages.

What excited Brunel, was the system's ability to cope with steep gradients and inclines, simply because it was lighter. This made it a perfect choice for the hilly terrain between Exeter and Plymouth. Building tunnels, embankments and cuttings were labour intensive, expensive and time-consuming. Brunel was convinced that this would counter the extra costs posed by installing and powering the pumping stations.

There's no doubt that the Committee felt completely justified in its eventual endorsement of the atmospheric railway system. After all, Brunel, an engineer of enormous repute, had championed the technology, giving the idea respectability. As the Committee reported on 22 April 1845, one of the main points in favour of the atmospheric principle was its superior safety record:

Your committee have no hesitation in stating, that a single Atmospheric line is superior to a double Locomotive line both in regularity and safety, inasmuch as it makes collisions impossible except at crossing places, and excludes all the danger and irregularity arising from casualties to engines or their tenders.

A particular fear among rail passengers was that the boilers on steam engines would explode.

With the endorsements of the Select Committee ringing in his ears, Brunel threw himself into his new project. Construction began and by May 1846 eight miles of track had been laid. The pumping stations housing the machinery were no simple sheds. Brunel was fond of Italianate design, and these utilitarian buildings were built of the local red stone, faced with cream Bath stone. With their pantiled roofs, square towers, and round-headed windows,

*Residents of Dawlish complained about the noise from the pumping station, seen here in a contemporary illustration, showing its distinctive square chimney.*

they echoed the style of the retirement mansion he planned to build near Paignton. Unfortunately the machinery they housed was simply not up to the job. The engines were modified and on 9 November 1847 the atmospheric railway took its first passengers from Exeter to Newton Abbot. By 2 March 1848, all trains on the line were moving thanks to atmospheric pressure. The *Devonshire Chronicle* was enthusiastic:

> This day witnesses the triumph of this great and important principle of propulsion!... As far as we can understand the apparatus and its appliances, there appears to be very little hazard of it getting out of order or causing any interruption to traffic.

The paper's editor gave his readers a first-hand account of the delights of the journey when he wrote:

> We enjoyed a pleasant trip to Teignmouth on Saturday last by the long and well-abused atmospheric power of propulsion. The pleasure of travelling is much increased by this mode; you hear nothing of the cry of 'Oh!' made by the locomotive as if it had asthma and was compelled to run uphill in spite of its short breath. To this is added the consideration of safety, accident being nearly impossible, while the motion of the carriages, from the position of the propelling power being under the carriage and of unvarying force gives increased ease when in motion; the oscillation is barely susceptible, you can write with ease while the speed is made from 40 to 50 miles an hour.

Another journalist tested the smoothness of the journey by placing a coin on the edge of the sash window. It stayed put for three miles. The editor of the *Chronicle* had a dig at those who were sceptical of the atmospheric principle:

> We shall be glad to see signs of honourable repentance among the Anties; we fear however, that they have not the candour to make a confession and allow that they did not know anything about what they were writing when they prognosticated the failure of the atmospheric railway.

The travelling public was happy but the investors were not. Where was the return on their investment? Fuel costs had tripled. The engines driving the system had been modified to run faster, and were therefore using more coal, but they were overstretched. Brunel had costed the project on the basis that the engines on the line would not need to run continually, but would be revved up when the carriages approached each pumping house. But this was based on the premise that the engineers at each pumping station knew when the carriages approached: information that would be sent along the line by telegraph. For some reason the telegraph was not up and running until the line was condemned as a failure.

Some fifty years later the Institute of Mechanical Engineers pinpointed this problem in a report on the South Devon Atmospheric Railway. It also referred to leakage as the other main reason the system proved more expensive than Brunel had calculated. As the carriages moved along the rails the valve opened in front of the arm, and was closed behind it by a roller. The valve had a leather cover, and if this did not close properly the engine pumped in vain, while the train waited helpless at the station. Rats have been blamed for chewing the leather covers, which would have hindered the valves efficiency. Certainly rats had to be flushed out of the tubes every morning before the line was used.

The winter of 1847–8 was bitter. These sub-zero temperatures followed a typically wet Devon autumn: the leather covering the valves froze. The following spring and summer, the South Coast bathed in glorious sunshine: the leather cracked and started to tear away. Brunel laid the blame on Joseph Samuda, who had patented the valve. He tried to insist that Samuda altered the valve to weatherproof it. Samuda refused.

At the half-yearly meeting of shareholders in August 1848, Brunel was forced to recommend that the atmospheric system be suspended until it could be made more efficient: the valve was failing along the entire length of the line. When shareholders then heard that the company's expenditure had exceeded income by £2,000, there was uproar. One shareholder ranted, 'We are exceedingly disgusted with that atmospheric bauble. If the matter had been discussed, I was prepared to have torn it into ribands'. Another attacked Brunel himself, saying it was:

> Unpardonable, indeed reckless, in Mr Brunel ever to give the least sanction to such a delusive, such an extravagant, such a deceptive system. Mr Brunel's reputation has been placed in jeopardy by this action.

By 9 September 1848, only ten days after the meeting, steam locomotives were in use on the entire line. The South Devon atmospheric railway had failed.

Isambard Kingdom Brunel still remains unchallenged as one of the country's greatest engineers, and was voted the second greatest Briton of all time in a national television poll in 2002. His mismanagement of the atmospheric railway is long forgotten. He was happy to lay the blame on the valve and its designer Joseph Samuda, and in so doing salvage his own reputation. In his defence, Brunel was managing twenty-four other projects at the same time, and he was not a mechanical engineer, which may explain why he failed to order larger engines to power the system. His failure to install a telegraph system in time, however, is inexplicable.

Brunel's Atmospheric Railway never reached its intended terminus in Plymouth. Pipe from the completed section between Exeter and Newton Abbot was torn up, and some of it was recycled as drainpipes on local houses. A section does survive in the museum at Newton Abbot. Beside the modern railway station at Totnes, is the building that was intended to be one part in the chain of pumping stations. Today it houses a modern dairy, but the style of architecture is instantly recognisable, although the distinctive square chimney has been demolished. At Starcross, on the modern line between Exeter and Newton Abbot, another former pumping station does retain its unusual chimney. These few remnants are testament to the development of the one-time rival to steam locomotives, hailed by some of the greatest Victorian engineering brains as capable of ousting steam-powered travel from the tracks.

## Cory's Chronicle

It is October 1896. A distinctive bearded figure is bent over his workbench. In one hand is the brass heel plate of a woman's boot, which he is shaping into the letter C. Close by is a motley collection of type, some of which has been made by him, some has been begged or borrowed. Forms lie set with type, ready for the wooden printing press which Cory Burrows has constructed himself. He is putting the first edition of the *Hartland and West Country Chronicle* 'to bed', a routine which he will go through for the next four decades.

A copy of the first edition of *Cory's Chronicle*, as it will soon be dubbed, survives in the archives in Barnstaple. That distinctive letter C crowns the front page in the masthead. Its contents include, 'Hints and Helps for Young Men', and a polemic entitled 'Why I Believe in Total Abstainence'. Hartland's own poet laureate, James Tailor, has even penned some verse for the first edition in honour of 'The Birth of the *Hartland Chronicle*':

A shout of mighty cheering is sounding in our ears;
O'd Hartland seems to tremble at the loud and lengthy cheer.
What's the meaning of this tumult; the town of it seems full;
T'is a salute in favour of the Hartland Chronicle.

Hartland's population of 1,600 may well have welcomed the infant community newspaper, but loud scoffing was heard in other quarters. So loud, in
fact, that the editor of the *Bideford Weekly Gazette*, was moved to write in
defence of this new addition to the newspaper fraternity:

> Some irreverent folk have been making merry over the shortcom-
> ings of the paper – they have pointed to its artistically mixed types;
> its advertisements overlaid each on top of the other; its erratic
> printing, and spacing, and general make-up. They are surely forgetting
> 'The Yellow Book', over which Aubrey Beardsley was wont to cast
> the radiance of his appalling genius.

This comparison with *The Yellow Book*, whose first edition in 1894 had scan-
dalised Victorian society, sets the tone of the letter. Aubrey Beardsley, notorious for his disturbingly erotic drawings, was *The Yellow Book*'s first art
editor. It was a magazine devoted to literature and the arts. Among its
contributors were Arnold Bennett, Walter Sickert and Max Beerbohm. The
22-year-old Beerbohm, a witty critic and caricaturist, had written an essay
called 'A Defence of Cosmetics' for the magazine. A harmless enough title
today, but it caused a furore that continued until the magazine folded in 1897.
*Cory's Chronicle* was to outlive *The Yellow Book* by forty years, despite the
shortcomings of its first edition. The letter continued:

> Our *Hartland Chronicle* has not an Aubrey Beardsley but it has a
> poet, native born, who contributes long stanzas to celebrate the birth
> of this new organ of Public Opinion. From what one can gather of
> this poem – some portion is illegible – it would appear that not
> Hartland alone, but the whole world held its breath while the
> Chronicle broke through its inky fastness into the light of publicity. I
> am not of the scoffers. Being responsible for a considerable waste of
> good ink – writing and printing – myself, I can approve and applaud
> the pluck of the man who has produced the new paper. He may take
> courage. *The Western Morning News* was once a little insignificant
> sheet, and time was when *The Times* was not! Even the *Bideford*

*Gazette* did not attain its present proud supremacy until some time after the Conquest. So take heart of grace, ye *Hartland Chronicle* and hope for the day when ye shall be an eight paged daily. It may be as well perhaps to hint to you as gently as possible, that the British Public does not like one page of its newspapers printed upside down. We have our own opinion of the great British Public, you and I, but still it is as well to humour them in those little details.

Cory Burrows was undaunted by these failings, and in the second edition, he encouraged potential advertisers by trumpeting, 'Our first, though so late, and so badly printed, sold completely out a few days after publication'.

Burrows had judged his potential market perfectly, but then he was very much a local boy. The son of a painter and decorator, Burrows had gone into his father's trade before venturing into business as an ironmonger. He developed a passion for printing and set up a small printing works in 1886, a business he ran in tandem with the ironmongery for a while. He was actively involved in the isolated community into which he was born in 1872. For two years he was clerk to the parish council and held the job of rate collector. As a staunch teetotaller he was a member of the Bible Christians and the Independent Order of Rechabites, both groups with a flourishing membership in North Devon at the time. The *Chronicle's* first issue was produced as a wraparound cover for the Methodist paper, the *Home Messenger*.

Despite its early teething troubles, *Cory's Chronicle* proved a success. Initially it was produced monthly, but by 1906 it was appearing weekly, packed with local news. Burrows was reporter, sub-editor, compositor, printer, advertising manager, and delivery boy. Soon he took on apprentices, and had a back-up team of willing friends and neighbours to help out. His entire operation was run from 46 The Terrace, Hartland, premises the *Chronicle* shared with his sister Beatrice's hat shop. From The Terrace, newspapers circulated to subscribers around the world: New Zealand, Ireland, Canada, South Africa, Italy, Germany, Denmark, and even Ahmednagar in India.

By 1905 the *Chronicle* was covering its costs, although earlier and later in its life, it was subsidised by Burrows's printing business. The 100th issue in January of that year gave a flavour of its coverage of the minutiae of Hartland life:

Thomas Beer, a lad of Hartland, summoned by PC Drew for using bad language, and fined 9s 6d inclusive. PC Drew said defendant came of respectable parents, but had been led away by Hartland

# A ONE MAN NEWSPAPER IN DEVONSHIRE

Setting up type.

The printing machine.

"Late news" machine.

As Press photographer.

Wiring the papers.

Mr. Burrow delivering his newspaper and standing outside his shop.

There is only a staff of one on the *Hartland and West Country Chronicle*, a paper published in a remote village thirteen miles from Bideford. He is Mr. Thomas C. Burrow, the proprietor, who fills the posts of editor, reporter, manager, printer, compositor, block-maker, photographer and publisher. The paper is published once a month, and though only intended for the surrounding villages, has subscribers in many foreign lands. Above, Mr. Burrow is seen performing some of his manifold duties. (*Daily Mirror* photographs).

*In 1913 the* Daily Mirror *featured Cory Burrows' one man newspaper.*

Youths. The Chairman said the defendant ought to be thoroughly ashamed of himself.

In the same issue condolences are offered to a gentleman for the death of his horse, and the sport of badger-digging is reported! But in keeping with Hartland's location, on a rocky headland on this coast notorious for shipwrecks, the *Chronicle* also carried reports of events at sea.

> December 30th – Schooner Jasper, Captain Quance, bound from Garston to Appledore with a cargo of coal was driven inshore at Clovelly. The crew rescued by the Lifeboat. The vessel was leaking badly and although in danger at the time was taken in hand when the gale moderated and taken safely into Appledore.

Cory also published an Almanac of 116 pages for the year 1905, in which tide tables were listed for all the important ports in the coastal trade: London Bridge, Greenock, Newcastle and Bristol. It also carried lighting-up times for cyclists and features covered topics to please all tastes and interests: 'My Fatal Social Blunder', 'Playing Cards with Strangers', 'A Sneezing Rhyme', and 'Memories of Newgate Prison'.

Hartland, a village that prided itself on being 'the farthest from the railways', also took great pride in its unique newspaper. The last issue appeared on 17 May 1940. Censorship prohibited any mention of preparations against imminent invasion, but Cory Burrows did mention the wartime paper shortage, which finally silenced the *Chronicle*. He died on 3 March 1956, at the age of eighty-three, reputedly without ever having shaved.

# CHAPTER 6

# THE PRIDE OF FORMER DAYS

English Heritage has 422 Grade I listed buildings in Devon, far more than in any other county in the South West. It is their architecture and associated history which merit them a listing, although often their past is lost or obscured.

Brunel Manor is not on that list despite its name. While Brunel was engaged in his 'atmosperic caper', he was obviously captivated by the beauty of Devon's South Coast and planned to spend his retirement by the sea. Between 1847 and 1858 he bought 100 acres of land near Torquay to build a retirement home. The foundations and cellars were complete when he died at the age of fifty-three in 1859. Subsequent owner, James Crompton, built the present house using Brunel's floor plan, but ditched his Italianate design in favour of a French style. Today Brunel Manor is a Christian Conference Centre, its association with one of the greatest men of the Victorian age, remembered in the name.

One of the most romantic ruins in England is Berry Pomeroy Castle, between Newton Abbot and Totnes, built by a family who arrived on English soil with William the Conqueror. The Pomeroys abetted the 1549 rebellion against the introduction of the English prayer book, and the castle passed to Edward Seymour, Lord Protector of England, whose family gradually abandoned it to nature after the Civil War. Another romantic ruin is the ivy-hung walls of Fowellscombe which stands in farmland near Ugborough, abandoned by its owners. Fire claimed Oldstone Mansion near Dartmouth, once a Victorian country house with a shell grotto, its ruined walls have since been used as a silage clamp.

### The Demise of Dunsland
The concert is over, artists and audience have left for home. The custodian switches off the lights, and locks the doors. Dunsland House, a victim of neglect and abuse, has been restored to its former glory. Intricate lime plaster

moulded ceilings have been rescued from damp and destruction. Festoons of foliage, built up over a core of wire snake once again across the drawing room ceiling: a rotting beam in the ceiling had formerly been collapsing under its weight. This ceiling was dubbed by the great historian, A.L. Rowse, 'the richest and finest in north Devon'. The chimneypiece is a riot of fruit, flowers and birds. The overmantel is of such quality that it was thought to be the work of Grinling Gibbons. But although the cherubs, pea-pods, partridges and pome-granates were among his favourite motifs, the craftsman was probably a local man. By day, light floods in through five tall sash windows. This has been the sitting room of Dunsland House for 300 years.

Next door is the parlour, a cosy room for everyday use. Down the corridor is the ballroom with doors opening out to steps down to the gardens. Over-heated dancers once took the air on these steps, sheltered from the weather

*Restored lime plaster cherubs, fruit and flowers garland the drawing room fireplace at Dunsland House.*

by a grove of Scots Pine, which were felled to satisfy the post-war need for timber. Upstairs in the Lattice Room, more fine plasterwork decorates the ceiling. The oak tester bed has been restored to its original home, after spending time in another country house nearby. To the left of the fireplace is a portrait of the last of the Arscott male line, restored to the house he knew. The Arscott family lived in Dunsland House for five generations. Although this was once a bedroom, it was also the place where ladies withdrew while the men sat below enjoying port and cigars.

The restoration of this North Devon gem took the National Trust thirteen years. Michael Trinick was the man charged with rediscovering the house's lost glory. He first visited in January 1954:

> Turning off the turnpike at Brandis Corner the house came into view, gaunt in the wintry landscape, with its most unclassical pediment appearing to overhang the valley below. Down the ruinous drive into this valley I was able to drive my car, thanks to the frost which had hardened the deep ruts, over the little bridge and steeply up. Not a soul was about, the windows shuttered, the doors bolted. I wandered forlornly until I found an oak door, iron studded, at the back of the house. I pushed, the door seemed to yield and then fell with a crash, forward into the house. As I wandered round the desolate rooms my heart sank. Such was the dereliction, so far gone did the house appear that I felt utterly unequal to my task, which was to try to bring it back to life for its new owners, the National Trust.

So how had this beautiful North Devon house fallen into a state of dereliction? The family heirs had not been killed in the trenches of the First World War like so many others. This was not a massive country house on the scale of Saltram near Plymouth, another National Trust property. This was a house that had been loved and lived in, passed down through inheritance by seven families.

The name first occurs in the Domesday Book, but the oldest part of the house to survive into the twentieth century was early Tudor. This was set around a courtyard, and designed to be defended if need be. The stone-flagged central room was used as a kitchen in later versions of the house. At one end was a bakehouse with two pottery ovens made nearby in Barnstaple. Lighting these ovens is described as rather like tending a bonfire, with attendant smoke. But once the coals were white hot, ashes were raked out and the oven filled with loaves. Upstairs the central bedroom of the master

*Dunsland House in its prime.*

and mistress of the house was lined with oak panelling. This led into a host of smaller bedrooms on either side, ensuring segregation of the sexes in times of greater propriety.

The long shoebox shape of this Tudor house was added to during the reign of James I. An east wing was added at right angles to the original building, although half of this was demolished sixty years later. After the restoration of Charles II in 1660, the owners enlarged Dunsland on a grand scale. The Restoration wing was three storeys high. Windows at ground level lit the enormous cellars where beer and cider were brewed. A still, hidden in a chimney, produced apple brandy. There were six granite salting troughs, each cut from a solid block of stone, large enough to salt an entire ox. Before the turnip was introduced in the eighteenth century, winter fodder was in short supply and beasts were killed and salted down for the winter.

The attics were lit by dormer windows, and the largest housed two powder closets, a relic from the days when hair was powdered. Long after the craze for powdered hair had gone out of fashion among the gentry, footmen still powdered their hair as part of their uniform. Each cupboard had a small, unglazed window, through which the footman put his head. A person inside powdered the hair without soiling the footman's uniform.

In a bedroom in this Restoration wing was another curiosity: a hiding place, large enough to conceal a seated man behind a hinged panel. This could only be bolted from the inside. Although it was known as the Priest's Hole, there is no evidence that the owners of Dunsland were recusants, Catholics who refused to recognise and adopt the Church of England. When the house was restored, two clay pipes dating from the seventeenth or eighteenth century were discovered inside.

These three distinct building phases survived, little changed, into the twentieth century.

Bickford Dickinson came to live in the house as a four-year-old and fell in love with it. His father Harvey had chosen a career as a barrister, so the Dickinson family let Dunsland to tenants. Harvey Dickinson had no particular interest in running a small country estate, nor did he have the expertise, until 1914. As the country staggered under the weight of the First World War, Harvey Dickinson spent increasing amounts of time at Dunsland. In the school holidays he was joined by his wife and youngest son, Bickford. These were working holidays: scything, ploughing, carting dung, and growing food as part of the war effort. Timber from the estate was also felled at this time of national emergency.

When the family came to live in the house full time at the end of the First World War, it was showing signs of neglect. Bickford and his parents ripped ivy from the walls, repainted and re-puttied windows, and replanted the walled vegetable garden. The leaking slate roof, however, defeated them. Short of the ready cash to put a new roof on the building, they grouted the slates with liquid cement. At last the building was waterproof. Bickford and his father had succeeded where many other country house owners had failed during this period of the depression. But the Second World War finished them off. A bomb that was dropped nearby blew a hole in the roof, which was patched with corrugated iron for the next twelve years. The demands of the home front took all Bickford's energy, and by this time his parents were really too old to make running repairs. The parkland, which had been decimated in the First World War, was once again plundered for timber. With one son in a German prison camp, and a grandson in the RAF, Mary Dickinson was worn out by the war. In the snowy winter of 1945 she died. Her husband was broken by her death and decided his only option was to sell the house and estate. He offered the house to the National Trust as a gift. They declined.

In 1947 Dunsland House, which had been handed down through seven families in the course of 900 years, was sold for the first time. It was bought as a commercial venture and the assets were stripped. Tenant farms were sold, ancient trees in the surrounding parkland were felled, and the leaking roof remained without repair.

Two years later an elderly architect, who specialised in restoring old houses, bought Dunsland and began a rescue attempt. But the Blitz had destroyed thousands of British homes, and as a result building materials were in short supply. There was no labour available, and he was too elderly to carry out the work himself. But he did patch up the roof and replace a slate water tank in the attic, which had been leaking. As his money ran out the architect, Mr Tilden, decided to reduce the size of the house to save what he could. He demolished the early Tudor wing, first stripping anything saleable. When he died the house was in the semi-derelict state described by Michael Trinick.

After the thirteen-year restoration, the National Trust had begun to use the house as a concert venue, as well as planning to open it to the public. Bickford Dickinson gave his few remaining family heirlooms, and a collection of old West Country books, including many first editions.

However, the crafted lime-plaster ceilings, the treasured family furniture, the idiosyncrasies of this beautiful Devon country house, were all incinerated in the early hours of 18 November 1967. The fire, which ate the house so greedily, almost cost the lives of the custodian and his mother, asleep on the second floor. John Manley Price and Enid Caffyn were saved by the barking of their Scottish sheepdog, Rover, at 3.15 a.m. Stumbling from his bed, John Price from his window in the east wing, saw the darkness broken by a fierce glow. As smoke started to fill the house, he and his mother escaped down the main staircase, blindly groping their way out into the night. The noise was terrifying as roof slates cracked and exploded in the intense heat.

Even if he had been able to reach it, the fire had put the telephone out of action, and John had to leap into his car and drive to the hamlet of Brandts Corner a few miles away to call the fire brigade. By the time he returned, his flat in the east wing was gutted. The framework of beams had been carefully soaked in wood preservative, which acted as an accelerant. Fire fighters from Torrington, Holsworthy and Hatherleigh attempted to douse the flames but by 7.30 the next morning, the roof was gone; the interior was a mess of charred, broken beams; the great sash windows which had lit the magnificent ballroom, were gaping holes. Roofless walls tottered above the fire fighters as they tried to investigate the cause of the fire. It remains a mystery.

In a few hours, 900 years of history disappeared. A beautiful house, evocative of a distant golden age, of faded grandeur and lost fortunes, was simply lost. Antiques worth more than £100,000 were destroyed. A pair of eighteenth-century Chinese ginger vases and two china candlesticks were all that could be saved. What little remained of the building was too dangerous to be left standing and had to be demolished. The location of Dunsland House is today commemorated with a plaque, although the parkland remains.

*A smoking ruin at first light on 18 November 1967.*

### The Long White Barrack By The Sea

A Victorian terrace of white stucco houses fronting Devon's Atlantic coast, owes its existence to three British writers – Charles Kingsley, Rudyard Kipling and John Betjeman. These twelve bay-windowed houses reign architecturally supreme above the developments of later villas and bungalows that line the coast at Westward Ho!. Standing five storeys high, the terrace is built into the steep hillside above the flat land that runs down to the pebble ridge and sandy beach stretching into Bideford Bay. But for the pen of Charles Kingsley it would not have been built; the early literary efforts of Rudyard Kipling were nurtured here; and John Betjeman helped to save it from the demolition ball.

The town of Westward Ho! was born in fiction. The eponymous novel by Charles Kingsley was a runaway success following its publication in 1855. His evocative descriptions of North Devon, and the exploits of his Elizabethan hero Amyas Leigh against the Spanish Armada, struck a patriotic chord with readers as Britain waged war against Russia in the Crimea. Visitors travelled to Bideford and Appledore, attracted by Kingsley's descriptions of the area.

*The imposing buildings of Rudyard Kipling's old school, still a landmark in Westward Ho!. Kipling's study was in No.7.*

Local entrepreneurs and speculators soon capitalised on this tourist boom, throwing up villas and boarding houses to cater for the tourists: so Westward Ho! was born. Among these entrepreneurs was George Molesworth a retired naval officer. Molesworth had retired from the navy in 1870, settling at Charles Kingsley's former home, North Down Hall in Bideford. Molesworth had a finger in every pie in the new town of Westward Ho! and it was thanks to him that Kipling's alma mater was founded in North Devon.

In the same year that Molesworth retired, Britain was in the grip of invasion paranoia. Bismarck's new united Germany was flexing its muscles, and had launched into a war with France (the Franco-Prussian War, 1870–71), which would culminate in the invasion of Paris. Aware of the needs of its far-flung empire, and the potential of Germany's militaristic ambitions, the British army was in the throes of reorganisation. Traditionally, officers were taken from the ranks of the gentry, and bought a commission in their regiment of choice. Regiments had a strict hierarchy, with cavalry regiments such as the Blues and Royals, the Guards, and the Royal Green Jackets among the most prestigious. The price of a commission in these regiments was commensurate with their status. Parliament abolished the system of buying commissions in 1871, recognising that the Empire needed to encourage a new breed of professional soldier, with the emphasis on brains and ability rather than wealth.

*Cormell Price, charismatic teacher and headmaster.*

It was the Duke of Cambridge, Commander in Chief of the Armed Forces, who instigated the birth of the United Services College. In 1873 he and a group of ex-army officers formed a limited company to found a school that would provide an inexpensive education for the sons of serving naval and military officers. It would prepare them for the notoriously difficult Army Entrance Examination, the passport to the officer training establishments at Sandhurst and Woolwich. The old-boy network swung into action, and Molesworth offered the twelve terraced villas, now known as Kipling Terrace in Atlantic Way.

His offer was not entirely altruistic. These twelve houses with their magnificent views across to the Island of Lundy, had been built as boarding houses, but had remained empty. With some adaptation they would easily accommodate 200 schoolboys. Walls were demolished to make dining halls, classrooms, a sick bay, and science laboratory. But it was the choice of headmaster that made the new United Services College such a success. Cormell Price was the man headhunted for the job. At the time he was a master at Haileybury College, in Hertfordshire, a public school with a strong tradition of educating boys from an Anglo-Indian background. He was so highly regarded, that he brought with him a coterie of boys whose parents were anxious that their sons remained under his tuition. The charismatic Price left his own account of the founding of the USC, or Coll as it was known among its old boys:

> In the early seventies there had been much talk in London Military Clubs and out in India of the need for a school where the education, while providing for those who were intended for the Universities or Civil professions, should in the main be adapted especially for those who aimed at entering the Army. The matter of cost was also a great consideration. It was true that Wellington College was a splendid foundation, with an endowment of a quarter of a million from subscriptions mainly contributed with a view to lessen the expenses of education for military parents of limited means. But Wellington College, so they considered, was not fulfilling its mission – at all events, it disappointed their hopes, the military element at the school was regarded as secondary to the University aspirants, and except for those who were on the foundation, the expenses were nearly as high as Eton or Harrow.

The United Services College opened in 1874. Recognising that many pupils would have fathers stationed abroad, it also offered bed, board and supervision in the holidays. The prospectus was keen to stress that while there was ample opportunity for fresh air in the surrounding grounds it was not completely out in the sticks:

> Westward Ho! has a telegraph and money-order office. Trains run through from Waterloo to Bideford Station, whence there are Omnibuses. Letters by the early morning dispatch from London are delivered at Westward Ho! the same day.

On 8 January 1878 a carriage pulled up at the rear of the school. Inside was a podgy twelve-year-old boy, with sallow skin and round glasses topped by beetle brows: Rudyard Kipling. The school was an obvious choice for his parents. Kipling's father was an artist and sculptor, who had gone out to India in 1865 as head of the School of Art in Lahore. John Kipling and headmaster Cormell Price were old friends, and moved in the same artistic circles: their friends included William Morris, Algernon Swinburne, Dante Gabriel Rossetti and other members of the Pre-Raphaelite movement.

Price was one of two men at the school who were responsible for nourishing the Kipling talent in their different ways. The other was William Crofts who taught Latin and English Literature and was the schoolboy writer's most constructive critic, and his housemaster. In his autobiography, *Something of Myself*, published posthumously, Kipling recalled Croft's 'gift of schoolmaster's sarcasm', which was 'a treasure trove to me':

> Under him I came to feel that words could be used as weapons, for he did me the honour to talk at me plentifully; and our year-in-year-out form-room bickerings gave us both something to play with. One learns more from a good scholar in a rage than from a score of lucid and laborious drudges.

But it was Cormell Price who is recognised as the foundation stone of the school's success. His attitude to his pupils was ahead of his time. Victorian adults were often distant and forbidding to children. In a tribute to Price when he died, one former pupil described the rapport established with Price within minutes of meeting him:

> Arriving late at night in a term which had already begun, my House Master himself led me down a dimly-lit dormitory to show me the Compartment allotted to me. The silence, the length of the room, the half light, are present to my mind as if it were yesterday, but, above all, there stands out the friendly companionship of my newly found Master. I had met him for the first time not ten minutes before we entered the dormitory, but he had already banished all shyness in the new boy, and the life-long friendship had begun. The key of his box hurriedly drawn from the boy's pocket sent a coin or two rolling along the floor of the House. In spite of protests, like an old comrade, the Master, the not-to-be-forgotten monocle in his eye, was straightaway down on all fours helping in the search, and by the trivial act, the foundation of friendship already laid was from that moment eternally cemented.

In the school holidays Kipling knew the headmaster as Uncle Crom, and it was he who offered Rudyard the job of editor of the school magazine, *The Chronicle*, which he edited for the last two years of his career at the USC. In *Stalky and Co.*, a fictionalized account of his school days published in 1899, Kipling wrote a loving description of the study inhabited by the man he came to idolise: he dedicated the novel to Cormell Price the headmaster of what

*The schoolboy whose pen gave us the Jungle Book and so much more. Rudyard Kipling in his last year at school.*

Kipling called 'the long white barrack by the sea'. In the book Kipling adopted the nickname Beetle, while the great friends who shared his study, Beresford and Dunsterville, he called M'Turk and Stalky. Like Kipling, Beetle was given the job of editor of the school magazine:

> Only the head took an interest in the publication, and his methods were peculiar. He gave Beetle the run of his brown-bound, tobacco-scented library; prohibiting nothing, recommending nothing. There Beetle found a fat armchair, a silver inkstand, and unlimited pens and paper. There were scores and scores of ancient dramatists; there were Hakluyt, his voyages; French translations of Muscovite authors called Pushkin and Lermontoff...

Price's study was on the ground floor of No. 7 Kipling Terrace, with a north-facing bay window looking straight out to sea. Kipling goes on to describe the head:

> Then the Head, drifting in under pretence of playing censor to the paper, would read here a verse and add here another of these poets; opening up avenues. And, slow breathing with half-shut eyes above his cigar, would he speak of great men living, and journals, long dead, founded in their riotous youth; of years when all the planets were little new-lit stars trying to find their places in the uncaring void, and he, the head, knew them as young men know one another.

This fictitious account of Price's teaching style, tallies with an account by another former pupil:

> The most interesting of my school time were the hours which I spent alone with him in the study of English literature and language. He never begrudged his time and the hour which was supposed to be devoted to me, often ran into two, while we branched off from Max Muller and Chaucer into subjects only remotely connected with either. Though he was in his day a leading expert in technical knowledge he taught far more than book lore to his pupils.

Kipling referred to the United Services College as 'the school before its time', when he wrote his autobiography. Cormell Price gave the boys huge freedom to roam over the surrounding countryside, and turned a blind eye to the fights and scrapping that went on between rival dormitories. He believed that boys who fell exhausted into bed at the end of the day would not have the energy or inclination to get up to any real misdemeanours, a form of muscular Christianity.

The United Services College did not have its own chapel, and Price, unlike that pioneering headmaster of Rugby and all-round educational role model, Thomas Arnold, was not ordained. Discipline was harsh, but it did not stop Kipling, Beresford and Dunsterville from getting up to all sorts of 'jolly japes'. Dunsterville was later to say that:

> Kipling, Beresford and myself shared a study and were generally at

*Left: L.C. Dunsterville, who appears as Stalky in Kipling's fictionalised account of his schooldays; and right, G.C. Beresford, whose fictional name was M'Turk, and who was the third boy in Kipling's study.*

war with masters and boys who incurred our dislike. Our various plots were quite ingenious and often hugely successful.

In *Stalky and Co.*, the boys make dens; break the rules; and even bury a dead cat under the floorboards of one of the school buildings. But amidst the antics of Beetle, Stalky and M'Turk, there seem to be genuine accounts of what the real-life characters may have got up to. The opening paragraph takes us right back to Victorian boarding-school life in a small North Devon town:

> In summer all right-minded boys built huts in the furze-hill behind the College – little lairs whittled out of the heart of the prickly bushes. Full of stumps, odd root-ends, and spikes, but since they were strictly forbidden, palaces of delight. And for the fifth summer in succession, Stalky, M'Turk and Beetle (this was before they reached the dignity of a study) had built like beavers, a place of retreat and meditation, where they smoked.

The boys' studies were at the back of the building, in the lee of this furze-hill, which was once the land between the college and its junior school on the ridge above. To a twenty-first-century reader the beatings and constant fights between dormitories fail to conjure a rosy picture. Yet Kipling is said to have looked back on his school days with some affection, although reputedly he was forced to entertain boys in his dormitory with stories far into the night during his early days at the school. In his autobiography he admits that his first few terms at the school were 'not pleasant':

> The most persistent bullying comes less from the bigger boys, who merely kick and pass, than from young devils of fourteen acting in concert against one butt. After my strength came to me about my fourteenth year, there was no more bullying; and either my natural sloth or past experience did not tempt me to bully in my turn.

The terrace of houses may have been built for holiday-makers but Kipling recalled that, 'Even by the standards of those days, it was primitive in its appointments, and our food would now raise a mutiny on Dartmoor'.

Although Kipling had relations in England, including his mother's sister who was married to Edward Burne Jones, he often had to board at the school during the holidays:

At the end of my first term, which was horrible, my parents could not reach England for the Easter holidays and I had to stay up with a few big boys reading for Army Exams and a batch of youngsters whose people were very far away. I expected the worst but when we survivors were left in the echoing form rooms after the others had driven cheering to the station, life suddenly became a new thing (thanks to Cormell Price). The big remote seniors turned into tolerant elder brothers, and let us small fry rove far out of bounds; shared their delicacies with us at tea; and even took an interest in their hobbies. We had no special work to do and enjoyed ourselves hugely.

Among the USC staff immortalized in *Stalky and Co.*, is Sergeant Major Schofield. He was the former army gymnastic instructor at Colchester Barracks, a distinctive figure at the school for nearly thirty years. With his red hair, mutton-chop whiskers, pipe, bowler hat and cane he was nicknamed 'the weasel' by Kipling and his confederates. In fiction he was allotted the soubriquet Foxy, who stalked the trio of schoolboys:

Nor did Foxy, the subtle, red-haired school Sergeant, trust them. His business was to wear tennis shoes, carry binoculars, and swoop hawk-like upon evil boys.

Foxy taught gymnastics in a separate building built to the east of the college. The boys also played golf and cricket on the flat land running down to the sea, an area that has long since been developed. There were strong links with the community, who were invited to concerts and plays performed by the boys. The school magazine, *The Chronicle* printed a review of *The Rivals* by Richard Sheridan performed in 1881, stating, 'Kipling's Sir Anthony (Aguecheek) was a capital performance, somewhat unfortunately marred by an obvious catarrh and a voice too slender'.

The USC is credited with introducing the game of rugby to North Devon, which was almost unknown there until played on the windswept college playing fields. Thanks to his bad eyesight, which earned him the nickname Gig-lamps, soon shortened to Gigs, Kipling was excused most sports. But he did enjoy swimming. A year after the school was founded, an outdoor pool was built above the beach. It was a hundred yards long, ten yards wide and eight feet deep, filled with sea water pumped in from the sea by a steam engine. The entire pool was tiled so that it could be drained and used as an ice rink in winter. Surrounded by a patio, swimmers were protected from the worst of the wind by high walls. It was inaugurated by a display of swimming skills given by Captain Webb, who six weeks later would achieve fame as the first man to swim the English Channel.

The school's patrons read like a military Who's Who of the late nineteenth century. They included General Lord Roberts, whose son would be killed in the Siege of Ladysmith, and Sir Redvers Buller who commanded the British Forces in the Boer War. The college's army links were strengthened by the annual return of Old Boys, who were accorded particular reverence. Kipling described this annual ritual in *Stalky and Co.*:

> With the last week of term the Old Boys began to arrive, and their welcome was nicely proportioned to their worth. Gentlemen cadets from Sandhurst and Woolwich, who had only left a year ago, but who carried enormous side, were greeted with cheerful 'Hullo! What's the Shop like?' from those who had shared their studies. Militia subalterns had more consideration, but it was understood they were not precisely of the same metal. Recreants who, failing for the Army, had gone into business or banks were received for old sake's sake, but in no way made too much of. But when the real subalterns, officers and gentlemen full-blown – who had been to the ends of the earth and back again and so carried no side – came on the scene strolling about with the Head, the school divided right and left in admiring silence. They would walk to and fro in the corridor with the little red school sergeant, telling news of old regiments; they would burst into form-rooms sniffing the well-remembered smells of ink and whitewash; or they would invade the gymnasium and make Foxy show off the new stock on the bars.

Ironically the school's most famous pupil was not destined for the army, but for journalism. The college roll grew, and a total of 1,200 boys passed through its doors, four of whom went on to win the Victoria Cross.

While establishments like Haileybury and Wellington College have survived into the twenty-first century as public schools to educate the children of the wealthy, the United Services College only just staggered into the early years of the twentieth century. Under the leadership of Cormell Price, the school became a victim of its own success. As Price wrote later, 'Its rapid success on slender means caused odious comparisons to be made'. Questions were asked about the merits of wealthier establishments, in particular Wellington College, which was compared unfavourably with the far cheaper

USC. This triggered a parliamentary inquiry into Wellington, and 'These reforms and the establishment of one or two other schools in rivalry, and, to a great degree in imitation, took the wind out of the sails of the USC'.

Despite its reputation, the United Services College began to have financial problems. Public schools near London, following its example, now offered classes to coach boys for entrance to Woolwich and Sandhurst. This competition, coupled with the fall in value of the Indian rupee, which made it more expensive for serving officers to send their sons to the school, spelt the end. At the close of the Easter term in 1904, the United Services College left Westward Ho! and remaining pupils were transferred to St George's School, Harpenden. Eventually in a remarkable circuitous twist, the remnants of the USC came to Haileybury, from where Cormell Price had been headhunted some thirty years earlier.

The college swimming pool survived long after the school had closed, as Great Nassau Baths – Nassau was the name of Molesworth's son. Tourists could buy a fourpenny 'bathing return' from Bideford Station to Westward Ho! before the First World War. Later the pool continued to be a tourist attraction, advertised as 'a sun trap [whose] high walls offer protection from any mischievous sea breezes'.

The baths became part of the Royal Hotel, with the addition of a large ballroom on the first floor. Both the baths and the hotel have been demolished. But if it had not been for that most English of literary men, Sir John Betjeman, the school buildings would have been lost. Betjeman was a great campaigner, saving many London landmarks from demolition. Likewise he stepped in when Kipling's old school was threatened with demolition in the 1950s.

*United Services College in Kipling's day, the junior school stands on the crest of the hill.*

## The Ignominious Death of Joseph Gandy

It is Christmas Day 1843. Charles Dickens latest book *A Christmas Carol* has just been published; civil servant Henry Cole has posted the first Christmas cards (designed in Torquay) to a thousand friends; and the country is experiencing a mini ice age, shrouding the country church of Plympton St Maurice with snow. All the components of our concept of a Victorian Christmas are falling into place. At Plympton House, a short distance from the church, a doctor and his family are sitting down to eat in the dining room of this beautiful Queen Anne House. Turkey and plum pudding are on the menu for their Christmas feast. But in a darkened windowless room in one of the outhouses, a 68-year-old man, hailed as a genius, lies dying. He is Joseph Gandy, an architect and Royal Academician, now regarded as the greatest perspective artist in British history. Plympton House is a private lunatic asylum, and will shortly become one of the most notorious mental hospitals in the country.

It was during the reign of mad King George III, that the subject of mental illness became a hot topic. Ironically it was not the illness of the King himself that brought it to the fore, but rather one of his subjects. On 15 May 1800, James Hadfield attempted to assassinate the King, but his bullet missed the intended target by a foot. Hadfield was detained as a 'criminal lunatic'. His assassination attempt sparked mass hysteria and fear of the mentally ill, but also a demand that such people should be securely locked away to protect society. Two months later, Parliament responded by bringing in legislation to ensure that such criminal lunatics could be locked up for the good of society. In 1808 local magistrates were given powers to construct county asylums.

Devon was slow to respond. Although not all English counties had public asylums, no other county without an asylum had as many 'pauper lunatics' in workhouses. Many of those who were mentally ill were looked after by families or friends, but there were still 500 people who were not. The workhouses could not cope, so private asylums sprang up. Demand for places outstripped supply, and it became a seller's market. Lunatic asylums were big business in the early eighteenth century, in the same way that nursing homes for the elderly are today.

But who were these lunatics? Unmarried mothers and epileptics were classed as lunatics; people suffering from depression were classed as lunatics; elderly men and women suffering from dementia were classed as lunatics. All these people were locked up in private asylums with others who were 'suffering from hallucinations' or what was termed 'chronic madness'. In the same way that some of those today who are mentally ill are violent, so were some of these patients.

Joseph Gandy was one of the eighty-four patients confined in Plympton House. The fifty-two men and thirty-two women, did not live in the mansion built by a former Lord Chief Justice of England, but were crammed into the dairy and outhouses. Sixteen of them were private patients and the remainder were paupers, sent there from Devon workhouses.

Joseph Gandy was once the darling of London society. He had risen from humble origins, as one of the twelve children of a waiter at White's Club, to recognition as an innovative and brilliant architect. As a teenage prodigy his potential was recognised and his future looked bright. But Gandy was bolshie, bad mannered and rude. The critics loved him, but he refused to alter any of his drawings to comply with the wishes of a client.

His saviour was Sir John Soane, who brought him into his architect's practice. While Soane designed the buildings, it was Gandy's brilliant realisation and embellishment of them on paper that sold them to the clients. He augmented his boss's designs with apocalyptic visions, visions that would be perfectly at home on the set of the Lord of the Rings film. Gandy became obsessed with death and incarceration and designed a cast-iron necropolis, in which the dead were housed in metal cylinders. After the fire that destroyed the Houses of Parliament on 16 October 1834, he designed a Graeco-Roman fortress as a replacement.

His grand designs were too way out for most. Few of them were built and fewer still have survived: offices for the Phoenix Fire and Pelican Life Insurance in Charing Cross, built in 1804, were demolished in 1924, though Storrs Hall, a country house on the shores of Lake Windermere, has survived. Gandy remodelled and enlarged an earlier house designing a central dome to bring light into the interior. His fantastical designs for a boathouse with Doric columns and a druidical temple, based on Stonehenge, were ignored by the client. He also designed a new wing for Lancaster Prison, to hold female inmates. It is a deep irony that the design with accommodation wings radiating out from a central hub is very similar to that of the Devon County Asylum, later known as Exminster Hospital, which was completed two years after Gandy's death.

Gandy was a friend of Samuel Taylor Coleridge and John Keats, and a visionary of the Romantic Movement. Despite his humble origins, he also wrote a seven-volume book on *The Art, Philosophy and Science of Architecture*, although it has not survived. Nevertheless one of his paintings for the book is in the collection at the Sir John Soane Museum in London. Painted in the last years of his life, it is a strange and unsettling vision of architecture and nature. Sir John Soane was Gandy's boss, friend and mentor, and had to bail him out on more than one occasion when Gandy was unable to support his wife and six children and was sent to debtor's prison.

The year 1830 was a low point in Gandy's life. On Friday, 12 November that year, *The Times* carried this sad advertisement for an auction of the household furniture and effects of J. Gandy esq.:

> The original and valuable Paintings and Drawings, including several beautiful specimens from the pencil of Joseph Gandy Esq, A.R.A., amongst which is a noble unfinished picture, A Contemplated View of the Heavenly Regions, a splendid composition; a very beautiful and highly finished picture, the Interior of a Palace, and other architectural designs in rich gilt frames, scene prints and a library of 400 volumes of books, chiefly on the fine arts, many very rare and scarce. The household furniture includes 4 post end tent bedsteads, goose beds and bedding, chests of drawers, dressing and pier glasses, a mahogany sideboard, pembroke, sofa, and dining tables, mahogany and Japanned chairs, kitchen requisites, excellent fixtures, and effects, at his residence, 15 Percy-Street, Bedford Square.

This was an inventory of Gandy's home: a comfortable, well-furnished house with a library of favourite books.

It was in 1839 that his family consigned him to Plympton House. No record has survived to give us details of his illness and its extent, but his wife must have been desperate. Eleanor had stuck with him through the birth of nine children, the death of three of them, and prolonged periods of poverty. Perhaps this was her last resort. Certainly the conditions in which Gandy spent the last four years of his life were close to his own apocalyptic visions. In the mini ice age of 1843 he was incarcerated in a damp, windowless outhouse. The building almost certainly had an earth floor. His diet was poor, and he was wracked with dysentery. His days and nights would have been punctuated with the cries and ramblings of the other eighty patients classed, like him, as insane. Whatever was wrong with these poor people when they were consigned to Plympton House, their neglect and treatment there cannot have improved their health.

In 1842 a team of government inspectors was appointed to investigate conditions in asylums. The 1844 Report of The Metropolitan Commissioners in Lunacy came too late for poor Joseph Gandy. But Plympton House was one of ten establishments throughout the country, picked out for particular criticism. On their visits to Plympton the inspectors were horrified by the

*Joseph Gandy's extraordinary vision of the fusion of architecture and nature.*

'Excessive and highly censurable degree of restraint'. The sixty-six paupers housed there were described in their report as 'the refuse of the workhouses'. What was even more scandalous was that Plympton was the second most expensive asylum in the country. An admission fee of 1 pound and 1 shilling (£1.05) was charged for every patient, with fees of ten shillings and six pence (52p) every week excluding clothing. While the proprietor and his family lived in the mansion, the patients were consigned to outbuildings. The inspectors were appalled at their condition, stating: 'It appeared that complaints had been repeatedly made of the state of the buildings, but apparently without any beneficial results'.

Incontinent male paupers slept in the former dairy, a badly ventilated room, with one small, unglazed window that was covered with a shutter at night. The inspectors described the building as 'damp and offensive' and their report revealed that some women lived in what was described as a cottage with three bedrooms:

> The wooden cribs were filthy, the floor was in holes and soaked with urine, and in parts covered with straw and excrement. It could not have been cleaned for some days. The windowless cells are as damp and dark as an underground cellar.

In these days before damp courses, the walls were running with condensation and smeared with filth. Although men and women slept in separate rooms, the inspectors obviously suspected a certain amount of abuse. In their report they highlight a male patient who slept in a room near several violent female patients, and he appeared to have access to the rooms where the girls slept. The only bedding was an old piece of carpet or straw.

In a dayroom the size of a cupboard, eight feet by four feet, three women were locked up, although there were two seats fastened to the damp wall. Another dayroom contained seventeen patients, but was so small that each person had only a square yard of floor space. In the room were ten seats, but no tables. In another room they found an even more distressing sight:

> In a state of furious mania, was a young woman who had been delivered of a child five or six weeks previously, confined by a straight waistcoat, and chained by an arm and a leg to a bench.

There is no mention of the fate of the child. According to the census return of 1841, the establishment had a live-in staff of a matron, four nurses and two 'keepers', hardly adequate for eighty-four patients. The inspectors were horrified to find that:

> Ten curable patients and two idiots were under the charge of a lunatic, who was himself confined by a chain from the wrist or ankle...principally to prevent him from escaping.

We do not know whether Gandy himself was restrained in any way, but it seems likely as twenty-one of the patients were chained to their beds at night. From the census return of 1841 it is possible to glean the names of some of his fellow inmates, but not whether they were private patients or paupers. They included Charles Everett, a retired soldier who from his age would have been a veteran of the Napoleonic Wars. Carpenters, shoemakers, builders, merchants, seamen and a preacher were all among the inmates. They lived on a meagre diet, and were given water and milk to drink, only 'if asked for'. Breakfast and supper consisted of bread, and milk or water. Their main meal was soup on two days a week; boiled rice and salt three days a week; potato pie on another; and for a treat, boiled beef on Sundays. But as there were no tables apparent, the inspectors were unsure how or where they ate.

One of the many criticisms levelled at Plympton House and the other nine private asylums picked out for their appalling conditions, was the management:

> The system of management appears to have been constituted less with regard to the cure of insanity, and the restoration of lunatics to health and society, than to their seclusion and safe custody.

The Victorian medical profession did have ideas for what was termed the 'most successful method of attempting a cure' of patients. These, too, are in the report, and a good diet is foremost among them:

> Warm clothing and bedding, and a moderately warm and dry atmosphere, are indispensable auxiliaries for promoting the comfort and cure of lunatics, in whom the circulation is languid, and who for the most part are chilly, and suffer much from exposure to cold and damp air.

Outdoor exercise and cleanliness were among the other common-sense suggestions 'generally found to promote the restoration of patients whose cases are of a curable description'. None of these prescriptions for the care of the mentally ill were found at Plympton House. Neglect seems to have been the watchword.

The inspectors visited Plympton House three times. On their second visit, it was a hot July day, and they discovered in the courtyard outside:

> Another woman in a straight waistcoat, was lying in a hole in the middle of the airing court, without covering to her head, or anything to shelter her from the broiling sun.

On their third visit they found 'the house was in even a worse state', yet astonishingly the asylum was not closed, or the proprietor's licence revoked. However, changes were afoot. The inspectors' report was based on the premise that insanity is a curable condition if treated early enough in a properly resourced and constructed asylum. The Devon authorities were in the process of doing just that. In 1842 building work had started on the Devon County Asylum, which would be known in the future as Exminster Hospital. The architect was Charles Fowler, whose main claim to fame is the design of Covent Garden. By 1845 the new asylum was built.

*The beautiful Queen Anne House which was once one of the most notorious mental hospitals in England. The wing to the right is a twentieth-century addition.*

At Plympton House, meanwhile, only thirty-three 'lunatics' are recorded on the census return of 1851. No longer do we know their names, only their initials. By this time the proprietors of Plympton House had made improvements.

Today Plympton House has been renamed and is owned and run by the Sisters of Saint Augustine. They bought the former asylum in 1934 and renamed it St Peter's Convent. Its residents are the elderly and those with dementia, but the successors of Joseph Gandy live within the beautiful Queen Anne House, and are cared for by a team of nursing staff.

It is reassuring to know that with more enlightened times comes a more enlightened approach to the treatment of the mentally ill. Devon may have the dubious honour as the site of one of the worst institutions for such patients, but it was also home to one of the best. Moorhaven Hospital was opened on 16 October 1891 on the southern edge of Dartmoor. Where the land slopes gently down to Bittaford, a purpose-built hospital was constructed for 203 patients. Initially known as the Plymouth Borough Asylum, the name Moorhaven was chosen by a ballot of staff. Over the years the building was extended, until in the 1950s it was home to 720 patients with 400 full- and part-time staff.

In its nursing of patients, particularly with schizophrenia, Moorhaven was at the forefront of a revolution in psychiatric nursing. This was masterminded by a trio: John Greene, chief male nurse, Belle Britain the matron, and Dr Francis Pilkington, the medical superintendent. In line with the thinking of its Victorian founders, male and female patients had been segregated by walls in the gardens outside: John Greene personally pulled the walls down. Residents were offered occupational therapy and were employed in workshops housed in Nissen huts. But John Greene also introduced a new concept – community psychiatric nursing – and ultimately this led to the revolution that closed old Victorian asylums all over the country.

The last patients left Moorhaven on 23 February 1993. Five years later the old asylum had been transformed into Moorhaven Village, a community of 100 homes with communal sports facilities. The dark days of Victorian prejudice and institutionalised mistreatment had been left behind.

### The Evolution of Endsleigh

It was Friday, 9 October 1953, and the 12th Duke of Bedford had gone out shooting before breakfast as usual. His targets were the hawks that preyed on the budgerigars and other birds on his Devon estate. The Duke had been staying at his holiday home Endsleigh House, near Tavistock, with its magnificent views over the River Tamar. For 140 years his family had been bringing guests to Endsleigh to shoot in the woods and fish on the best salmon river in England.

But the Duke did not return. Once the alarm was raised, estate workers, helped by soldiers and men from the Royal Marines, began to comb the grounds of the 9,000-acre estate. It was two days before his body was found below the quaint Swiss Cottage built for his ancestors. The unconventional and eccentric Duke was found with his gun beside him. Although police ruled out foul play, rumours and gossip abounded, but at the inquest the coroner gave a verdict of accidental death. It was only thirteen years since the Duke had succeeded to the title, and Endsleigh House and its grounds had to be sold to cover death duties. But the house which had been a second home to the Dukes of Bedford for 140 years proved difficult to sell, and finally changed hands fourteen years later.

Tavistock and much of the land around it had been granted to the Russell family after the Dissolution, and it was in 1810 that Endsleigh House and its magnificent gardens were designed for the 6th Duke of Bedford and his second Duchess, Georgina. The Bedfords were among the wealthiest aristocrats in the country, so naturally they employed two of Britain's top designers, architect Jeffrey Wyatville, and the father of landscape gardening, Humphry Repton. Both men had worked at the Bedford family seat at Woburn Abbey and were part of the Picturesque Movement. The

*The Swiss Cottage, built in the grounds of Endsleigh House, it is now a holiday cottage.*

Picturesque had evolved from the eighteenth-century idea of 'nature over artifice' and, as defined by the originator of the term, William Gilpin, was, 'That kind of beauty which is agreeable in a picture'.

The Duchess was the darling of Regency Society. Her long-suffering husband put up with her open affair with the most famous artist of the day, Edwin Landseer. Despite being twenty years his senior, Georgina obviously entranced the young man, and bore him a child. And she also bore her husband twelve children, ten of whom survived.

Endsleigh House was designed as a cottage orné, purposely quaint and irregular. Rachel Evans published a book of walks round the Tavistock area in 1846, called *Home Scenes*, in which she describes the house and its grounds:

> The contour of the building is irregular, gradually receding from the front towards the wings. Rustic verandas adorn the front, containing odoriferous plants and flowering shrubs, and supported by trunks of oak trees as columns, around which cling the clustering scotch rose, the ivy and the honeysuckle, forming natural festoons above the windows. One portion of the wall is covered with a far spreading magnolia; every year this plant unfolds its rich blossoms

and sends a delicious fragrance through the air. By its side blooms the flowering myrtle and scarlet geranium, while the flaunting passion flower sends down its brilliant petals to them from above.

The book is dedicated to the Duchess for 'allowing her honoured name to be inscribed on this simple page'.

A handsome bracket supports the bust of Francis Duke of Bedford, the eminent patron of agriculture, whose early demise was deeply lamented by all who were sensible of his worth... The chimney piece is of polished granite of a handsome dark grain.

In fact the chimney piece, which still stands in the hall, is made of concrete designed to look like granite. In the same way, what appears to be oak panelling is in fact pine that has been painted with fake oak grain. Not because the Bedfords had gone over budget, but all in keeping with a cottage orné!

To complement the cottage, the gardens were designed by the Dan Pearson of his day. Humphry Repton coined the phrase landscape gardening, believing that the garden should enhance the house and set the building in the landscape. In his book *Observations on the Theory and Practice of Landscape Gardening* (1803), he outlined his principles:

The perfection of landscape gardening consists in the four following requisites. First, it must display the natural beauties and hide the defects of every situation. Secondly, it should give the appearance of extent and freedom by carefully disguising or hiding the boundary. Thirdly, it must studiously conceal every interference of art. However expensive by which the natural scenery is improved; making the whole appearance the product of nature only; and fourthly, all objects of mere convenience or comfort, if incapable of being made ornamental, or of becoming proper parts of the general scenery, must be removed or concealed.

Here we have some of the fundamental principles of modern garden design, such as the use of borrowed landscape, whereby a gap in the boundary hedge can reveal a beautiful view, or a church tower. When television gardeners show viewers how to conceal a compost bin behind trellis, or to disguise it as a beehive, they are following these Repton principles.

It was the gardens that drew visitors to Endsleigh; even Queen Victoria visited and although the Duke was not in residence she was shown round by the head gardener. More lowly visitors bought a ticket at the estate office, in nearby Tavistock. The garden was still entrancing tourists by the end of the century. John Lloyd Warren Page, in his book *The Rivers of Devon*, rhapsodised in 1893:

> It is not the house which brings so many visits to Endsleigh; it is the dells, the dingles, the beautifully-laid-out gardens, the grottos, chalets, and what not. For which it has been the delight of the former noble owners to plan, not only for their own delight, but for that of others. For the grounds immediately adjacent are thrown open to duly accredited parties, and I fancy, indeed know, that the estate office at Tavistock is at times pretty well besieged for cards of admission. Endsleigh is, in fact, the happy hunting-ground of picknickers from all over the neighborhood round – from Launceston, from Lifton, from Tavistock, and exacting indeed must be the individual who cannot enjoy a very satisfactory 'dolce far niente' in this retreat so 'far from the madding crowd'.

These gardens, which drew visitors for so many years, were actually Humphry Repton's last commission. In 1811 he had an accident while travelling back

*Endsleigh House with the garden in full bloom in August 1833.*

from a ball with his three daughters on the night of 29 January. Snow had drifted across the road, their carriage overturned, and he received serious spinal injuries from which he never entirely recovered. He was confined to a wheelchair until his death seven years later. Frustrated that he was unable to garden, or even pick flowers from his wheelchair, he invented the raised bed, another concept familiar to all modern gardeners.

In the pre-television era, this garden tourism offered an opportunity to peep through the keyhole at a house that belonged to one of the most famous and wealthy aristocratic families in the country. Endsleigh House is now a hotel, and the 'cabinet' referred to by Rachel Evans is used as a bar today:

> From the windows of all these rooms which open on the terrace, many lovely peeps of the woods and river are gained, but the most beautiful view is from a tiny cabinet adjoining the library. The large pane of glass enables us to discern, without interruption, the verdant lawn stretching far away, with the winding Tamar foaming over its rocky bed, until lost to sight amid the depths of wormwood.

One of Repton's great design principles was that a lawn should act as a foreground to the house, where terracing was vital. He also reintroduced the idea of flowerbeds, which had gone out of fashion. Rachel Evans was entranced:

> As we proceed the hand of cultivations is more apparent; arches of twisted osier entwined with the wild clematis and woodbine; shade the walk; wooden bridges cross small rivulets, and at length the garden gate opens on the desired paradise of sweets. A grotto on the left is the first object to be seen. This, perfect in its kind, is ornamented with beautiful specimens procured from the various mines in the neighbourhood, as well as other more distant regions; while shells and corallines help to fill up the interstices. Seats of polished marble from Plymouth, are laced in the recesses; a gurgling stream swelling from a small fountain in the centre, enlivens the place with its ever chiming music... It has been justly remarked that the perfect solitude and retirement of Endsleigh forms its principal charm. It offers a delightful and soothing retreat from the busy world, presenting such an enticing home scene as England alone can boast; and gladly must the wearied statesman and active noble retire to this spot to enjoy the quiet of such undisturbed seclusion.

Here is a delicate allusion from Rachel Evans to just how well connected the Bedford family was. When she visited in 1846, Lord John Russell had just become Prime Minister. He was Duchess Georgina's stepson, the 6th Duke's third son by his previous marriage, and had been elected MP for Tavistock in 1813. No wonder Rachel Evans is almost breathless in her excitement:

> Near the offices a flight of steps conducts to the rock garden, where a number of stones are arranged so as to mingle with the natural rock, and form supporters for the rocks which spring up between. In the centre are mimic ponds whose waters slip away unseen, and again ooze out at some little distance, from so many dropping wells from the overhanging rocks. Leaving the green-houses on our right we are conducted by a subterranean alcove and a flight of steps cut in the rock to the dairy dell.

There were several rustic buildings dotted round the grounds, including a Swiss Cottage and a Fisherman's Hut, its porch built to resemble a boat. Reputedly servants had to keep a fire lit in the hearth of the Woodman's rustic cottage, whatever the weather, so that its curling smoke could seen rising above the encircling trees.

Morris Taylor, who was the last head gardener to the Dukes of Bedford, had a team of men to care for this landscape. Their duties had included tending to the walled garden, which grew produce for the house when the family came down to stay. Usually this was for six weeks in May and June at the height of the fishing season. When the fish were not rising, the 11th Duke had a small fleet of canoes specially built for expeditions on the river. Made of oak to withstand stones, they were unusually narrow to squeeze between rocks. Apparently they were also rather unstable. In her diary of 5 June 1912, the 11th Duchess described one of these expeditions:

> Canoed from Endsleigh to Latchley Weir, the Duke and Miss Green in a double canoe and I in a single. As the river was in flood, and the Duke has had it narrowed in places for his salmon fishing, I ship-wrecked handsomely on two occasions. The first time was rather a shock, as the water was so cold that it took all my breath away, and the current is too strong to allow of standing, even if you are in your depth, which I was not. The second time I saw shipwreck was inevitable and was prepared, as I had already been under, head and all. It takes about 1 hour 40 minutes to canoe to Latchley (6 miles) in

a flood, allowing for upsets and emptying of canoes.

The Bedfords had a boathouse downriver at Morwellham Quay, for those who would rather take to the water in a more decorous manner. The Duchess certainly did not let the restraints of pre-First World War fashion prevent her from enjoying herself. In fact she took up flying after the First World War at the age of sixty, and broke records by flying to India and Africa. However, she went missing off the East Anglian coast on a solo flight in 1937.

In the years since the death of the 12th Duke, the gardens that had been carefully designed to make the best of nature were taken over by nature. Death duties forced the family to sell the estate piecemeal. The dairy, which Rachel Evans described in her book in 1846, has been restored by The Landmark Trust:

> Crossing a rustic bridge, we follow a path which leads to the dairy – a simple building, containing one room and a small vestibule, paved with marble. The milk is received in marble basins, around which are small canals of water, and an ever-bubbling fountain in the centre assists in keeping the place cool. The walls are lined with tiles of white porcelain edged with a wreath of green vine leaves; china vases are disposed around, ornamented with a corresponding pattern. The place, we believe is more for show than use, but it is a pretty toy for the world's favourites.

*The Landmark Trust has restored the fanciful dairy.*

*The dairy interior.*

Endsleigh House became the home of a salmon fishing club after it was sold, and in 2004 Olga Polizzi bought the house and 100 acres and converted it into a hotel, and the gardens designed by Humphry Repton are gradually being restored.

# CHAPTER 7

# THE BLAST OF WAR

The roll of honour begins with Achey and ends with Zemple: 946 American servicemen who died on the Devon coast in rehearsals for the D-Day landings. But for the unstinting research of Ken Small their names and their fate would have been forgotten. The disaster happened in April 1944 as German E-Boats stumbled on Exercise Tiger in the months running up to D-Day. Some men are still listed as missing, but most were found floating in the water the following day. Such is the nature of war that survivors were sworn to secrecy and the bodies were hastily buried. Some may still lie in the fields surrounding the villages of Slapton, Chillington, Stokenham, Strete, Sherford, Torcross, East Allington and Blackawton.

It was on 20 December 1943 that the villages surrounding Slapton Sands were evacuated, to enable 30,000 Americans to use the area for military manoeuvres. The American visitors were to train on Slapton Sands because of its similarity to the beaches of Normandy. The exercise began in the early hours of 28 April 1944, as the naval convoy, carrying assault troops and landing craft, cruised off the Devon coast. Nine German E-boats were out hunting in the English Channel and attacked. There were failures in communication on the side of the Allies, as well as possible friendly fire. The German E-Boat commander was awarded an iron cross, but the Allies' plans for D-Day were not rumbled despite the disaster.

It was the dog tags, regimental insignia and wedding rings found by beachcomber Ken Small which led him to uncover the lost story of Exercise Tiger. War is a byword for sacrifice, and its losses are to be found both above and below ground. At times even the link to war has been forgotten.

**Bloody Sunday**
In the pre-dawn cold of 3 December 1643, 400 Royalist soldiers waded across the creek. As the estuarine mud clung to boots and clothes, their breath clouded the air with the exertion. One slip, and a soldier's musket would

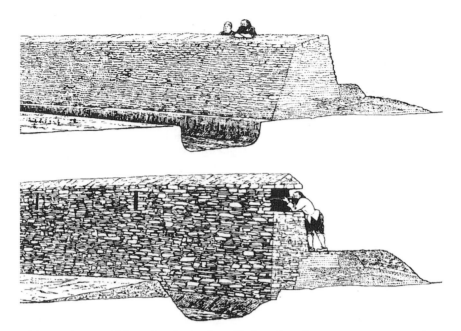

*Excavations at Friary Goods Yard enabled archaeologists to reconstruct the Plymouth's civil war defences. Top: Turfed rampart of late 1642. Above: The stone fronted rampart of 1643.*

become wet and useless. Besides, in the pre-dawn silence sound would carry clearly across water, and a splash would alert the enemy on the far side. Their aim was to steal through a gap in the trenched outer fortifications protecting the city of Plymouth.

Successfully across the creek, they slipped through the defences, past the enemy fort. As they marched towards Laira Point, these men knew they had right on their side. They were fighting for the King, in a war which had destabilised the entire country, A King who ruled by divine right, anointed with holy oil, a King who had the right to call people to arms, and to ask them to finance his mistakes. It is the latter, which had upset the people of Plymouth. In the 1620s Charles I launched abortive forays against Spain and France, but the expeditions were poorly planned and supplied. When the fleet returned to port, it was the people of Plymouth who picked up the bill. The King expected the remnants of his army to be fed, watered and housed by the people of Plymouth at their own expense. In 1643, King Charles was not popular in this city.

With the waters of Sutton Pool to their backs the Parliamentarians of Plymouth had already withstood two sieges. They had three strong points: the castle at the entrance to Sutton Pool; the Elizabethan castle on the Hoe; and the fort on St Nicholas Island out in Plymouth Sound. The English Channel was controlled by their navy, so supplies of arms, money and men had sailed up through the Sound. Royalist guns had bombarded this supply line but had been unable to stop the ships getting through. Royalist troops set up camp to the north, west and east of the city. But the men, women, and children of Plymouth, according to oral tradition, dug ditches, and built earth banks topped by stone for the city's defence. They may have been unwilling to pay the costs of King Charles's foolish forays against the French, but they did pay to defend their homes against him. By 1643, the remains of the town's medieval wall near the castle had been extended to circle the town. Forts stood every 250 to 500 metres along the wall, with names such as Terrour, St George, Charles and Resolution. Under modern Plymouth the remains of these defences survive: limestone and shale foundations fronted by a ditch, defensive banks and walls, with a further ring of fortifications beyond, on the outskirts of the city.

Further east, the Parliamentarians also defended Dartmouth Castle at the mouth of the Dart but once this fell the King's western army had moved on to concentrate on Plymouth. By late September, Plymouth was sandwiched between Royalist Cornwall and an army ranged along its north side. It was also cut off from the main Parliamentary army to the east.

John Syms, a puritan minister, recorded in his diary the relief felt in the city when a ship carrying 500 reinforcements arrived in Plymouth at the end of September that year. The city's defenders were short of provisions and ammunition, and guards were exhausted from an eight-day stretch of defending the walls against a Royalist assault. Despite this brief reprieve the Royalists went on to take the Fort at Stamford across the Cattewater to surround the city. In November 1643 Syms wrote that the people of Plymouth resolved to burn the town to the ground rather than 'the Enemyes of God and his cause should possess it'.

During lulls in the fighting Syms recorded how teams of people were:

...being busyed in mending of some Hedges that were formerly pulled down between the works [earthworks]; the only line of communication we have scarce defensible against the stormings of horse, yet such places we must resolve to defend upon equall terms with the enemy; for the works are of such a distance each from other, and the grounds far narrower, that an enemy may in some places approach within the works without any molestation by them.

His words were prophetic. But the dawn attack on that Bloody Sunday of 3

December 1643 could not have happened without a little help. It is easy to think that a city under siege is filled with a people united against the enemy and, indeed, Plymouth was packed with Puritan refugees from Cornwall. But those living through such events had no knowledge of the final outcome, and a significant number did not have the strong convictions of men like John Syms. In his siege diary, Syms recorded how 'two malignants' were accused of plotting to blow up Maudlin Fort in the outer ring of defences. The two men fled to the enemy, and on 3 December it was they who guided the musketeers round the Parliamentary defences.

Caught off guard the garrison at Laira 'works' was overwhelmed and, as Pym wrote, it was hardly a fair fight, 'The works is but a half moon and the guard there placed only to give the alarum if the enemy should approach Lary-point over the fields when the Tyde is out'.

The Royalists advanced further – up the steep hill to Lipson – but by dawn the Roundhead defenders were ready to rally for a counterattack. At this point the Royalist cavalry arrived. At the head of five cavalry, and four infantry regiments, is Prince Maurice, the less glamorous younger brother of dashing Prince Rupert. The cavalry drove the Parliamentarians right back to the city walls. According to tradition, a mounted cavalier, dodging pistol

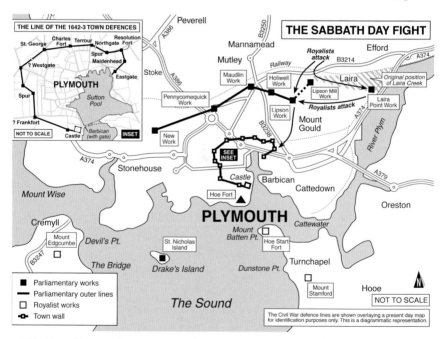

*The Royalist attack on 3 December 1643, reconstructed from contemporary sources and plotted on a modern map.*

shots from the walls, plunged his sword into the wooden town gate. But this proved to be a futile gesture, and the closest the Royalists came to victory.

On the outer defences at Lipson, the Parliamentarians kept the rest of the cavalry at bay so that by mid-morning the Royalist cavalry had been routed, and the Battle of Freedom Fields was over. Soldiers were hacked down as they retreated and some drowned whilst trying to escape back across the creek (when they crept across at dawn the tide was out, but later in the day it was high). Victory for the Parliamentarians was costly too – burials in the graveyard of St Andrew's Church peaked in the months following the Battle of Freedom Fields.

The monument to the events of that Bloody Sunday was built on the spot where the Parliamentarian defenders stood firm, on the high ground at Lipson to the north-east of the city walls. The words give some indication of the civic pride still felt 250 years later.

Upon this site on Sunday December 3rd 1643, after hard fighting for several hours the Roundhead garrison of Plymouth made their final rally, and routed the Cavalier Army which had surprised the out-works and well nigh taken the town. For many years it was the custom to celebrate the anniversary of this victory long known as the 'Sabbath Day Fight', and recognised as the 'Great Deliverance' of the protracted siege successfully sustained by Troops and Townsfolk on behalf of the Parliament against the King under great hardships for more than three years.

But Plymouth's struggle against the Royalist army continued for another two

*Monument to the Parliamentarian victory on the site of the battle in Freedom Fields Park.*

years. Each time they repulsed the Royalist forces, the besieged gathered up the firewood, tools, arms and ammunition left behind. Throughout 1645 the Roundheads conducted a scorched earth policy, turning the area north of Plymouth into a wasteland, destroying any Royalist fortifications, and even burning villages to the ground. But by the end of the year the outcome of the war was still uncertain, and the inhabitants were tired of living under siege. In a newsletter sent to the speaker of the House of Commons, the Governor of Plymouth Colonel James Kerr, summed up the problem:

> Those of the Enemy party in the Town (as it must be expected in all places are some) began to get courage, our own friends doubtfull; and I believe the Nutralists [neutrals] do desire that the Town might be delivered up.

On 3 December 1645, the second anniversary of that bloody Sunday, Colonel Kerr was offered an incentive to surrender the city. The bribe, which he referred to as 'this temptation', was a reward of £10,000, the command of a cavalry regiment of 500 men, 'with what honours you yourself shall desire'. The Royalists had underestimated Governor Kerr. His scornful reply, which survives in the city archives, begins, 'Your motion to Treason I have seen, and detest it'. To reinforce his stance, Kerr added that, 'The messenger who brought this letter to Colonel James Kerr, hath since received his reward, and is executed by Martial Law'.

Kerr's morale must have been boosted by the knowledge that the New Model Army was already in Devon, and by January 1646 was close to Plymouth. As Cromwell's Roundheads advanced, the Royalist army fled to Cornwall, and ultimately surrendered in Truro in March 1646. The successful stand of the Parliamentarians in Plymouth is recognised as vital to Cromwell's eventual victory in the English Civil War. The defence of Plymouth was the key to the South West.

## Battles and Beaches

Devon's modern tourist industry was indirectly triggered by the birth in 1769 of a Corsican lawyer's son, Napoleon Bonaparte. Three decades later he had become a charismatic, glamorous, and brilliant little general. With much of the continent under his belt, Napoleon set out to destroy the great British navy. And it was this ambition, in a round about sort of way, that brought holiday-makers to the Devon Riviera and transformed humble fishing villages into holiday resorts.

Britain had gone to war first with her erstwhile colony, America. Soon

France, then Spain, and finally Holland joined the melée. In the light of later wars it is easy to forget the danger in which Britain found herself at the end of the eighteenth century. The physical peril posed by these wars, was exacerbated by their economic impact. Warring neighbours no longer provide an export market. Privateers from all sides regarded war as a licence to board ships, throw the crew overboard and steal ship and cargo. Lloyd's List records the fate of the sloop *Adventure*, a Brixham ship, which sailed from London in early 1801. Although the *Adventure* made it through the Channel and out into the Atlantic, she was seized by the French before reaching her destination in the Azores. An Exeter-based smack, the *Dart*, was burnt out by an American privateer in the Bay of Biscay on 1 December 1814. But this ungentlemanly behaviour worked both ways. *L'Heureuse Marie Adele*, was not so lucky when she was seized as a prize on 4 February 1814, and spent the next twelve years as a British coaster until she was lost at sea.

As one of the counties facing the French coast, Devon towns and villages had traded raiding parties with the French for centuries. A French raid at Blackpool Sands near Dartmouth was, according to tradition, defeated by men and women who – quite literally – fought them on the beaches. In 1779 the threat was rather more serious, when a combined French and Spanish fleet lay off Plymouth.

Devon was a heavily fortified county with troops stationed at towns such as Kingsbridge, Modbury and more major centres such as Plymouth and Exeter. When Napoleon came to power in 1793, Britain was once more on red alert. Bony, like Hitler over a century later, was determined to invade Britain, even investigating plans for a Channel tunnel in his desperation. The spectre of Bony and his invasion resurfaced in 1797–8 and again throughout the years 1801 to 1805, until like Hitler, Napoleon was diverted by the obsession of invading Russia.

Recent excavations by archaeologists revealed that during the tedious and anxious hours watching for signs of enemy invasion during this period, a

*An artilleryman's button with three field guns lost during the Napoleonic Wars.*

member of the Royal Artillery lost a single metal button from his red uniform. The watcher was at his post on Beer Head, one of a string of gun batteries along the Devon coast. From this outpost a team of gunners aimed cannon with a range of over a mile out to sea. Nearby was a signal mast, one of a chain of semaphore posts, which transmitted messages from Plymouth to Admiralty headquarters in London. There were thirty signal posts in this shutter telegraph system, nine of which were in Devon. Telegraph Hill at Kennford, just outside Exeter, is so named because it is the site of one of these telegraph stations. And there is Telegraph Cottage close to the modern television mast close to the A38 at Plympton. Two centuries later, email delivers messages in less than a minute but during the Napoleonic Wars a message was sent from Plymouth to London and a reply was received in just twenty minutes.

The crushing of Napoleon's army at the Battle of Waterloo brought peace to Britain at last. The spectre of Napoleon Bonaparte no longer hung over the green and pleasant fields. When the bogeyman himself was brought into Plymouth Sound on the *Bellerophon*, en route to his exile on St Helena, crowds gathered in a scene more reminiscent of the arrival of a modern movie star. A crush of small boats set out from the town, as people struggled to catch a glimpse of the little figure on deck. One man was drowned in the crush, and women reportedly fainted at the sight of the most famous man in Europe.

Britain may have won the war with France and her allies, but peace was

*Sightseers flock to see the most famous man of the day, a small black silhouette on the deck of the* Bellerephon.

not followed by prosperity: two decades of war had blighted foreign trade. But some recompense had been drawn from the thousands of soldiers stationed in Devon: local economies had been boosted by the supplies inevitably required by troops, their families, as well as prisoners of war.

The holiday industry, which has become a lynchpin of Devonian life and economy, was kicked off by Napoleon's designs on the navy. Much of the Royal Navy was based in Devonport, the booming war town to the west of Plymouth. But naval commanders found Plymouth Sound an exposed anchorage and preferred to drop anchor in Tor Bay, which was more sheltered and large enough to take the entire fleet. In medieval times a hamlet had sprung up round the wharf that served Torre Abbey, and during the Napoleonic Wars, the Mansion House at Torre Abbey became the headquarters of the naval commander. The picturesque little village soon attracted a fleet of camp followers, as officers' wives and families arrived to visit their men whose ships were at anchor in the bay. They took rooms in pubs and farmhouses – Torquay's tourist industry had begun. With Napoleon lurking on the other side of the Channel, foreign holidays were out of the question, so the more leisured classes chose to holiday at home. Military men came to convalesce in the benign climate of the South West. By the end of the Napoleonic Wars in 1815, the idea of Devon as a holiday destination was established, even if the tourist infrastructure was not.

Soon Tor Quay had earned a reputation as a gentile watering place. Convalescent soldiers were followed by convalescent consumptives, when it was realised that the balmy summers were followed by mild winters. Property developers began to build the villas so typical of that sweep of coast, and the arrival of the railway in 1848 finally put Torquay firmly on the tourist map. A public holiday was declared. Townspeople walked in procession to the station and a feast was organised for the inhabitants, when the line opened in December that year. By 1850 Torquay had earned itself the soubriquet 'Queen of the Watering Places'. A century later 6,000–7,000 visitors a week arrived at the station to start their seaside holiday in Torquay.

The Earl of Devon must have had the transformation of Tor Bay in mind, when in the 1850s he encouraged his tenants in Hope Cove to 'take in visitors'. This South Hams village housed a fishing community, who supplemented their income by also working as farm labourers. Thatched cottages with cob walls still huddle around the village square in Inner Hope, not far from the withy beds that provided the raw material for crab pots.

When J.C. Hook 'discovered' Hope Cove in the 1870s the villagers had taken the exhortations of their landlord to heart, and he had no difficulty finding a place to stay. Soon his artist cronies were drawn to the unspoilt village where local fishermen like William Thornton and his son James Edward, were happy to pose for their paintings. The visitors brought in extra pennies, supplementing village incomes in the same way that agriculture had in the past. This was a welcome boost. Agriculture was in the doldrums, and in 1879 and 1880 farmers were ruined by the worst harvests in living memory. Throughout Devon agricultural workers and their families moved or starved.

Enterprising carriers brought each 'crop' of tourists from the closest railway station. Those travelling to Hope Cove stopped at Kingsbridge Road Station in the village of Wrangaton until 1893, when the railway extended a finger further down the South Hams to Kingsbridge itself. As the village began to attract more tourists, so more houses were built. The wealthy did not want to slum it in the pokey bedroom of a fisherman's cottage. Upper-middle class families, with a clutch of children, along with an appropriate number of servants, needed hotels.

At the mouth of the Kingsbridge Estuary the little fishing village of Salcombe had soon grown enough to be reclassified as a town, its population of chandlers, shipwrights and fishermen, being swelled by the owners of elegant estuary homes on the adjacent cliffs. Just as the visitors benefited from the scenery and sea air, so the local economy was boosted by the pounds, shillings and pence, which jangled in the tourists' pockets.

With the invention of the internal combustion engine, the summer population of Devon soared. Signs offering 'Bed and Breakfast' and 'Cream Teas' sprang up at farm gates as farmers followed government exhortations to diversify. Fast money made elsewhere quickly snapped up country cottages as self-catering became the mode.

Exmouth was the first holiday resort in the county. It was patronised by townies from Exeter looking for some fresh air, rather than trippers from further afield. In 1871, when Elias Tozer wrote his book *Devonshire Sketches* under the nom de plume 'Tickler', it was still a thriving resort, but the beach looked very different from those early days:

> There is every facility for bathing here, under certain Local Board regulations. The proprietors, or 'proprietresses' of the bathing machines are permitted to occupy a portion of the beach, from which bathers, who do not hire a machine, are not allowed to dip. Outside a certain point however, persons may bath to their hearts' content. Some mistakes are now and again made; and woe betide the unlucky wight who ventures to trespass on the ground allotted to the reticent

'proprietresses' of these bathing machines. I was peacefully engaged in floating on the 'ocean waves,' one fine morning, when I was suddenly made aware of a great stir in my vicinity. Looking about I saw the stalwart figure of a man, who had presumptuously [sic] undressed near the machines, who was floundering about like an innocent porpoise, thinking, I suppose, that the sea was 'free to all.' He was not permitted to indulge in this happy hallucination long, for the 'female proprietresses' were down upon him; and he was very soon glad to escape from the sea to his clothes, into which he quickly got and 'bolted.' Ambitious bathers sometimes come to grief. A facetious tradesman of Exeter, not a hundred miles from Queen-street, being unable to swim, and not relishing the taunts of small boys, hired a boat for the purpose of bathing 'out to sea.' He had provided himself with a 'belt'; which was warranted to sustain an elephant in any water. Unbounded faith in this apparatus led our adventurous friend to descend into deep water. If the 'belt' was capable of sustaining an elephant, it could not float him, so down he went to the bottom. The boatman, alarmed, instantly thought of the mussel dredger, an article having several sharpish prongs attached to it. With this instrument of torture our poor friend was raised from a 'watery grave,' and he is now the bearer of marks very similar to those which used to be borne by heretics in the 'good old times' of torture and persecution.

## The Prisoners of Princetown

While there was fun to be had on the beaches of the South Coast, elsewhere in the county the direct impact of war was felt in a very different way. In the mid-1800s travel writer Rachel Evans wrote wistfully of the impact prisoners of war had on her home town of Tavistock:

> During the course of many years from the commencement of the last war with France, Tavistock was a depot of prisoners, who were chiefly naval and military officers, on their parole of honour. It had then much the appearance of a foreign town, as the inhabitants were induced to converse with those strangers in their respective languages, French, Spanish and Italian. This increase of residents advanced the interest of trade in the vicinity, and at the same time tended to soften the asperities, previously felt, against those who were liable to be considered as national enemies, while in fact they proved themselves on the broad scale of humanity, worthy of being treated as neighbours and friends.

Just as trade in Tavistock suffered once the POWs left for home, so the main prisoner-of-war camp on Dartmoor suffered. The town of Princetown had grown to service the prison, providing accommodation and supplies for the 1,200-strong garrison. The enormous granite buildings, built by the prisoners themselves, were falling into disrepair when Rachel Evans visited in 1845; she was shown round the guardroom by an Irishman, as she described in her book *Home Scenes*:

> In one of these, is a number of inscriptions in French, intimating the feelings of the poor captives, who waited to be confined or released, by order of the recording officer. An inner court contains a covered piazza, furnished with gratings, through which the prisoners, on certain days, were permitted to traffic with such small articles, as their ingenuity led them to produce, from the apparently incompetent materials afforded by old bones, waste paper, and slips of straw. By

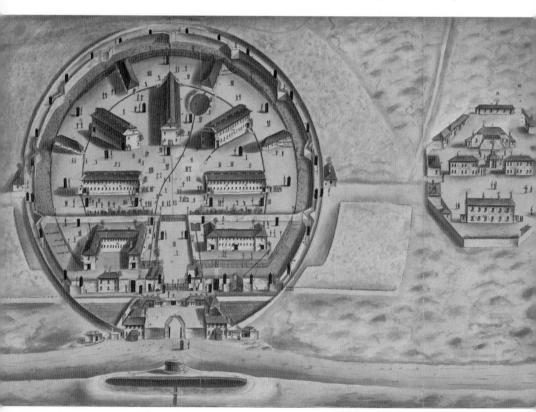

*A plan of Dartmoor Prison drawn shortly after it was built.*

apt contrivance they constructed from these, boxes, dinner mats, and various ornaments, suited to the taste of the fair inhabitants of the nearest towns, who crowded to make purchase of the prisoner's wares.

These prisoners were also a captive labour force and, indeed, during the economic slump of 1811–12, one Plymouth businessman supplied straw to POWs, which they wove into hats. These were then exported to the Channel Islands, the West Indies and Spain.

Rachel Evans also described the POWs' graveyard on the east side of the prison walls, where the bones of the dead had been exposed by the hooves of cattle and horses. But she was shocked at the tumbledown state of the prison buildings:

It appears unfortunate that they should be allowed to fall into decay. The repairs which have been recently commenced, will it is feared, be insufficient to prevent the destruction of the woodwork. The floors in many places have entirely fallen in, which must necessarily be the case, while the houses are subject to the ravages of time in a moist climate, without being defended by wholesome heat, from the hearth fire of any inhabitants...

Five years later the prison did receive its first consignment of convicts. It housed men of a very different persuasion during the First World War: conscientious objectors.

When Britain declared war on Germany on 3 August 1914 there was a rush of volunteers to enlist at recruiting offices up and down the country. But as the casualty lists lengthened, and a state of stalemate developed in the trenches, the army grew short of men. Conscription was introduced in Britain for the first time in March 1916, and a new class of people was born. These conscientious objectors were a nuisance and a mystery to the army, which had no mechanism to deal with them. 'Conchies', as they were nicknamed, went to tribunals with others asking for exemption from military service. Very few won exemption. Instead they were deemed to be in the army, and hence as soon as they disobeyed an order, they were court-martialled and sent to an army prison.

Within a few months, the government realised the need for some alternative, and started the Home Office Scheme. This offered conscientious objectors 'work of national importance' based in a handful of centres round the country: the largest was at Dartmoor Prison.

Eric Dott, a socialist and a Christian, was one of the thousand conscientious objectors who came to Dartmoor. He wrote to his sister Kathleen shortly after he arrived in 1917:

> At first I was a little surprised to find it was a proper prison where we were to stay – but I was soon put right about that – I picked up with a very nice young man almost at once (they appear all very nice men here) and he undertook to show me all around. In the first place we went to my cell, which we prefer to call a 'room', and I found that all the doors have their locks screwed up and that there is nothing to keep us in our rooms. In the course of conversation with my new friend, I learned that there are only two or three warders in the whole place, that it is practically 'run' by the COs themselves, that nothing is ever locked, except the big outside door at night, and that after working hours are over at 6pm we can wander anywhere within about five miles round, so long as we are inside the prison by 9.30pm! Some prison! More like a well- arranged holiday camp.

Eric Dott was young, fit and a born optimist. His impression had been coloured by the three months spent in solitary confinement in Wormwood Scrubs:

> All this after the solitary seclusion and severe restriction of Wormwood Scrubs is indeed enough to carry us off our legs a bit – and so far as I saw last night there seems to be a good deal of wasted time in the evenings – excited talking and playing at games constantly – I can't be sure how others find it but I feel that I will need to take great care to get some good sound reading done and to substitute self-discipline for prison discipline.

Classes were started by the conchies to keep themselves occupied. These included French, English, Shorthand and Logic. Plays and musical evenings were staged.

Among the 'work of national importance' done by these political prisoners, was digging ditches in the vicinity of Mis Tor. Looking back on this later, Eric Dott found the term 'work of national importance' to be a complete misnomer:

> We were supposed to be laying a pipeline or something and it was of no importance. We had two wardens who stood over us and saw that we dug the trench, and nobody took it very seriously at all and we'd

dig slowly and the wardens were very friendly and as long as they saw we were doing some shovelling they didn't take any other interest in us, and we'd break off at intervals at lunchtime and then we'd have meetings there and have learned discussions on philosophy and socialism and religion and all that kind of thing. Lively meetings that we exchanged views in.

That traditional task of convicts, stone breaking, was another form of work. Eric Dott was exempted from this after a few days, because he wore glasses. Instead he sewed mailbags in his cell, a welcome alternative.

The conscientious objectors at Dartmoor came from many different backgrounds. About a quarter were from religious groups such as the Plymouth Brethren, Salvation Army, Quakers, Jehovah's Witnesses, Christian Scientists and Methodists, but they were forbidden by the Bishop of Exeter to worship in the prison chapel. They were released in the spring of 1919.

## Profit and Loss

Evelyn Patey was eighteen years old, and worked as a housemaid in Salcombe. On Saturday, 27 January 1917 she had come home to Hallsands to see her family on her day off. She remembered:

*Evelyn Patey in her early twenties.*

My father and brother had been to Start Farm that day. They hurried home because the sea was so rough. Father went to the scullery to wash his hands, and the walls collapsed around him. He held on to the frame of the door to get to us, we were in the kitchen. We could see the white foamy waves under the stone floors and the coal house and the front passage. We had a back door but it was not safe to open it onto the road because of waves coming over the tops of the houses...

The storm represented just the combination of circumstances that villagers in Hallsands had been dreading: a severe south-easterly gale combined with an unusually high tide. The ninety-four villagers of Hallsands covered their doors and windows with shutters and settled down to wait for the storm to pass, as they had so many times before. The experience was still fresh in the memory of Evelyn Patey, when she wrote down her memories forty-five years later:

We had seen so many storms, we just watched and waited as we had before, never dreaming or thinking of all our homes going like they did. We were born and bred there, and our elders came of generations of fisherfolk and were made of stern stuff, not one of them panicked either man or woman, they were always ready for any emergency, and we always felt safe with them. We felt safe in our kitchen corner on this night until daylight came. We saw that half of our cottage had gone into the sea with the rock it had been built on, the left half of it, which was the scullery, the coal house and half of a bedroom had gone. We had to move out quick before the other half followed.

Evelyn Patey's home was the first to go. The storm lasted three days, by the fourth morning, twenty-four families were homeless and only one house was habitable, but incredibly there had been no loss of life. Many villagers had scrambled up the steep and crumbling cliff in the dark, to find shelter in the chapel and coastguard cottages. They had lost everything. Fishing boats had been wrecked, crab pots carried off by the waves, and furniture and possessions bobbed in the waters of the bay.

But the demise of Hallsands was not due just to the vicious storm. Across the Channel men were dying in the trenches of Verdun and the Somme, as two great Empires struggled for supremacy in the First World War. Arguably Hallsands, too, was sacrificed on the altar of British Imperialism; its existence was quite literally undermined by the great naval arms race that contributed to the onset of war.

Start Bay is a magnificent sweep of Devon coastline between Start Point in the west, and Dartmouth to the east. Villages perched above its shingle beaches have lived on the brink for centuries. Fertile farmland rolls inland, buffeted by south-westerly gales pushed up the Channel from the Atlantic. Hallsands is the most southerly of the villages on this exposed bay, the scene of many wrecks.

On the night of 9 March 1891 five ships were wrecked at Start Point including the *Lizzie Ellen* from Chester. Evelyn Patey's grandfather, John Patey, was one of six men from the village who went to the rescue. In the teeth of an easterly gale and hampered by a blizzard, they lowered themselves down rocks near the village to rescue the crew. They managed to get a line out to the ship and saved the mate and a seaman, although the master drowned as he tried to persuade the cabin boy to jump from the ship into the sea. The Hallsands men were all awarded the RNLI award for bravery.

Access to the village of Hallsands by land is along narrow single-track lanes that meander around ancient field boundaries. When the census enumerator visited in 1841, he must have ridden west along the coastal path from Beesands and Slapton, rather than taking the road. What he found was a village of twenty-five households, with eighteen families making a living from fishing. This was a skilled occupation, with the secrets passed on from father to son, and indeed from husband to wife and daughters. There were two fisherwomen living in the village that year, Elizabeth Trout aged fifty and her fifteen-year-old

*Hallsands fishermen at work.*

daughter. Widowed Elizabeth took the oars of her husband's boat after his death, and supported her family by fishing until she was well into her sixties. By the time she was seventy-one, she was living with two unmarried children and two grandchildren. She had given up fishing and was 'on parish pay', the fate of the elderly poor in this era before the state pension.

The Hallsands villagers were inshore fishermen, catching mullet and mackerel, which in turn were used as bait to catch gurnard, which was used as ideal bait in crab pots. The fish were caught by seine-nets: boats were rowed or sailed to the shoal and the net was lowered into the water surrounding the fish. The catch was then hauled in from the beach by men, women, and children. Crab and lobster were sent by road, then by rail to Billingsgate Market. Alternatively the catch was kept in tanks to await collection by a ship that came every two weeks. Although most of the fishermen could not read or write, they were informed by telegram of the price the catch had made at market and were, inevitably, sometimes swindled.

Other villagers, both male and female, were employed on local farms. In this county of thatched cottages, there was the village thatcher, William Perrott, who had no son to take over his business. As he grew older Perrott must have found thatching too arduous and supplemented his income by becoming the village grocer. By 1861 his business was actually registered as the Hallsands' Grocers Shop. His coffin would have been made by village carpenter William Adams, whose two daughters were both milliners, for this was an era when it was unseemly to leave home without a hat. Fifty-year-old bachelor William Gillard was a tailor who probably sought company at the London Inn run at that time by Susan Pearse. The pub had been serving the village since the 1750s, but there was little passing trade so seventy-year-old Susan supplemented her income by taking in three lodgers, including the village blacksmith. By the end of the nineteenth century the Patey family ran the London Inn, brewing the White Ale, which attracted visitors brought to the bay by steamer from Brixham and Torquay.

Nearly all the villagers were born in the parish, but among the neighbours were three families of incomers. Thomas Blarney, one of three coastguards stationed in the village in 1841, was born in Cawsands in Cornwall. The Coastguard Service had been founded in 1822 as part of the battle against smugglers, so it was the practice for men to be posted away from home for fear of collaboration or collusion.

In common with many communities of the time, the village was made up of a handful of principal families, among them Steer, Pepperell, Patey and Trout. There were six branches of the Stone family, and confusingly three fishermen named John Stone, two of whom were the same age! Family fortunes varied. For example Henry Patey was recorded as a fisherman in 1841, and twenty years later in 1861. But in 1851 he had become an agricultural labourer, a lowly occupation, but one that many fishermen took up in times of bad weather or poor catches. The men worked the boats in pairs, but none could swim. Fishermen and their boats were regularly lost at sea, sometimes their bodies were never found. Evelyn Patey's grandfather was drowned off Start Point in May 1897 at the age of fifty-three. The whole village turned out to his funeral, first gathering round the coffin that rested on two stools outside the Patey home, to sing a favourite hymn. The coffin was then carried the three-and-a-half miles inland to the church at Stokenham for burial. Fishermen from Beesands joined the procession en route at Beeson Pool.

In an era when most of the wider population were tenants, all the cottages at Hallsands were owned by the inhabitants as the death of a philanthropic local landowner, Sir Robert Newman in 1857, had given them the chance to buy their homes. The houses themselves lay on both sides of a single village street. The most northerly cottage, lived in by the Barber family, was wedged between rock and cliff using the cliff as a side wall. But most houses were built upon a rock terrace several metres above sea level, the remnant of the ice-age shoreline. As the village expanded, space on this rock shelf ran out. New houses were built above sand-filled gullies, and rough retaining walls were built out on to the shingle beach as foundations. This beach was where the fishermen pulled up their boats and it provided anchorage for washing poles where clothes and fishing nets alike were hung to dry. It was also the village's natural defence against the greedy sea. But the beach, like so much else, was at risk as two empires marched towards the slaughter of the First World War.

By the last decade of the nineteenth century the British Empire was at its zenith. Other European powers could not match the territory and riches acquired by the British over the previous hundred years. Queen Victoria ruled over four hundred million people, a quarter of the world's population. The Indian sub-continent was largely under British rule, although the border with Afghanistan was a constant trouble spot. In South Africa, the Boers were agitating against British rule, and in northern Africa there were problems in the Sudan and Egypt. In the scramble for power the European powers had carved up the entire African continent between them. These African acquisitions were of enormous strategic importance, lying as they did midway between the mother country and the riches of India. Policing such vast territories required naval superiority, but here British supremacy was threatened by that other rich and strong European nation – Germany.

It was Count Otto Von Bismarck who had finally unified the vast estates of fertile Prussia in the east, with the galaxy of individual princedoms to the west. The militaristic tradition of Prussia was combined with the natural resources that abounded in the industrial powerhouse of the Ruhr. Germany considered itself unstoppable, but in order to create an empire on a par with Britain, it would focus on European neighbours rather than exotic territory far from home.

Plymouth Sound lies thirty miles west of Hallsands. The Royal Naval Dockyard at Devonport had been extended throughout the nineteenth century, and the final building phase began in February 1896. A year later, as the fishermen went about their work, hauling up crab pots in the bay, a line of dredgers appeared out to sea. Sir John Jackson, head of one of the largest building firms in the country, had applied for and been granted, the right to extract shingle from the seabed to the north of the village. It was to be used as aggregate in the building of the last phase of Devonport Docks.

One landowner, whose land adjoined the coast to the north of the village, had been asked for his views and raised no objection. The villagers of Hallsands and neighbouring Beesands had not been informed or consulted, but they immediately recognised the dangers. Under the terms of the licence, the Board of Trade, which 'owned' the shingle, had stipulated that, 'dredging must be carried out in such a way as not to expose the land above [the] high water mark to encroachment by sea'.

The fishermen called for help. The Devon Sea Fisheries Committee asked the Board of Trade to stop the dredging, but it was not until the local MP asked a question in Parliament that there was a public inquiry. It was held in the coastguard station on the cliff above the village. The fishermen told the inspector of the reduction in their catches, caused by the noise and disruption from the dredgers. They expressed the fear that a south-easterly storm would carry away the shingle beach protecting their homes.

The dredging was moved further north, and the fishermen were given a derisory amount of compensation for their loss of income. But some months later a November storm damaged the London Inn. In February 1901, the grocer who delivered twice a week from nearby Kingsbridge, wrote to the local authority about the dangerous state of the road between Beesands and Hallsands. A month later the quay walls along the seaward side of the village street were undermined, and the state of the village was attracting lurid headlines from the press. The Plymouth-based *Western Daily Mercury* trumpeted that Hallsands was a 'Devon Fishing Village in Peril'. This was not alarmist; the beach at one end of the village had dropped by seven feet.

Frank Mildmay, their hardworking and conscientious MP, campaigned for the Board of Trade to inspect the area, and in September 1901 an inspector recommended that the dredging be stopped. In fact 1,600 tons of shingle was still being sucked up four months later. Folklore maintains that it was the fishermen themselves who stopped the dredgers in January 1902. The men of Hallsands and Beesands certainly did march to confront the dredgers, and appeal to the better nature of their crews. The ships did not set out for the dwindling shingle reserves again, but it was because the Board of Trade had finally revoked the licence. It was 8 January – nearly four years after work had begun.

It was a Pyrrhic victory. The pebble beach that had protected the village had now dropped by twelve feet. Fishing boats could no longer be left safely on the beach, but had to be pulled right up into the village street.

As 1902 progressed the beach began to reform. It seemed that the claims made by Sir John Jackson, that the sea would replenish the pebbles, would be vindicated. Sir John turned his attention further up the coast in his search for suitable shingle to complete the docks. After negotiations with the local landowner, Sir John began to dredge shingle from the coast at Strete Gate at the northern end of Slapton Sands. Dredging went on for three months before he discovered it was the wrong type of shingle. His gaze returned to the coast off Hallsands.

It was tradition for the villagers of Hallsands and its sister village Beesands, to take part in what must qualify as the most unusual cricket match in the world. At the lowest spring tide, families armed with picnics rowed out to a spot near the Start Point Lighthouse known as Skerries Bank. As the tide receded, a sand and shingle beach caught between an outcrop of rocks was revealed, and this was the site for the annual cricket match. In 1902 there would be no cricket match. Without a licence, Sir John Jackson began to dredge sand and shingle from the Skerries. Work continued for two years.

On the evening of 26 February 1903, the House of Commons debated a call to restrict immigration, while some 200 miles away in Devon a massive storm hit the coast. As George Stone emerged the next morning to check the damage, the quay in front of the London Inn collapsed beneath him. Two nights later, at the other end of the village, Ann Trout was forced to move in with her niece, as one side of her house collapsed along with the quay and part of the road. Next door John Gillard and his wife and two children had to move in with a neighbour as the sea swept away the foundations. The following night they were homeless again as the sea undermined that neighbour's cottage. Two more cottages collapsed in the ensuing weeks, and villagers made a desperate appeal to their MP by telegram.

Mildmay came to see the damage at Hallsands for himself, and called in local geologist Richard Hansford Worth to investigate. It was Worth who laid the blame for damage squarely on the wealthy shoulders of Sir John Jackson. And it was Worth who predicted that the village would succumb to the sea.

For the rest of 1903, houses were in turn damaged and repaired. Sea walls were built in the middle and to the south of the village, in an attempt to keep out the sea. But the village had been cut in half and houses to the north of the village could only be reached at low tide via a thirty-foot ladder. By spring the following year, five more houses had collapsed plus the remains of the quay. When waves tore off the thatched roof from her cottage, seventy-year old Mrs Login had to knock drainage holes in the cottage walls to let the sea out. Cavities in the village street had to be bridged with makeshift planks.

Family and friends took in the homeless as repairs were made, but the villagers remained in their battered homes; they had nowhere else to go. The *Western Morning News* started a relief fund, and four new houses were built on the cliff above the village. With the help of the campaigning MP Frank Mildmay, the *Western Morning News* took up the cause. Finally the six Hallsands families who had lost their homes were paid £65 compensation. Only a few years earlier cottages at Hallsands had been valued at £100.

*Villagers salvage furniture from their wrecked homes after the storm.*

For the next thirteen years life at Hallsands continued. Children walked to the little school at Huccombe; families worked the allotments at the top of the cliff; willow was harvested from the withy beds to weave the crab pots; nets were mended. It seemed that the village had been reprieved. But the winter of 1916/17 brought fresh disaster. The lifeboat at nearby Salcombe, crewed by many relatives and friends of those at Hallsands, was capsized by an enormous wave as it returned across 'the bar'. Only two of the fifteen-strong crew survived. The same October storm saw two more of Hallsands' cottages evacuated.

When the storm of January 1917 struck, it broke up a community. Some families were re-housed in Fordworth Cottages, built with money raised by a public appeal in the next cove, now known as South Hallsands. Others moved to Beesands or other villages nearby. Many had to leave South Hams altogether.

The lost village of Hallsands, an improbable casualty of war, became a place of pilgrimage and recreation for many of the new generation; its tragic tale the stuff of folklore. Faded snapshots survive of bleached summer days, paddling off the shingle beach, with the ruins of their grandparents' village stark in the background. Today, the one habitable building, which still stands high above the shrunken beach, was home to Evelyn's aunt Elizabeth Prettejohn, until her death in 1964. Newspapers relished the story of the eccentric old lady living alone with her chickens; talking to her friends the gulls; reliving the past as she happily guided visitors among the ruins of her village.

## Defence and Defiance

It is from the trenches of the First World War that the term 'pillboxes' originated. These small concrete forts are believed to have been built first by the Germans, towards the end of the war. But it was as part of Britain's defence strategy in the Second World War that over 18,000 were built in Britain. Many of these were built in what has been described as the Hadrian's Wall of the twentieth century. This started at Seaton on the South Coast and ran north to Bridgwater, on the coast of North Somerset. There are 280 surviving pillboxes known in this defensive line.

Pillboxes were also built all along the coastline as the threat of invasion gripped the nation during the late spring and summer of 1940. Some are brick built, but most were thrown up in concrete, and the marks of the wooden concrete shuttering can still be seen on the outside. They were carefully placed in areas vulnerable to attack, often built into the cliff or camouflaged by surrounding vegetation. These would represent the last line of defence when the anticipated invasion began. From the small loopholes, members of the Home Guard could cover a wide stretch of the beach. Each loophole or window had sides

*Coastal pillbox at Thurlestone.*

angled at about 45 degrees to give the maximum breadth of sight. Some had a small wooden shelf fixed beneath this window with iron bars, on which the gunner could rest his elbow while taking aim. Entrances were covered with camouflage netting pegged into place. Inside, these forts were cramped, being only ten feet square with a ceiling height of about six feet. As the Directorate of Fortifications and Works outlined in its instructions to local authorities, 'The lower the roof, the greater is the chance of concealment'.

Astonishingly there were more than twenty-six different designs. Some Second World War defence sites are merely heaps of rubble, or have vanished altogether. Home Guard veteran Percy Moysey was part of a team whose tactics in the event of an invasion are evocative of a scene from a James Bond film. The men guarded the road between Kingsbridge and the neighbouring town of Dartmouth. On the hill above Bowcombe Bridge, just outside Kingsbridge, the Home Guard dugout stood next to two enormous 400-gallon oil tanks. The oil fed down the hill onto the bridge, and into a narrow pipe, which had been drilled with small holes. As the Germans approached, the oil would be turned on, ignited, and become a huge arch of fire designed to create havoc among the approaching enemy!

Despite such Home Guard precautions Devon was considered a place of relative safety, playing host to thousands of children evacuated from London, and other major cities. In February 1941, 6,000 children were evacuated from Bristol alone, following raids on the Avonmouth docks and the city centre. As a result Devon schools were overcrowded, so teachers taught classes in shifts, leaving pupils free to work on farms or school allotments. Children were encouraged to pick rosehips for jam and syrup; acorns, which they could sell to farmers as pig fodder; and in spring, bunches of primroses, which were carefully packed up in moss and sent to those in hospital.

Dartington Hall took in 300 children, and some evacuees even camped in the bailey of Totnes Castle. The magnificent Ugbrooke Park, near Chudleigh designed by Robert Adam was, like many other stately homes, used as a school for evacuees.

Great Torrington's largest house, built by wealthy Victorian glove man-ufacturer William Vaughan, had been turned into a Red Cross Hospital during the First World War. In 1939 the doors of Sydney House were thrown open for the war effort once again, this time for sick evacuees from London. But on the bitterly cold night of 19 February 1942 fire broke out in the linen cupboard on the top floor, close to the boys' dormitories. Fire ripped through the building despite the efforts of the fire brigade and local volunteers. By morning five of the fifty-nine boys were dead. A memorial stone was unveiled on the site, now the entrance to South Street car park, during a service taken by the Bishop of Exeter in 2002.

A factory manufacturing de-icing systems for the RAF was evacuated from London to Bideford, complete with its 300-strong workforce. Enemy aliens, Germans and even Jews who were in Britain when war broke out, were housed in an internment camp in Paignton. Lorries rumbled through Devon lanes with bitumen and concrete, to construct airfields from Okehampton to Upottery – the home of 'Easy Company' from the 101st Airborne Division. From airfields near the village of Hemyock, Spitfires and Hurricanes flown by Polish, Czech, and British pilots, protected aircraft crossing the Channel and shot down enemy bombers. From Smeatharpe, United States long-range Liberators cruised the skies hunting the German submarines that threatened Atlantic convoys. Civilian workers such as female mechanics were also billeted near these air bases. Fifty thousand air cadets trained in Torbay, and in the run up to D-Day American troops camped on the site of playing fields at Torquay Community College.

The Hoe at Plymouth has been a symbolic spot for defiance in the midst of war. Sir Francis Drake's apocryphal game of bowls remained uninterrupted by the Spanish Armada, and the city's wartime MP Lady Astor organised daytime dances in the space to boost morale during the Blitz. Half a million explosive devices were dropped on the city in a total of thirty-one air raids. The highest number of casualties in one night was on 20 March 1941, when

336 people were killed. A month later, just before midnight on 22 April, seventy-six people were killed in a direct hit on the Portland Square air-raid shelter. Many casualties could not be identified, so strong was the blast. The site is now in the centre of the Plymouth University campus. The distinctive mounds of some of the city's air-raid shelters can still be spotted today in Devonport Park and Morice Square where the entrance has been filled with concrete. Plymouth was said to have been the worst bombed city in Britain, and as a result many travelled out to the countryside by train, to sleep under hedgerows for the night, rather than risk another night of bombing.

Among the buildings lost in the raids were the Guildhall, the pier and the Pannier Market. The market continued to run in a series of temporary buildings throughout the war, and the present market is a Grade II listed building to mark this.

Devonport Docks were the target of many bombs, and the rebuilding of Plymouth was taken up with glee by post-war city planners. It was considered an opportunity to replace the old crowded city with planned housing separated by open spaces, but criticisms followed that Devonport had been 'sliced up' and 'cut off'. Certainly today it is apparent that the modern city, and its sister Exeter, lost far more than ancient buildings, quaint streets and unlucky civilians, due to the deadly aim of the Luftwaffe bombers.

**The Lost Devons**
On Saturday, 27 January 2007, Drum Major Tony Cox and his fellow bandsmen played the regimental march for the last time as they marched past

*Officers beside their makeshift mess during the siege of Ladysmith.*

Exeter's Guildhall. This was a medley of tunes, 'We Lived and Loved Together', 'Maid of Glenconnell', and of course 'Widecombe Fair', put together when the Devons were amalgamated with the neighbouring infantry-men in Dorset in 1958. Band members sported their scarlet uniforms and white helmets, as the regimental colours carried by the standard bearers were laid in Exeter Cathedral, where they will remain. In the new modern army, Devon's county regiment is now an echo from the past.

Traditionally the British Army had relied on the Irish for the bulk of its canon fodder, but in 1782 regiments were encouraged to recruit in particular counties. The 11th Foot were told to 'Cultivate an intercourse with the county of Devon so as to create a mutual attachment between the inhabitants and the regiment'.

That attachment between Devonians and their regiment was only too plain as they marched through their 'home' town. Cheers and clapping resounded from the crowds lining the streets, particularly when the old comrades marched past. For the marchers, this was a last 'family' gathering. While the army has traditionally fostered a sense of family, the county regiments have been more like a close-knit family, moving to postings around the world as a family group. As of February 2007, these men and women marching through the streets of Exeter became known as the 1st Battalion The Rifles.

The origins of Devon's county regiment stem back to the volunteer militias raised by various Devon worthies to stamp out the Duke of Monmouth's rebellion of 1685. This bastard son of Charles II tried to claim the throne on the death of his father. As a protestant he was popular with Devonians, and 400 of them joined the Pitchfork Rebellion as it became known. These men, mainly from East Devon, were part of the 6,000-strong rebel army, but they were poorly armed – many only had agricultural implements. Hopelessly defeated at the Battle of Sedgemoor, thirty-three were brought to trial at the Exeter Assizes in September. The boiled and tarred quarters of the thirteen rebels who were hanged, were dispatched for display in Devon towns.

The regimental colours hang from the walls of Exeter's ancient cathedral, alongside battle honours won all over the British Empire, during the Indian Mutiny, the wars with Afghanistan, and the Boer War. These are the flags that hundreds of Devon men have followed to the death. The regiment won the nickname 'The Bloody Eleventh' during the Peninsula Wars as Britain and her allies chased Napoleon over the Spanish/Portuguese peninsula. On 22 July 1812, at the Battle of Salamanca, the 11th Foot went into action with 412 officers and men. By the end of that hot and dusty day there were just 72 survivors.

In the autumn of 1899, the Devons sailed for South Africa as part of the force sent to crush guerrilla attacks by Dutch settlers, the Boers. Among them was Drummer E. Boulden. Soon after the Devons set sail, the Boers began the siege of Ladysmith, which was to last 118 days. During those three-and-a-half months there was only one serious attempt by the Boers to take the town, at the Battle of Wagon Hill. The hill lay to the south-west of Ladysmith, in a key strategic point above the town, which was within gun-shot range below. The battle began in the small hours of 6 January 1900. By five o'clock in the afternoon it was hailing steadily, as the Devons prepared for a charge with fixed bayonets. At the order 'Company, double charge!' they ran up the side of Wagon Hill. Drummer Boulden described what he saw of the battle, in a letter home to his father:

> With dear old Captain Lafone leading on in front we charged up over the hill and the Boers were only 15 yards away from us and I sounded the charge with another drummer and then we joined the charge... I was nearly mad, in fact all of us was.

As they charged, men fell on all sides under the barrage of bullets from the Boers. On the crest of the hill, the Devons had to follow the ground to the right and complete the charge across 130 yards of flat ridge. The Boers, who were renowned marksmen, were firing at them from three sides; those killed were all shot in the head. Popular officer, Captain Lafone was among them. Drummer Boulden wrote home:

> When we returned off the hill to the town all the civilians came out and meet us and gave us a nice hot cup of tea and patted us on the back and said my dear brave men. Well I carried poor Captain Lafone's belt and sword and haversack back to camp and the Colonel gave me his

*Survivors after the Battle of Wagon Hill, among them Drummer Boulden.*

silver mounted pipe to keep in rimemence [sic] of him as he knows that the captain knew our family at Hanworth the Captain had told him so, and well what do you think his dear old mother done, she sent a quarter of a pound tin of Players Navy Cut tobacco to every man in the Captain's company. That was Mrs Lafone and we had not had a smoke of tobacco for 4 months and we used to smoke dried tea leaves and sunflower leaves and we did treasure that tobacco.

The Devons' charge was the climax of the Battle for Ladysmith. The Boers, a hidden enemy that specialised in guerrilla warfare, had been repulsed on open ground. It was a much-needed morale boost for the British nation in this expensive and ultimately futile war. Amongst the regimental treasures, are four silver side drums that commemorate the Devonshire Regiment's bravery at Wagon Hill. The inscription reads:

Presented by the men and women of Devon to the 1st and 2nd Battalions the Devonshire Regiment to record the county's pride in the valour of her sons, 1900.

The graves of 5,787 officers and men from the Devonshire Regiment, who died in the First World War, are to be found scattered over what was then the British Empire. Men of the twenty-five battalions who served in the county regiment, lie in France, Belgium, Germany, Italy, Greece, Egypt, Iraq, Palestine, India and

*War memorial in Exeter Cathedral to the First World War casualties from the Devon Regiment.*

Russia. But the most celebrated action in which the Devons took part, was in the last months of the war, at a hill known as Bois Des Buttes. It's a landmark not found on any local map, and has been roughly translated as Hillocky Wood. Bois Des Buttes was a mile behind the British front line to the north. Interconnected tunnels ran through the hill, with gas curtains at the entrances. It was here on the night of 27 May 1918 that the 2nd Battalion sheltered as they prepared for the German guns to open up.

At 1a.m. the hill appeared to shake as the German bombardment of gas and high explosives began. At first light, the Devons emerged from the tunnels into a cloud of dust and smoke so impenetrable, that they had to hold on to the coat tails of the man in front. The men of the Middlesex and West Yorkshire regiments closer to the British front lines had suffered tremendous casualties, and the Germans had penetrated their lines. The Devons were surrounded. The trenches, in which they tried to take cover, had been 'blown to blazes' as one survivor put it. So few men survived, that a complete picture of the stand of the 2nd Battalion, is hazy. In his last letter home, before dying in hospital, twenty-year-old Private Ambrose Borne left a snapshot of an early part of the battle:

> I was with the Lewis gun team and we were first in action. All my pals in the team [became] casualties... Lads were falling left and right... I was firing steadily at the German hordes... I looked about and I seemed to be all alone... Then when they were about a hundred yards away things got a bit too warm so I picked up the gun, ran back about a hundred yards and had another go.

This was Ambrose Borne's first and last battle. He was taken prisoner by the Germans and died in hospital after repatriation. An eyewitness, watching further back in the British lines, described the 2nd Devons that morning as 'Merely an island fighting with perfect discipline and by the steadiness of their fire mowing down the enemy in large numbers.'

The battle at Bois Des Buttes began at 4a.m. and ended shortly after midnight. The 2nd Devons suffered overwhelming casualties: 23 officers and 528 men were missing or dead, among them the Commanding Officer, Colonel Rupert Anderson-Morshead. A Battery commander came across him shortly before his death:

> At a late hour in the morning I with those of my men who had escaped the enemy machine guns and his fearful barrage, joined the CO of the 2nd Devonshire Regiment and a handful of men holding onto the last

trench north of the Canal. They were in a position in which they were entirely without hope of help but were fighting on grimly. The Commanding Officer himself was calmly writing his notes with a perfect hail of high explosive falling round him. I spoke to him and he told me that nothing could be done. He refused all offers of help from my artillery men, who were unarmed, and sent them off to get through if they could. His magnificent courage, dauntless bearing and determination to carry on to the end moved one's emotions.

Many were wounded; some were captured; others escaped and made their way back to British lines; others who survived the battle and capture, were shot as they tried to escape and rejoin the remnants of their regiment. Two officers and ninety-men regrouped, and in the relentless fashion of war, went on to fight at Bligny Ridge.

As the Devon Regiment paraded through the streets of Exeter for the last time, the old comrades were a reminder of all those who had died in the service of their country in the Second World War and other theatres of conflict in the twentieth century. The last name on the Devon Regiment roll of honour was that of Corporal 'George' Cosby shot during an operation against insurgents in Iraq on 16 July 2006.

*Borne in battle, hanging in peace, regimental colours in Exeter Cathedral.*

# PICTURE CREDITS

Dick Bird (page 87)

Courtesy of the Trustees of the British Museum (page 18)

David Clarke (page 60)

Alan Denbigh (pages 4, 6, 9, 10, 11, 12, 16, 30, 62, 77, 80, 94, 96, 97, 123, 138, 139,
140, 168, 186, 195, 214, 219, 221)

The Devonshire Association (page 51)

Courtesy of Exeter Archaeology (pages 11, 192)

Felicity Goodall (page 194, back cover)

Basil Greenhill Collection, Barnstaple (pages 125, 128)

Bill Horner, Devon County Council (page 197)

Colin Humphreys, South West Archaeology (page 56)

The Landmark Trust (pages 184, 189, 190)

Library of the Institute of Mechanical Engineers (pages 149, 150)

Tony Manley (page 157)

Courtesy of the Master of Haileybury (pages 167, 170, 171, 175)

Morwellham Quay Museum (pages 90, 91, 92, 124)

Courtesy of Museum of Barnstaple and North Devon (page 111)

Courtesy of the National Trust (pages 160, 165)

Ron Patey and family (front cover picture and pages 205, 207, 212)

Courtesy of Plymouth City Museum and Art Gallery (pages 113, 118, 198)

Chris Preece (pages 54, 57)

Courtesy of the Regimental Museum, Dorchester (pages 216, 218)

St Peter's Convent (page 182)

Courtesy of the Trustees of the Sir John Soane Museum (page 179)

Courtesy of Torquay Library Services (pages 42, 46)

Courtesy of the West Country Studies Library (pages 32, 34, 35, 66, 70, 75, 116, 132,
136, 137, 143, 145, 151, 162, 165, 202)

Peter Webster (pages 100, 102, 104, 105)

Anne Whitbourn, Dartmoor Tinworking Research Group (page 68)

# BIBLIOGRAPHY

*Abridged Report From the Select Committee on Atmospheric Railways*, House of Commons

Aggett, W.J.P., *The Bloody Eleventh, History of the Devonshire Regiment, Devonshire and Dorset Regiment*

Armstrong, John (ed.) *Coastal and Short Sea Shipping* (Studies in Transport History), Scolar Press

Booker, Frank, *Morwellham*, Dart Publication No. 2

Bramwell, Frederick, *The South Devon Atmospheric Railway*, extract for the Institution of Mechanical Engineers Proceedings, 1899

Brewer, Kath, Railways, *Quarries and Cottages of Foggintor*, Orchard Publications

Bridbury, A.R., *England and the Salt Trade in the Later Middle Ages*, Clarendon Press

Carrington, Charles, *Rudyard Kipling*, Macmillan

Chitty, Jean, *Paper in Devon*, thesis

Chope, R.P. (ed.) *Early Tours in Devon and Cornwall*, James Commin, Exeter, 1918

Clayton, Howard, *Atmospheric Railways*, Howard Clayton

Collyer, Graham (ed.), *Hope Cove, Galmpton and South Huish, The Story of a Devon Parish*, Hope Archive Group

Defoe, Daniel, *A Tour Through England and Wales*, J.M. Dent and Sons

Dickinson, Bickford H.C., *The Dunsland Saga*, James S. Porterfield

Dickinson, M.G., (compiler and ed.), *A Living From the Sea*, Devon Books

Duffy, Michael, *New Maritime History of Devon*, Conway Maritime Press

Dunsford, Martin, *Historical Memoirs of the Town and Parish of Tiverton*, 1790

Dunsland House, *National Trust Guidebook*

Evans, Rachel, *Home Scenes*, Simpkin and Marshall

Finberg, H.P.R., and Kelley, Augustus M., *Tavistock Abbey*, New York

Freeman, Ray, *Dartmouth and Its Neighbours*, Phillimore and Co.

Gallacher, Ian, *A Hard Living, West Country Seafarers in Victorian England*, Whistlestop

Goodall, Felicity, *A Question of Conscience*, Sutton Publishing

Grant, Alison, *North Devon Pottery: The Seventeenth Century*, University of Exeter

Gray, Todd, *Early Stuart Mariners and Shipping*, Devon and Cornwall Record Society

Harris, Helen, *Industrial Archaeology of Dartmoor*, David and Charles

Haynes, R.G., *The Care of Rabbits on Dartmoor Warrens*, Devonshire Notes and Queries

Hemery, Eric, *The Historic Dart*, David and Charles

Hoskins W.G., *Devon*, Devon Books

Kipling, Rudyard, *Stalky and Co.*, Macmillan and Co.

Kitton, F.G., *A Visit to the Eddystone Lighthouse*, Plymouth City Council

Majdalany, F., *The Red Rocks of Eddystone*, Longmans

Marshall, William, *Rural Economy of the West of England*, G. Nicol, 1796

Maxted, Ian, *Papers on the History of Books in Devon*, Devon County Council

Melia, Steve, *Hallsands, A Village Betrayed*, Liverton Forest Publishing

Minchinton, Walter, *Devon at Work*, David and Charles

Minchinton, Walter, *Devon's Industrial Past, A Guide*, Dartington Centre for
    Education and Research

Nix, Michael, *Maritime History of the Ports of Bideford and Barnstaple*, thesis

Murch, David, *Wreck and Rescue on the South Hams Coast*, David Murch

Overton, Mark, *Agricultural Revolution in England, The Transformation of the
    Agrarian Economy*, Cambridge University Press

Parkinson, Margaret, *The Axe Estuary and its Marshes*, Transactions of the
    Devonshire Association

Patrick, Amber, *Morwellham Quay, A History*, Morwellham Quay Museum

Pennington, Robert R., *Stannery Law*, David and Charles

Pilkington, F., *Moorhaven Hospital, Ivybridge, South Devon*, Historical Review

Polwhele, Richard, *A History of Devonshire*, Kohler and Coombs, 1977

*Report of the Metropolitan Commissioners in Lunacy*

Richardson, P.H.G., *Mines of Dartmoor and the Tamar Valley*, British Mining Vol. 44,
    Northern Mine Research Society

*Risdon's Survey of Devon*, Rees and Curtis, Plymouth, 1811

Rowse, A.L., *Economic History*, 1932

Selleck, Douglas, A., *Cookworthy, A Man of No Common Clay*, Baron Jay

Slade, W.J., *Out of Appledore*, Percival Marshall and Co.

Small, Ken, *The Forgotten Dead*, Bloomsbury

Stephen, John (ed.), *Ancient Religious Houses of Devon*, Sydney Lee Ltd

Storrs Hall, Windermere, *The Georgian Group Journal Vol. XV*

Sturt, John, *Revolt in the West: The Western Rebellion of 1549*, Devon Books

*Strong's Industries of North Devon*, David and Charles (reprint)

Swete, Reverend, *Travels in Georgian Devon*, Halsgrove Publishing

Veale, Elspeth M., *The Rabbit in England*, Agricultural History Review

*White's Directory*, 1850

Windeatt, E., and Watkin, H.R., *Priory for Nuns of St Mary, Cornworthy*, Devonshire

Williamson, Tom, *The Archaeology of Rabbit Warrens*, Shire Archaeology

**Newspapers:**

*Trewman's Flying Post, North Devon Journal, The Times*

**Devon Archaeology Society reports:**

Gaskell Brown, Cynthia, *Morwellham an Archaeological Survey,*

Stoyle, Mark, *Exeter in the Civil War*

Stoyle, Mark, *Plymouth in the Civil War*

*Tavistock Abbey*

# INDEX